Barrie Gunter is Emeritus Professor in the Department of Media and Communication, University of Leicester. He was a founding professor of the Department of Journalism Studies, University of Sheffield, and then, as Professor of Mass Communications and Head of Department, led the re-launch of the Centre of Mass Communication Research at the Department of Media and Communication, University of Leicester.

Mokhtar Elareshi is Lecturer in Media and Communication Studies at the University of Tripoli, Libya, and was also former Head of the Department of Media at Azzaytuna University, 2003–2006.

Khalid Al-Jaber is Assistant Professor of Political Communications in the Gulf Studies Programme at Qatar University. He is also Editor-in-Chief of the *Peninsula* newspaper published in Doha, and works as Principal at Global Media Consultants Organisation, Atlanta, GA, USA.

'This is an important book that fills a gap in the literature on the new and social media in the GCC states. The edited volume showcases how digital telecommunications technologies influenced the social and media landscape in the GCC region, which is considered a more stable part of the Arab world following the recent upheavals. This collection of essays, the majority of which written by Arab scholars, provides an indispensable source for a broader understanding of the Gulf societies and how they were influenced by social media as well as the recent political tensions. It is an invaluable read for anyone interested in understanding digital communications in the GCC region and how these can conflict with the current regimes' strategies.'

Professor Noha Mellor, Creative Arts, Technologies & Science Faculty, Bedfordshire University

'This edited volume fills a huge gap in the academic literature by shedding light on the social media role in the Arabian Gulf countries during the course of the Arab uprisings in 2011. The volume includes several studies authored by esteemed scholars who utilised various theoretical and methodological approaches to scientifically assess whether new media have mobilised the public in the GCC countries.'

Professor Mohammed el-Nawawy, James L. Knight School of Communication, Queens University of Charlotte

'There has been much debate about the role of social media in the spread of public protest and political activism in the Middle East that began in 2011. Here at last is a book that brings together the results of original empirical research from scholars from across a wide range of disciplinary backgrounds to provide some thoughtful reflection on the "Arab Spring", to dispel many of the myths that have emerged around the associated events, and to offer some well-founded insights into the social and political processes that gave rise to them. The editors are to be congratulated not only for the breadth of their survey of academic work on the topic but also for their own worthy individual contributions to this collection. Together these chapters offer an invaluable guide to this complex and still-unfolding episode in world history.'

Roger Dickinson, Reader in Media and Communication, University of Leicester

Social Media in the Arab World

Communication and Public Opinion in the Gulf States

EDITED BY

Barrie Gunter
Mokhtar Elareshi
Khalid Al-Jaber

I.B. TAURIS
LONDON · NEW YORK

Published in 2016 by
I.B.Tauris & Co. Ltd
London • New York
www.ibtauris.com

Library of Modern Middle East Studies 189

ISBN: 978 1 78453 578 0
eISBN: 978 0 85772 866 1
ePDF: 978 0 85772 835 7

A full CIP record for this book is available from the British Library
A full CIP record is available from the Library of Congress

Library of Congress Catalog Card Number: available

Printed and bound by CPI Group (UK) Ltd, Croydon, CR0 4YY

MIX
Paper from responsible sources
FSC® C013604

Table of Contents

List of Tables

About the Contributors

Samah Ahmed is a media advertising professional currently based in London, UK. Samah spent her early childhood in Doha, Qatar and Khartoum, Sudan, before settling with her family in the UK. After discovering a passion for science, she pursued a degree in Biomedical Sciences and worked in the Pharmaceutical sector. Having always been interested in exploring different countries, she moved to Dubai, UAE, and made a career change from science to media. Outside work, Samah enjoys being involved and contributing to sociopolitical changes. She is a passionate member of the Sudanese diaspora, keen to contribute to the progress of Sudan, especially in the areas of youth development and education.

Fatima AlSalem is Assistant Professor in the Department of Mass Communications in Kuwait University, where she received her BA in Mass Communication (she also has an MA from Florida International University and a PhD from Indiana University). She has attended several training programmes and conferences in Turkey, Lebanon, Greece, the US, the UAE, Qatar and Japan. AlSalem joined the United Nations digital training programme run by the United States Mission to the United Nations and the Department of State. Among her research interests are online political participation, Arab public opinion, and the influence of digital media on the Arab world. She has also conducted several internationally recognised public opinion polls and online analyses for Kuwait's leading newspaper *Alqabas*.

Omair Anas has a PhD from the School of International Studies, Jawaharlal Nehru University, New Delhi, where he has worked on transnational Arab media. He has published several papers on the use of social media during anti-Hosni Mubarak protests in 2011.

James Buie is a graduate of the School of Journalism at the University of North Carolina at Chapel Hill; he also has an MA in Journalism and Public Affairs from the American University in Washington, DC. He started his career as an editorial page and general assignment reporter in Fayetteville on daily newspapers in North Carolina, then as arts and entertainment reporter in Durham, and later as a writer of personality profiles and features for *The News & Observer* of Raleigh. After graduate school, he periodically taught journalism as an adjunct for The Washington Center for Internships and Academic Seminars and the Washington Internship Institute. He worked as a reporter and editor for *Church and State* magazine, as an education reporter and editor for Capitol Publications, as senior reporter for the American Psychological Association's monthly publication, and as a publications editor for the National Alliance on Mental Illness. He was an early adopter of internet technology and managed websites for the public relations firm of Barksdale Ballard in Washington, DC. His clients included Bill Moyers' Public Affairs Television, PBS, and the Robert Wood Johnson Foundation.

David W. Bulla is Associate Professor in Communication and Media Sciences College at Zayed University, Abu Dhabi. His research focuses on the history of journalism, examining limitations on press performance. He concentrates on nineteenth-century newspapers, particularly the US Civil War. His first book, *Lincoln's Censor*, was published by Purdue University Press in 2008. Much of his research has been devoted to the Peace Democratic journalists of the Civil War. He also conducts research on international and scholastic journalism topics. He is a frequent contributor as a book reviewer to several scholarly journals, including *Journalism History* and *American Journalism*, as well as H-Net Book Review in the *Humanities and Social Sciences*, which is web-based. He earned a PhD in Mass Communication from the University of Florida, an MA in Journalism from Indiana University, Bloomington, and a BA in English from the University of North Carolina, Greensboro. Before moving to the UAE, Dr Bulla taught at Iowa State University for seven years.

Shubhada Chaudhary is a PhD candidate at Jawaharlal Nehru University, New Delhi, and researches topics related to Arab traditional and social media in the contemporary developments of the 'Arab Spring'. Her MPhil dissertation focused on the 'Role of Arab Media in the Uprisings of Bahrain and Syria: Case Study of Al-Jazeera and Al-Arabiya'. Chaudhary has previously worked in South Africa, researching political developments in the West Asian Region, and has pursued her MA degree in International Journalism from the University of Westminster, London. Chaudhary also writes for Gulf-based magazines on West Asian politics.

Mokhtar Elareshi is Lecturer in Media and Communication Studies. He has taught at the University of Tripoli, Libya, when he was also former Head of the Department of Media at Azzaytuna University 2003–2006. In 2012, Elareshi earned his PhD at the Department of Media and Communication, University of Leicester. He is the author of *News Consumption in Libya* (Cambridge Scholar, 2013) and the co-author of *The Future of News Media in the Arab World* (Lambert, 2013). He has written and reviewed several journal articles in Arabic and English. His research interests include news consumption, young adults' media habits, new media and satellite TV.

Barrie Gunter is Emeritus Professor attached to the Department of Media and Communication, University of Leicester, UK. A psychologist by training, he spent the first part of his career in the broadcasting sector where he worked in audience research for a media regulator before moving into the academic world. He was a founding Professor of the Department of Journalism Studies, University of Sheffield, and then, as Professor of Mass Communications and Head of Department, led the re-launch of the Centre of Mass Communication Research at the Department of Media and Communication, University of Leicester. He has published nearly 60 books and more than 300 journal papers, book chapters and other reports in media, marketing, and psychology. His special interests include media and violence, audience reception of news, digital health communication, advertising and children, celebrity studies, and the impact of the internet. He is a fellow of the Academy of Social Sciences, UK.

Khalid Al-Jaber is Assistant Professor of Political Communications in the Gulf Studies Programme at Qatar University. He is also Editor-in-Chief of the *Peninsula* newspaper published by Dar Al-Sharq Press, Doha, and works as principal at Global Media Consultants Organisation, Atlanta, GA, USA. Al-Jaber earned his PhD from the University of Leicester, UK. He also holds an MA and Diploma from Fordham University, NY, Stanford University, San Francisco, CA, and Georgetown University, Washington, DC. Al-Jaber is a scholar of Arab and Gulf studies whose research focuses on global media organisations, political science, and international communications. He has published scholarly works in several academic and professional journals including the *World Press Encyclopedia* and *Gazette.*

Marc Owen Jones is a researcher studying political repression in Bahrain at Durham University. In addition to teaching Middle East politics, Jones is a member of the advocacy NGO Bahrain Watch. He has written academically on Bahrain, on topics from policing to social media. He has also written for outlets such as CNN, Democracy Now, Index on Censorship and the Economist Intelligence Unit. In 2011, Jones helped exposed the fake journalist Liliane Khalil and appeared on Al-Jazeera and France 24 to discuss how PR companies are able to use such figures to spread government propaganda. He is the co-editor of the forthcoming book *Bahrain's Uprising*, published by Zed Books Ltd.

Abdul-Karim Ziani is Assistant Professor in the Department of Media, Tourism and Arts at Bahrain University, Bahrain. He is the author of *Conflict of Wills: Gaddafi's Image in the* Washington Post *Newspaper in the Era of President Reagan* (Talta Publishing House, 2007) and *American Press: Developing, Philosophy and Treatment* (Talta Publishing House, 2005); he has also written several journal articles, book chapters and other scholarly publications on journalism and political communication. Among his special areas of interest are international political communication, new media and politics, and news coverage.

Note on Sources, Citations and Bibliography

Two methods were used for citing sources in this book. Primary sources such as newspapers, interviews, internal reports, magazine articles, press releases, speeches, talks, blogs, Facebook and Twitter information were treated as archival material and cited in full in the endnotes but not in the bibliography. Books, monographs, conference papers, journal articles, academic theses and dissertations, and published reports were cited in both the endnotes and bibliography. Finally, where copyright material was reproduced, the editors made every effort to check and obtain permission from the copyright holders.

Acknowledgements

The idea for this book originated at a workshop organised in August 2014 at the University of Cambridge under the auspices of the Gulf Research Conference, entitled 'Social Media and the Changing Context of Politics in the Gulf', led by Douglas Boyd and Yousef Al Failakawi. Without their support it would not have been possible to gather together such a range of scholarly contributors covering the GCC region. We would like, therefore, to express our appreciation to the Gulf Research Conference for allowing us to go ahead with the book.

The chapters making up this book are mostly based on studies presented at the workshop. The chapters written by Marc Owen Jones and by Fatima AlSalem did not derive from material presented at the workshop. The first and last chapters, written by the volume's three editors, were also drafted after the workshop specifically to set the scene and draw some general conclusions.

We are deeply grateful to Professor Noha Mellor (Create Arts, Technologies and Science Faculty, University of Bedfordshire, UK), Professor Naomi Sakr (University of Westminster, UK), Professor Mohammed el-Nawawy (James L. Knight School of Communication, Queens University of Charlotte, USA) and Dr Roger Dickinson (Media and Communication Department, University of Leicester, UK) for their comments and advice in improving the overall quality of this book, although the editors and authors assume ultimate responsibility for any errors that occur. We also wish to express our gratitude to I.B.Tauris Publishers, especially to Maria Marsh and Sophie Campbell, who assisted us during the editorial process involved in publishing this book.

1

The Significance of Social Media in the Arab World

Barrie Gunter and Mokhtar Elareshi

The events of the so-called 'Arab Spring' have their genesis in public discontent with their ruling classes and the social and economic opportunities provided for ordinary people in their societies that had festered over many years. New technologies linked to the internet and mobile phones played a critical role as communication platforms that enabled formerly disparate individuals to become organised swiftly into groups with a common purpose.[1] In this context, there has been a great deal of discussion and speculation and some research among academics and practitioners alike about what role the new media, especially social media, are currently playing and what impact they will have in future social and political developments in the Arab world.[2]

This edited book is designed to shed new light on these matters. It focuses on social media usage in the Gulf Cooperation Council (GCC) region and the links between these and the traditional media. The GCC states comprise Bahrain, Kuwait, Qatar, Oman, Saudi Arabia and United Arab Emirates. The book covers the different roles played by social media across a range of social, cultural, political, economic and religious contexts in the region. The GCC cannot be considered in isolation from the remainder of the region. Developments in the use of online social media in the Gulf States form part of a wider sphere of technological revolution spanning the entire Middle East and North Africa (MENA) Arab world. Although the world's attention was drawn to the events that occurred in these countries from 2011, seeds were being sown for a number of years before then. The growth in the use of blogs, micro-blogs and social media sites was observed from 2005, and these technologies quickly became adopted as tools of political activists.[3]

The analysis of 'social' media forms part of a wider interest in the role allegedly played by 'new' media in shaping political activism and outcomes. It is important to be clear about the definition of these terms because there has been much loose writing about new media. We can take our cue from the work of Sean Aday and his colleagues who identified three major categories of 'new' media: Blogging, 'social' networks such as Facebook, hosting services such as YouTube, micro-blogging services such as Twitter, and short text messaging primarily via mobile phones and email.[4] These various services provide platforms for interpersonal communication and information exchanges that can take place between one individual and another or between one individual and many others.

In a political context, these different communications channels can provide sources of information that supplement or displace the mass media as sources of reporting and debate.[5] They might also be used by specific individuals and groups to forge and maintain links with like-minded others and to organise live events. Because 'new' media channels are under the control of the users, they can publish whatever they want whenever they choose without facing the usual restrictions of professional gatekeepers who determine news agendas in the mainstream media.[6] As we see in Chapters 4 and 10, when numerous arrests were taking place in the GCC region following the recent 2011 Arab uprisings, online users were jailed for their online activities, especially when these were linked to views about political oppression.

There is, of course, a risk attached to the use of new media sources in that recipients of their messages cannot always be sure about the authenticity of the information they contain or the credibility and agenda of the sources – if the sources are known at all. The online community, however, tends to engage in self-policing of content particularly in regard to the accuracy and balance of new media messages that are posted to mass recipients – a phenomenon that has been referred to as 'gatewatching'.[7]

Even in the online world, and despite its democratic goals as far as information production and reception are concerned, elite content providers emerge. Some bloggers, Facebook and Twitter users attract more followers than do others.[8] This is true regardless of whether the bloggers in question are specialists in political affairs or write about celebrity, fashion and lifestyle issues. Some bloggers can achieve an almost celebrity-like status if they command the regular attention of millions of followers. They may also come to dominate the setting of specific agendas among those followers on a scale that matches old-style mass communication. For some writers, this phenomenon has called into question whether the internet is a site of true democracy or has in fact been hijacked by dominant information providers and opinion leaders.[9]

The debate about whether digital democracy really exists has been further fuelled by the observation that most internet users are not political activists and their online consumption patterns tend to be dominated by content generated by the mainstream news media that also operate in online settings. In the United States, for example, some of the most widely-accessed political blogs have close links to traditional media organisations.[10] Even independent bloggers depend heavily on mainstream news media sources for their source materials.[11] Network analysis of communications links and information flows between different categories of websites in the UK revealed the dominance of the major news media as principal 'hubs' from which multiple other sites retrieve content. The presence of independent bloggers with this kind of hub status was rare.[12]

What is clear is that the 'new' media have reached a point of parity with the 'old' media (newspapers, magazines, radio and television) in some communities. Some confusion is caused by the migration of old media into new media environments where they actively cross-promote between their 'old' and 'new' media outputs.[13] Nevertheless, the gatekeeping controls that the old media were able to exert over the flow of information have been diluted or can be circumvented by the many new media channels that now have mass reach. This is a significant development in non-democratic countries in which governments have traditionally exerted centralised control over the media and their outputs.

New media have given citizens of those countries opportunities to speak out on issues of their choosing and to reach large numbers of other people at home and abroad with their opinions and personal observations of events. These same new media channels also provide the citizens of non-democratic nations with opportunities to obtain news from uncensored sources and, hence, to absorb different news agendas from the ones promulgated by their own government-controlled media.[14] One term that has been coined to describe this process is the 'disintermediation' of the mainstream media. The digitalisation of interpersonal communication between private citizens has scaled up these communications from the highly localised to the highly public on a mass scale.[15]

Based on the previous discussion, there are several reasons for producing this book at this time. It has already been well documented that online social networking platforms played an active part in the different national uprisings collectively grouped under the 'Arab Spring' in 2011. Much has been written about these events in the Western world, but a variety of perspectives on their form and impact exist among scholars and commentators in the Arab world. The current volume represents a 'one-stop shop' collection of writings from within the Middle East and North Africa region.

Further, there has been an increased academic research focus on the growth and use of online social media in the GCC countries that have adopted a variety of theoretical and methodological perspectives.[16] This burgeoning body of work is also represented here. As social media use has become more widespread across the Arab world, not only as a toolkit for political activists but also as important communications devices for ordinary citizens in their regular professional and private lives, there is a growing need to understand their longer-term implications for Arab societies. This book aims to gather together the latest research evidence alongside what is also known from extensive research conducted in the West and to provide a fresh overview and critical analysis of the field. The contributing authors are all active experts in the field currently engaged in conducting their own research or analysis of the spread and impact of digital communications technology in the Arab world.

This book is different from other books in the market because it represents the first overview of its kind that covers the GCC region. As events continue to unfold in the Middle East that may lead to the redrawing of geo-political maps and radical changes in the ways in which some

Arab societies function, new media technologies remain centre stage. It is important, therefore, to consider not only what has already happened but what is likely to take place in the future and how social media use has evolved among specific user groups with their own vested political, religious, cultural, social and military agendas. More stable parts of the Arab world, such as the GCC, have closely observed the changes taking place in less stable areas and the mediating role that digital communications technologies have played. There is a need for a deeper understanding of the power of social media and of how the use of these platforms can and should be controlled for the greater good. This understanding must not grow out of prejudice or from anecdotal experience alone. It is best based on systematic and objective empirical inquiry and evidence. The status of such evidence and the establishment of an effective research agenda for the future are desperately needed. It is the aim of this book to facilitate this process.

As well as the preceding considerations, the evolution of social media has occurred alongside dramatic changes to the wider media landscape of the GCC region. Some of the latter changes have been catalysed by the adoption of social media by ordinary citizens who have begun to seek a broader news agenda than that provided by traditional government-controlled news media operations. News media in the GCC region, as in other parts of the world, have embraced social media as part of their news-gathering and delivery mechanisms.[17] This greater collusion between professional journalists and news consumers has changed traditional news delivery dynamics. The implications of such developments for the future of the GCC news media represent a further important feature of wider social changes in the region that needs to be better understood. This subject will also be covered by this edited collection.

Digital Expansion in the Arab World

The role played by digital media technologies and platforms in the events linked to the recent political upheavals in the Arab world should really come as no surprise. Investment in online infrastructures has advanced more rapidly in this region than anywhere else in the world.[18] Digital technology tracking showed that the annual rate of internet penetration growth in the MENA region between 2006 and 2011 (23 per cent) far outstripped the worldwide figure (14 per cent).[19]

Research among young people across the MENA region has shown that their involvement in the internet and other digital platforms, not least the blogosphere and social media, has led many to question traditional forms of governance, politics, economics and cultural values. Although they may not necessarily be seeking a complete overhaul of the rules according to which they live their lives, they do seek greater government transparency, more vibrant and open economies that provide more commodity choices, more job opportunities and a better standard of living, and better health-care and education. Many young people in the Arab world were found to believe that current education systems leave graduates ill-equipped for the job market. Many also seek to run their own businesses and want to be free to trade beyond local regions and national borders.[20]

It is not surprising that young people across the MENA region sought politico-economic change since, in 2011, when the events of the 'Arab Spring' first gathered force, more than one in four of those aged 15 to 24 years were unemployed.[21] In a survey of young adults aged 15 to 35 years in nine countries (Algeria, Bahrain, Egypt, Jordan, Kuwait, Lebanon, Qatar, Saudi Arabia and UAE), only around half were working.[22]

The importance of the internet to the news landscape of the Arab world is well known.[23] It is also an important and widely used medium of entertainment. In particular, YouTube has emerged as an extremely popular entertainment source. Around four in ten young adult internet users in the MENA region were found to be accessing this video site. The proportion of national internet users who watched YouTube videos every day in Saudi Arabia (42 per cent) and UAE (34 per cent) outstripped European countries such as France and the United Kingdom (15 per cent each) and Germany (12 per cent).[24]

The Growth of Social Media

Internet access underwent dramatic growth in the Arab world from 2005 onwards. At that time, penetration across MENA countries was just 13 per cent but by 2011 it had reached 40 per cent. By 2014, nearly half the people living in Middle East countries (48 per cent) had internet access, a growth rate of more than 3,300 per cent from the year 2000, placing it well ahead of the average for the rest of world (42 per cent). Gulf countries such as Bahrain (99 per cent), United Arab Emirates (96 per cent), Qatar (95 per cent), and Kuwait (93 per cent) had achieved near universal access, while others such as Oman (80 per cent) and Saudi Arabia (67 per cent) enjoyed widespread penetration.[25]

After the introduction to the region of Facebook and Twitter, both tools were adopted rapidly by political activists. By December 2012, there were 23.8 million Facebook users in the Middle East.[26] While many Arab social media users communicate in English, the introduction of an Arab interface for Facebook in 2009 boosted users of the site in the MENA region by 3.5 million over the next 12 months.[27] By 2014, there were 6.5 million users of Twitter in the Arab world, producing 10 million tweets a day. Saudi Arabia had a Twitter penetration of 33 per cent, the highest in the world.[28] Twitter was a popular tool for linking political activists to journalists in mainstream media. Six in ten Twitter users in the region were found to tweet in English to the media.[29]

The expansion of social networking has also been boosted by the growth in mobile broadband penetration across the Arab world. Mobile social networking, as we will see in Chapter 5 of this book, is growing rapidly around the world, but it has been promoted in particular in the MENA region by the enthusiastic adoption of smartphones and the growing young and increasingly literate population. Mobile broadband penetration in MENA in 2009 stood at just five per cent but was expected to reach 58 per cent by 2015.[30]

The use of online social media has varied between MENA countries. Usage tended to be less widespread in North African countries, with the exception of Egypt. While penetration in countries such as Libya, Morocco and Tunisia tended to lag behind that in the Gulf States, users there were still very active.[31] Egypt, however, led the way in terms of activating online social media as a political tool. This phenomenon was no doubt driven by the high proportion of young people in Egypt – where the median age is 24 – and the higher level of unemployment among them. The prospect of being unable to find employment, coupled with a high level of computer ownership among Egyptian youth, created a social cocktail that promoted their political activism.

In Egypt, Facebook emerged as the tool of preference for online political activism, with four million users by the end of 2010. Activists readily attracted tens of thousands of followers to their Facebook sites, sometimes within days of their launch. Combining Facebook with Twitter, Egyptian activists were able to communicate quickly with one another, disseminate messages to large numbers of remote supporters to organise events, and reach out to people and the media beyond their national borders. Blogging and micro-blogging across the region displayed signs of widespread discontent among young people in Arab nations, but in Egypt there were also clear signs that they were actually seeking to orchestrate a change of government. Arab bloggers were more likely to criticise than praise their own leaders. This did not necessarily mean they wanted leaders like those in the West. Analysis of message contents revealed that they were also often just as critical of foreign leaders. There was widespread support for Palestine, but equally widespread criticism of terrorism.[32]

Not all blogging in the period running up to the 'Arab Spring' sought the overthrow of existing national governments. There were clear early rumblings of discontent with current leaders in the Egyptian blogosphere well before 2011, but in countries such as Bahrain and Kuwait bloggers engaged with political debates, particularly around election times, without wishing to instigate wholesale change in the existing political system.[33]

The Applications of Social Media

Leaving aside the direct wishes of young people for political, economic and social change, there has been a more subtle undercurrent of influence flowing from young people's use of social media. Young Arabs do not need to state openly that they want more social and cultural freedom: their behaviour online provides clear demonstrations that they are already acting differently and moving away from traditional social relationships or are at least supplementing these relationships with new ones that operate quite differently.

The events of the 'Arab Spring' focused the world's attention on the use of social media by political activists. To assume that this is principally where the interest in online social networking lies in this region gives rise to a misleading impression of the much wider scope of internet adoption, especially by young Arabs. There is a political dimension to social media activity, but this centres as much on the use of online tools to promote civic engagement and political participation as on the overthrow of governments. It is true that, during the first three months of 2011, there was a dramatic surge in Facebook and Twitter traffic in the Arab world. This occurred as these sites were used to organise the mobilisation of people in support of anti- and pro-government civil protests and the dissemination of information about these events throughout local communities and to the wider world.[34]

Undoubtedly, sites such as Facebook and Twitter served as valuable tools that enabled a more regular flow of uncensored information about events taking place in countries such as Egypt and Tunisia in 2011 and also facilitated the organisation of geographically dispersed activists in ways that would not have been possible otherwise. Yet, the adoption of social media pre-dated these events and has continued since their occurrence, driven by a wider span of important political, economic, social and cultural applications. The internet and, more specifically, online social media have played a range of increasingly important social and business roles that have significant economic and cultural implications for the region.[35]

Research with young Arabs across the MENA region has shown that their adoption of digital media has changed the way they interact with one another and with their families.[36] The use of online technologies has become more tightly integrated into the everyday lives of young people in the Arab world, and as a result changes have occurred in the way they interact with family members. There is more use of online social media to communicate with family and friends. This does not mean that face-to-face contact has been lost, but there are clear signs that, for significant and growing minorities of young people in this region, remote contact has replaced some direct physical contact. Perhaps of even greater significance, in terms of the potential cultural impact of social media, is that larger proportions of young Arab women than of young Arab men have made reference to the use of online and mobile communications to maintain contact with family and friends. However, there remain some reluctant users of social media who readily admit they only take part because their friends do and who believe that the world will not be enhanced if people resort primarily to remote communications with others who are close to them.[37]

Taking the online social relationships further, there have been interesting and potentially important cultural shifts in the acceptance of the internet as a means of finding a spouse. Traditionally, in the Arab world, marriage and the discovery of marriage partners follow strict religiously-underpinned cultural rules. These rules differ for men and women. Families tend to be closely involved in the selection process and approval of marriage partnerships. Yet, the emergence and widespread popularity of online dating in the West has also reached the Arab world. Even highly conservative Arab societies such as Saudi Arabia have accepted the use of specialist internet sites for the search for and discovery of marriage partners.[38] Public opinion among young Arabs across North Africa and in Jordan and Lebanon found that over half (55 per cent) felt it was acceptable for a woman to search for a husband online, with a substantial minority (41 per cent) in the GCC states in agreement.[39]

The same survey found that a clear majority of young Arabs (between two in three and three in four) across MENA countries felt that, far from being a threat to traditional cultural and religious beliefs, the internet represented a site through which they could get closer to their religion, increase their knowledge of it and strengthen their beliefs.[40] In spite of the role played by the internet in the political uprisings in the Arab world, it was widely regarded by young Arabs as a tool for enhancing political transparency. Rather than being used simply to overthrow unpopular governments, the internet could be used as a channel through which a country's government and, most especially, its leaders could reach out to their citizens. Following the example of the West, government services could increasingly be rolled out online. This electronic or 'e'-governance might enable people to feel more engaged with government processes.[41]

Social media provide distinctive new social experiences, but in the Arab context these have been found to still have close links to everyday social interactions and relationships. At the same time, there is a sense, particularly among young people, that social media can also bring about social, economic and, possibly, political change. In a survey of internet users in Bahrain, Egypt, Jordan, Kuwait, Lebanon, Oman, Saudi Arabia and UAE, evidence emerged that social media were perceived by significant minorities of people as having the ability to empower them to influence change in their community. More than four in ten respondents agreed with this point of view in six out of the eight sampled countries in this study. The two exceptions in which endorsement was lower were UAE (33 per cent) and Saudi Arabia (32 per cent).

Perhaps another factor that shaped this perception of the potential for change through social media was the further observation, endorsed by between 47 and 65 per cent in these eight countries, that Arab internet users felt more open to tolerating different points of view. While this openness to other belief systems might be regarded by conservatives as a threat, this is clearly not the sense in which it is meant by most Arab internet users. The same survey of online adopters from eight Arab countries found that significant majorities (between 66 per cent and 85 per cent) claimed that using social media strengthened their sense of national identity and made them feel that they had stronger links to their fellow citizens.[42]

In the aftermath of the 'Arab Spring', social media use has continued to rise in the Arab world; this has not been driven by continued political activism but has arisen from the array of other applications that have been adopted. Social media continued to be regarded as having a role to play in domestic politics, especially in the context of promoting wider civic engagement.[43] Social media have also been acknowledged as agencies for social change driven by more open discussion of opinions and ideas in which everyone can get involved. Online social discourses can both reinforce existing national, religious and social identities and introduce alternative identities. In this setting, it is more likely that any social and cultural changes flowing from such discourses will be evolutionary rather than revolutionary.

New Media and the Spread of Unrest

What part did 'new' media play in the Arab uprisings that began in 2011? There is much anecdotal evidence that political activists benefited hugely from blogging and micro-blogging tools and social networking sites such as Facebook. It has even been claimed that, without these tools, the uprisings would not have taken place at the pace they did and in some instances might not have been possible at all. More reflective analyses have acknowledged that blogs and social media played some part in the mobilisation of large-scale support for political uprisings, particularly in places such as Egypt.[44]

Evidence also emerged that localised activism on the ground also depended on more direct face-to-face communications as well as online mediated social networks.[45] Online networks were useful for the sharing of intelligence both to inform debates and to guide the planning of events on the ground.[46] When protestors on the ground in Cairo were questioned about why they were there and how they found out where to go, only a few mentioned Twitter, whereas virtually all referred to news reports in mainstream media and direct interpersonal communication with people they knew.[47]

A further important role played by social media in the context of the Arab uprisings was their provision of channels for communication of news to audiences outside the region. The significance of these events had often been played down by the local media, but the unfettered reports of 'citizen' journalists via blogs, micro-blogs and social media posts, which often included a mixture of spoken and written reports supplemented by video images, presented alternative perspectives on the fast-moving events to an increasingly interested international audience.[48]

An analysis of users of Twitter feeds during uprisings in Tunisia, Egypt, Libya and Bahrain found that information consumers were predominantly (Libya – 92 per cent; Tunisia – 86 per cent, Egypt – 76 per cent and Bahrain – 62 per cent) from outside the countries in which these events took place. The proportions of users inside these countries were small (14 per cent in Egypt; seven per cent in Tunisia and Bahrain, and virtually zero in Libya). The proportions of information consumers across the remainder of the Arab region tended to be smaller than those within the national boundaries of the political uprisings, except in the case of Bahrain (31 per cent). The researchers here concluded that there was little evidence that Twitter was a major factor in driving the political uprisings.[49]

Despite the growing presence of bloggers in Tunisia, there were few advance signs of disquiet among the people. If anything, Tunisia was a somewhat unexpected site for the initiation of the political unrest that spread rapidly across the MENA region from 2011. It was activists in Egypt who were the first to learn from the unexpected fall of the Tunisian government. The size and status of Egypt in the Arab world meant that it represented an important tipping point that encouraged others to follow suit. Within weeks, the overthrow of President Mubarak triggered other waves of popular protest against authoritarian regimes in Bahrain, Libya and Yemen, while even in other Arab countries that were known to have more open governments, such as Jordan and Morocco, people still sought political reforms.

The adoption of online communications technology facilitated these orchestrated demands for political change by enabling activists to link up with one another more quickly and on a larger scale than ever before. There was also a generational factor at play here. The most dissatisfied citizens were young people, who sought more economic and social opportunities that could only be achieved through changes to the existing political systems. These same young people were also the most enthusiastic early adopters of the internet and its communications systems.

Moreover, in countries where free speech was suppressed, the blogosphere and online social networks provided open platforms for the exchange of views that were difficult for governments to control. These sites also provided channels of largely uncontrolled communication with the outside world. This meant that online activists could communicate to the rest of the world what they were doing, and what their government was doing to them in return, without being curtailed by government-imposed censorship. Such tools have proven invaluable to those who seek to promote free speech.[50]

While there is evidence that the rapid spread of political unrest across the Arab world from 2011 had links with the use of internet-related tools such as blogging, micro-blogging and social media sites, there is further evidence that the internet and online social media had spread rapidly in popularity in the MENA region some years earlier and also that these communications channels have been adopted in service of a wide range of applications, especially for young people in this part of the world. Their apparent role in supporting the orchestration of political unrest does not define the significance of social media in Arab countries for everyday users.

At the time of the first political uprisings in North Africa, research among young people in nine MENA countries (one of which was Egypt) found that significant proportions of young people aged 35 and under sought greater freedom to choose their own direction in life. Two thirds of young people (68 per cent) questioned in Algeria and Egypt endorsed the view that 'I should be able to do what I want so long as it does not affect other people'. Clear majorities of young adults in Jordan and Lebanon (65 per cent) and across Bahrain, Kuwait, Qatar, Saudi Arabia and UAE (61 per cent) endorsed the same point of view. At the same time, far fewer in these three parts of the Arab world (47 per cent, 45 per cent and 29 per cent respectively) believed that they 'could express [their] opinion without fear of the consequences'.[51]

Varied Pace of Change across the Region

The MENA region has the distinction of being populated by Arab peoples, but there the similarities often end. Arab countries across the MENA have substantial differences in their populations, strengths of their economies, political stability (or instability), physical infrastructures and social systems. There are also variances between Arab nations in the availability and adoption of broadband internet and social media. In some instances these differences are substantial. Within countries that have widely adopted the internet and its different applications can be found age and gender divides in online behaviour. If digital media are to play a part in enhancing the political and economic stability of the region, it is essential that they be available to and used by all. The 'digital divide' that was found at the turn of the twenty-first century in early Western digital communities, explained by national differences in relevant infrastructures that were in turn underpinned by the nature of the politico-economic systems in place,[52] can still be found in the Arab world.

Among the Middle East Arab nations in mid-2014, all but four had internet penetration levels of 80 per cent or higher. The Gulf States enjoyed the highest penetration rates of all. The exceptions were Palestine (West Bank) (62 per cent), Syria (26 per cent), Yemen (20 per cent) and Iraq (9 per cent). The North African Arab nations generally had much lower internet penetration rates: Morocco (61 per cent), Egypt (53 per cent), Tunisia (46 per cent), Libya (22 per cent), and Algeria (17 per cent).[53]

By mid-2012, there were 45.2 million Facebook users in the Arab world. This was a threefold increase from two years earlier. Facebook penetration was highest in Jordan (39.1 per cent), Lebanon (38.4 per cent),

UAE (37.3 per cent), Palestine – West Bank (35.4 per cent) and Qatar (31.6 per cent). Penetration exceeded one in five of the population in Kuwait and Saudi Arabia. Other countries in the Middle East (Yemen – 1.9 per cent, Bahrain – 3.1 per cent and Iraq – 7.8 per cent) had much lower Facebook penetration rates. In North Africa, the highest Facebook penetration was found in Tunisia (30.4 per cent), whereas the other Arab countries in the region had much lower rates of penetration ranging from 10 to 15 per cent.[54]

The internet has been most enthusiastically adopted in the Arab world by young people. This has also been true of the adoption of social media sites. Facebook in the Arab world is a young person's environment, with seven out of ten users being aged between 15 and 29.[55] The adoption of social media by young Arabs has been regarded as an enabler of political empowerment of youth. Regardless of whether the use of social media was the primary driver of the 'Arab Spring' – and, as we have seen, there has been disagreement on this point – there is a perception among young Arabs that online social networks have enabled them to become politically engaged and to be heard.[56]

As well as empowering youth, there has been further debate about whether social media in the Arab world have empowered women. Two thirds of Arab Facebook users were male and one third were female. This compared with a 50:50 split across most of the rest of the world. Yet, the changes to political and social systems that have occurred in different parts of the Arab world have been characterised in part by increasing efforts to eradicate the oppression of women.[57] The impetus for a shift in cultural and social values relating to women derived in part from the prominent roles played by female activists in the events of the 'Arab Spring', as we see in Chapter 7 of this book. Despite the promise shown by their recent participation in political activism, women still lag far behind men in the Arab world as users of sites such as Facebook.

Even so, Arab men and women often agree about the way social media sites should be used by women. There is growing recognition that social media can play an important role in the empowerment of women, perhaps by creating a platform on which they can perform equally. In an analysis of the reasons why Arab women lag so far behind their fellow women in other parts of the world, public opinion has identified, as explanations, women's lack of relevant information technology skills, lack of confidence online, and the relative absence of content that is relevant to them. However, outweighing all of these rationales is the perception that cultural and societal stereotypes actively discourage women from going online, often enforced within the family.[58]

The Book

This book is divided into eleven chapters. Chapter 2, by Shubhada Chaudhary, examines the role of social media as a decisive actor in Saudi Arabia and the impediments to political transition within the region due to the existence of neo-patrimonial state structures and dogmatic social contracts. It discusses how social media, as a decisive factor, have played an integral role in confronting the egregious dominations within these rentier state economies in spite of the failure of inter-subjective and cognitive theorising of their function. The chapter also investigates the gaps that exist in the understanding of the theories of modernity, resource mobilisation, network societies and their relationships with conceptual knowledge of GCC societies that make it impossible to situate social media in their contextualisation. There are questions about what led to the emergence of social media, their engagement with interpersonal communication and the evolution of multi-generational political dialogue, and how social media have been caught in the dichotomy of techno-realists and digital evangelists, thereby reducing their essence to technological determinism and cultural exceptionalism. In order to defend the arguments made, very specific examples from the context of Bahrain are incorporated. The comparative scenario-building process contrasts the situation in Bahrain with the non-GCC state of Syria to differentiate how the same stimulus in social media caused different results.

Chapter 3 by Omair Anas examines social media use in the Arab world after the 'Arab Spring' and the implications of a cyber-public-sphere for GCC public opinion with the emergence of Arab social media in the region. The chapter also highlights the importance of social media and their challenges in the GCC region by discussing whether an Arab online public sphere has the dynamics of a Western online public sphere.

Chapter 4 by Marc Owen Jones examines social media and the unethical peer-to-peer (P2P) diplomacy in the Bahrain uprising of 2011. The chapter presents an overview of the ethical P2P diplomacy that has been undermined by the intimidation, incarceration and killing of those citizens more likely to advocate the promotion of social justice and Global Public Goods (GPG). This chapter analyses how the local government attempts to improve the image of the country through propaganda, psychological operations, information intervention and strategic public diplomacy, posing questions for the ethical act of diplomacy that involves the encouragement and upholding of GPG. Jones argues that many of the democratic challenges to a strategic ally away from the public gaze have been played out on social media, which has demonstrated another front to P2P diplomacy. Without meaningful pressure from outside powers such as the US with regard to the exchange of GPG, Bahrain will have little incentive to radically alter its diplomatic strategy.

Chapter 5 by Abdul-Karim Ziani and Mokhtar Elareshi reports a study of mobile phone and internet use by young Arabs in the GCC region. It examines how GCC university students obtain local news and information about their communities using mobile devices. With the expansion of mobile phone penetration in the region, some evidence has emerged that the mobile phone is being used as a local news reception device. The chapter attempts a systematic analysis of this phenomenon. It presents new data from a young, well-educated population drawn from across the GCC region on their news interests and consumption habits and the sources to which they now turn for their information.

Chapter 6 by David W. Bulla and James Buie addresses the use of social media by political dissidents, bloggers, satirists and videographer bystanders to crime, and the serious legal problems they have encountered, including prison sentences and a social media usage policy proposed by the federal government. The chapter also examines the UAE's cybercrime law, as well as the broad definition of defamation, and how these laws have been applied in specific cases. This chapter investigates how stakeholders perceive the function of social media in UAE society, including young people and communication professionals. This chapter therefore examines how different groups use social media and how they see them in terms of their potential and their overall usefulness as they negotiate their lives in Emirati society.

Chapter 7 by Fatima AlSalem examines Kuwait's political system and the appropriation of social media by female online users by looking at the influence of the technological revolution on the Kuwaiti political and social structures. The chapter explores the backdrop of active political life in Kuwait, which is appropriate for investigating the dynamic of social media effects, especially Twitter. There is, however, a dearth of data on the relationship between social media use and women's political participation in Kuwait online and offline, the factors that influence women's online political participation, and how social and political systems affect the way in which social media are used in the Gulf region, especially the effects on marginalised groups such as women and youth, and the roles of social media in such events. This chapter is designed to shed new light on these matters.

Chapter 8 by Khalid Al-Jaber and Mokhtar Elareshi examines the findings from two surveys of three GCC countries' respondents' perceptions of consumption patterns of new media sources in 2009 and 2013 to understand the extent to which Arab audiences have taken up an expanded and more diverse supply of news through specific channels such as satellite TV and social media. What is the significance of online social network sites as 'news sources' and communications channels for ordinary people? What role can and do they play as part of a set of information-gathering channels for consumers? How have these platforms been used to produce and present their own 'perspective'? How important are they as information sources for mainstream media and as platforms for mainstream media to disseminate their 'information'? The chapter seeks to provide a more recent comparative analysis of social media use and other traditional consumption habits in three GCC countries in an attempt to provide more details on the Gulf region, its audiences and its media.

Chapter 9 by Marc Owen Jones examines social media, surveillance and spying in the 2011 Bahrain uprising. This chapter argues that, using the aforementioned methods, government agents and government supporters alike have been able to preserve the status quo by extending the means by which they conduct surveillance. Such methods are attempts to impose normative forms of behaviour in spaces that allow the performance of identities that challenge the hegemonic order. The political regime has been challenged and changed as citizens, including Shi'i people, have acquired greater freedom to express their views, especially through online formats. The capacity of social media to function as a space of resistance did not go uncontested in Bahrain, and hegemonic forces also used it to enhance and 'mobilise identities to facilitate the extraction of resources from the society to confront the external (and in Bahrain's case, internal) threat'. Thus, while social media allow activists to 'overcome the powerlessness of their solitary despair… and fight the powers that be by identifying the networks that are', they also allow hegemonic forces to resist change. For the regime, these are all spaces of crisis, transformation and change or heterotopias. Social media are no different and can also be regulated and controlled. As the struggle for democracy continues in urban space, so it does in cyberspace. In many ways, the battle is *for* cyberspace, for it is a battle between the principles of empowerment and control, the continuation of which underlines the argument that social media are a tool of both emancipation and repression.

Chapter 10 by Samah Ahmed looks at how the role of social media in political discourse in the Gulf region has been widely reported on across the media and by academics in a vast array of studies highlighting the evolution of internet consumption in the GCC and the wider Middle East. The GCC online community is clearly becoming increasingly politicised. In this chapter, Ahmed argues that many people, frustrated by the lack of political debate in traditional media, are going online to voice their issues and concerns. People's transition to social media as a 'news source' is driven by their preference for eyewitness accounts of news and citizen journalism-reports from people via Twitter, Facebook updates, Flickr photographs, and other real-time updates to their own networks. The increasing use of social media by news producers themselves suggests that those who make the news as well as those who consume it want less intermediary and more direct access. While social media have no doubt played a significant role in anti-government movements and politics in parts of the GCC, such as Bahrain where online forums and blogs have been utilised extensively for nearly a decade, it will require more than social media alone to put the concept of democracy into practice.

Finally, in Chapter 11 Mokhtar Elareshi and Barrie Gunter draw together what has been learned from the analyses provided in the earlier chapters of the book. Elareshi and Gunter look at the development of social media in the MENA and Arab world during the recent Arab uprisings of 2011 and consider the potential future of social media in the region.

Notes

1 Barrie Gunter, *Television versus the Internet: Will TV Prosper or Perish as the World Moves Online?* (Oxford: Chandos Publishing, 2010); El Mustapha Lahlali, 'Arab Media Discourse: Breaking Taboos', *International Journal of Afro-Asiatic Studies*, 13 (2011), 157–166; Alfred Hermida, Seth C. Lewis and Rodrigo Zamith, 'Sourcing the Arab Spring: A Case Study of Andy Carvin's Sources on Twitter during the Tunisian and Egyptian Revolutions', *Journal of Computer-Mediated Communication*, 19 (2014), 479–499.

2 Fadi Salem and Racha Mourtade, 'Citizen Engagement and Public Services in the Arab World; The Potential of Social Media', *Arab Social Media Report*, 2014 <http://www.mbrsg.ae/getattachment/e9ea2ac8-13dd-4cd7-9104-b8f1f405cab3/Citizen-Engagement-and-Public-Services-in-the-Arab.aspx>; Fadi Salem, Racha Mourtade and Sara Alshaer, 'Transforming Education in the Arab World: Breaking Barriers in the Age of Social Learning', *Arab Social Media Report*, 2013 <http://www.arabsocialmediareport.com/UserManagement/PDF/ASMR_5_Report_Final.pdf>.

3 Courtney Radsch, 'Blogosphere and Social Media', in *Seismic Shift: Understanding change in the Middle East* (Washington, DC: The Henry L. Stimson Center, 2011), pp. 67–83.

4 Sean Aday and others, 'Watching from Afar: Media Consumption Patterns around the Arab Spring', *American Behavioral Scientist*, XX (2013), 1–21 <doi:10.1177/0002764213479373>.

5 Mokhtar Elareshi and Barrie Gunter, 'News Consumption among Young Libyan Adults: Are New Satellite TV News Services Displacing Local TV News', *Arab Media & Society*, 2010.

6 Pamela Shoemaker and Stephen Reese, *Mediating the Message* (White Plains, NY: Longman, 1996).

7 Axel Bruns, 'Gatewatching, Not Gatekeeping: Collaborative Online News', *Media International Australia Incorporating Culture and Policy: Quarterly Journal of Media Research and Resources*, 2003, 31–44; Axel Bruns, *Gatewatching: Collaborative Online News Production* (New York, NY: Peter Lang, 2005).

8 Eric Lawrence, John Sides and Henry Farrell, 'Self-Segregation or Deliberation? Blog Readership, Participation, and Polarization in American Politics', *Perspectives on Politics*, 8 (2010), 141–157; Shaomei Wu and others, 'Who Says What to Whom on Twitter', in *Paper present at the 20th International Conference on World Wide Web* (New York, NY: ACM, 2011), pp. 705–714.

9 Matthew Hindman, *The Myth of Digital Democracy* (Princeton, NY: Princeton University Press, 2010).

10 Mark Leccese, 'Online Information Sources of Political Blogs', *Journalism and Mass Communication Quarterly*, 86 (2009), 578–593; Mark Tremayne and others, 'Issue Publics on the Web: Applying Network Theory to the War Blogosphere', *Journal of Computer-Mediated Communication*, 12 (2006), 290–310.

11 Linda Kenix, 'Blogs as Alternative', *Journal of Computer-Mediated Communication*, 14 (2009), 790–822; D Travers Scott, 'Pundits in Muckrakers' Clothing: Political Blogs and the 2004 US Presidential Election', in *Blogging, Citizenship and the Future of Media*, ed. by Mark Tremayne (New York, NY: Routledge, 2007), pp. 39–57.

12 Barrie Gunter and others, 'Blogs, News and Credibility', *Aslib Proceedings*, 61 (2009), 185–204.

13 Mokhtar Elareshi, *News Consumption in Libya: A Study of University Students* (Newcastle: Cambridge Scholars Publishing, 2013); Hindman.

14 Sharon Meraz, 'Is There an Elite Hold? Traditional Media to Social Media Agenda Setting Influence in Blog Networks', *Journal of Computer-Mediated Communication*, 14 (2009), 682–707.

15 Manuel Castells, 'Communication, Power and Counter-Power in the Network Society', *International Journal of Communication*, 2007, 238–266; Manuel Castells, *Communication Power* (New York, NY: Oxford University Press, 2009).

16 Some of the current chapters were conference papers that were presented at the 5th Gulf Research Meeting at the University of Cambridge. See, for example, Hermida, Lewis and Zamith; Everette Dennis, Justin Martin and Robb Wood, 'Media Use in the Middle East: An Eight-Nation Survey', 2013 <http://mena-mediasurvey.northwestern.edu/>; Racha Mourtada and Fadi Salem, 'Social Media, Employment and Entrepreneurship: New Frontiers for the Economic Empowerment of Arab Youth?', *Arab Social Media Report*, 2012 <http://www.dsg.ae/en/publication/Description.aspx?PubID=307&PrimenuID=11&mnu=Pri>; Salem and Mourtade; Jeffrey Ghannam, *Social Media in the Arab World: Leading up to the Uprisings of 2011* (Washington, DC: Center for International Media Assistance, 2011).

17 Khalid Al-Jaber and Barrie Gunter, 'Evolving News Systems in the Gulf Countries', in *News Media in the Arab World: A Study of 10 Arab and Muslim Countries*, ed. by Barrie Gunter and Roger Dickinson (New York, NY: Bloomsbury, 2013), pp. 21–40; Khalid Al-Jaber and Barrie Gunter, 'News Developments and Changes to News Consumption Patterns in the Arab World', in *News Media in the Arab World: A Study of 10 Arab and Muslim Countries*, ed. by Barrie Gunter and Roger Dickinson (New York, NY: Bloomsbury, 2013), pp. 135–152.

18 United Nations, 'E-Government Survey 2012: E-Government for the People', *UnitedNations*,2012<www.unpan1.un.org/intradoc/groups/public/documents/un/unpan048065>.

19 Jeffery Cole and others, 'World Internet Project: International Report', 2012 <www.digitalcenter.org/wp-content/uploads/2013/01/2012wip_report4th_ed>.

20 Karim Sabbagh and others, *Understanding the Arab Digital Generation* (Dubai: Booz & Company and Google, 2012).

21 Ibid.

22 Ibid.

23 Barrie Gunter and Roger Dickinson, 'The Changing Nature of News and the Arab World', in *News Media in the Arab World: A Study of 10 Arab and Muslim Countries*, ed. by Barrie Gunter and Roger Dickinson (New York: Bloomsbury, 2013), pp. 1–20.

24 Sabbagh and others.

25 Internet World Stats, 'Internet World Stats, Usage Population and Statistics', *Miniwatts Marketing Group*, 2014 <www.internetworldstats.com>.

26 Internet World Stats.

27 Grail Research, 'Mobile Social Networking in MENA: Opportunities and Implications', *Grail Research*, 2012 <http://www.integreon.com/pdf/Blog/Grail-Research-Mobile-Social-Networking-in-MENA_237.pdf>.

28 Karine Jazra, '15 Stats about Social Media in the Middle East That You Need to Know', *Social4ce*, 2014 <www.social4ce/blog/2014/07/01/15-stats-about-social-media-in-the-middle-east-that-you-need-to-know>.

29 International Labour Organisation, *Global Employment Trends* (Geneva, Switzerland: ILO, 2008).

30 Grail Research.

31 Radsch.

32 Bruce Etling and others, 'Mapping the Arab Blogosphere: Politics, Culture and Dissent', *Research Publication No. 2009-06* (Cambridge, MA: Harvard University, 2009) <www.cyber.law.harvard.edu/cyber.law.harvard.edu/files/Mapping_the_Arab_Blogosphere>.

33 Global Voices Online, 'Kuwait Bloggers to Play Leading Role in Elections', 2008 <www.globalvoicesonline.org/2008/04/02/kuwait-bloggers-to-play-leading-role-in-elections>.

34 Fadi Salem and Racha Mourtada, 'Civil Movements: The Impact of Facebook and Twitter', *Arab Social Media Report*, 2011 <www.unpan1.un.org/intradoc/groups/public/documents/dsg/unpan05080>.

35 Salem and Mourtada, 'Civil Movements: The Impact of Facebook and Twitter.'

36 Dennis, Martin and Wood.

37 Sabbagh and others.

38 Several sites have been launched for dating and marriage services such as singlemuslim.com and Saudi Arabia Dating.

39 Ibid.

40 Ibid.

41 Bahjat El-Dawicke, Milind Singh and Sandeep Ganediwala, 'Digitization and Prosperity', *Strategy+ Business*, 2012 <www.strategy-business.com/article/00127?gko=efe69&cid=20120904enews>.

42 Salem and Mourtada, 'Civil Movements: The Impact of Facebook and Twitter.'

43 Ibid.

44 Nahed Eltantawy and Julie Wiest, 'Social Media in the Egyptian Revolution: Reconsidering Resource Mobilization Theory', *International Journal of Communication*, 2011, 1207–1224; Eike Rinke and Maria Roder, 'Media Ecologies, Communication Culture, and Temporal-Spatial Unfolding: Three Components in a Communication Model of the Egyptian Regime Change', *International Journal of Communication*, 2011, 1273–1285.

45 Victoria Newsom, Lara Lengel and Catherine Cassara, 'Local Knowledge and the Revolutions: A Framework for Social Media Information Flow', *International Journal of Communication*, 2011, 1303–1312.

46 Eltantawy and Wiest; Melisssa Wall and Sahar El Zahed, '"I'll Be Waiting for You Guys": A YouTube Call to Action in the Egyptian Revolution', *International Journal of Communication*, 2011, 1333–1343.

47 Christopher Wilson and Alexandra Dunn, 'Digital Media in the Egyptian Revolution: Descriptive Analysis from Tahrir Data Sets', *International Journal of Communication*, 2011, 1248–1272.

48 Habibul Khondker, 'Role of the New Media in the Arab Spring', *Globalisations*, 8 (2011), 675–679; Gilad Lotan and others, 'The Revolutions Were Tweeted: Information Flows during the 2011 Tunisian and Egyptian Revolutions', *International Journal of Communication*, 2011, 1375–1405; Marc Lynch, 'Political Science and the New Arab Public Spheres', *Institute for public knowledge*, 2012 <http://publicsphere.ssrc.org/lynch-political-science-and-the-new-arab-public-sphere/>.

49 Aday and others.

50 Dan Gillmor, *We the Media: Grassroots Journalism by the People, for the People* (O'Reilly Media, 2006).

51 Sabbagh and others.

52 Pippa Norris, *Digital Divide: Civic Engagement, Information Poverty, and the Internet Worldwide* (Cambridge, UK: Cambridge University Press, 2001).

53 Internet World Stats.

54 Ibid.

55 Fadi Salem and Racha Mourtada, 'Social Media in the Arab World: Influencing Societal and Cultural Change', *Arab Social Media Report*, 2012 <www.arabsocialmediareport.com/userManagement/PDFD/ASMR 4 updated 29 08 12>.

56 Ibid.

57 Ibid.

58 Ibid.

2

The Role of Social Media as a Decisive Actor in Saudi Arabia

Shubhada Chaudhary

The Arab uprisings continue to have a long-lasting and unfolding impact on the politics of the Arab world countries, especially Saudi Arabia. The emergence of social media which created political upheaval in countries such as Egypt, Tunisia and Libya had a limited impact in the context of Saudi Arabia. This chapter discusses this anomaly in three concrete steps. First, it reveals the fundamentals of the neo-patrimonial set-up in Saudi Arabia, its functioning, and its impact in creating a coherent political culture, and eventually predicts the case scenarios that may cause rupture in the state's machinery in the coming decades. Secondly, it looks at the role of social media in Saudi Arabia and the political and cultural maturity of the Saudis, examining how the use of social media reflects public opinion in this oil monarchy, if at all. Thirdly, after understanding the reasons for the failure of social media to pose a threat to the House of Saud, the chapter attempts to bridge the gap between democratisation and use of social media in Saudi Arabia with reference to Alexander Wendt's social theory of international politics.

Pro-Democracy Protests in Saudi Arabia: Defining the 'Arab Street'

Incessant scholarly debates on the phrase 'democratisation of the Arab world' are not an impulsive and topical product of Arab uprisings. In fact, it was the newly-launched Qatar-based Al-Jazeera channel in 1996 that first coined this phrase, thereby targeting the authoritarian regimes in West Asia.[1] Thus, it must be noted that the need for democracy had been felt long before the Arab uprisings took place. Nonetheless, the outburst of pro-democracy uprisings in the Arab world added a new momentum to how the world envisaged the power of people, language and violence.

The self-immolation of Mohammad Bouzazi in December 2010 did indeed send shock waves across West Asia. A mere act, which usually went unnoticed, especially in rural districts and towns, suddenly had the power to galvanise people. Meanwhile, the emergence of social media, which provided a platform for representation and the voicing of one's opinion in the virtual online sphere without restrictions, also simultaneously reduced the power of authenticity and credibility of traditional Arab media channels that, over time, had come to resemble propaganda tools. Thus, the leverage of the antipodal existence of social media was further triggered, as people believed these media had bestowed on them virtual platforms to engage in and process their long-tapped catharsis. Simultaneously, it also started the debate, questioning whether or not social media played a pivotal role in causing the 2011 Arab uprisings and, if so, why certain countries such as the Kingdom of Saudi Arabia were untouched by their influence. Taking these trajectories into consideration, this chapter introduces a new lens for understanding these pro-democracy protests, their impact and the role of social media in the context of Saudi Arabia by using Alexander Wendt's social theory of international politics.

Social media transformed the passive vision of defining 'Arab Street' from the prevalent neo-orientalist perspective that had tried to deprive the Arab world of a more focused term such as 'Arab public sphere' or 'Arab public opinion'. With the sprouting of social media, the 'Arab Street' no longer denoted an 'abnormal mindset'. Rather, it revealed the opinions of dissent, voiced in a coherent manner by the citizens of the Arab world, who had their own identities and interests. Additionally, they demanded concrete changes in the political governance of their respective countries and mobilised well-organised protests to vent their emotions, demands and challenges.

It further validated the perspective that political attitudes in the West Asian context are often hidden from Western view not merely through the existing barriers of language but also through metaphors that betray prevalent stereotypes rather than reveal reality.[2] Such a nomenclature with a jaundiced point of view starting from the very embryonic definition of Arab society was eventually also involved in the context of democracy in this region.

Thus, the pro-democracy uprisings and how social media portrayed them revealed another process – the simultaneous struggle which continued in the theoretical analysis of the progress of democracy in such governance systems, which for decades had been considered incompatible with Western liberal values. Autocratic rule within countries such as Saudi Arabia in the Gulf region stems from several factors such as the integral role of the state in the economy, the restrictions imposed on the freedom of the population in return for promised prosperity, and the catalysed action taken by Western powers to prefer stability over democracy.[3] This is reflected in the integration of dogmatic social contracts and neo-patrimonial state structures that hinder the very questioning of the lack of political transition in Saudi Arabia. Moreover, the survival strategies of the ruling elites in this oil monarchy sustained them because the protests failed to be homogenous, indigenous and constant.[4] A slight furore had also been created in the mid-1980s when international oil prices seemed likely to collapse. Industrial growth based on import substitution had started to reveal its deep-seated fractures. But the authoritarian state machinery of Saudi Arabia witnessed and overcame it.

Due to the type of social contract being practised, the rentier-state model eventually started to handicap the very freedom of speech and expression of common individuals in Saudi Arabia. Nevertheless, from the beginning of the 1990s, Saudi Arabia witnessed political activities that, although not directly questioning the Islamic foundation of the royal family, did call for changes in the way the Kingdom was being governed.[5] But the House of Saud continued to control public order by countering dissent, challenges and any questioning of its authority. In the same way, the violence and chaos – often unreported – merely led to a stricter grip by the oil monarchy. To bring a cultural twist to this entire paradigm, Islam was declared to be incompatible with democracy even though no substantial quantitative analysis and empirical research had been conducted in this matter. In the wake of the 2011 Arab uprisings, it was still uncertain whether the theories of democratisation that preached causal outcomes of development and modernity were now becoming increasingly uniform or whether the utopian optimism of these pro-democracy uprisings was a mere mirage and not a 'new kind of newness'.[6] Hence, was the 'white man's burden' now ready to be shed or was a new occidental perspective of democratisation and development emerging to carve the white man's ideas as a burden in themselves by confronting their political hegemony?

Since scholarly acumen lacked theoretical and conceptual developments of activism in the Arab world, especially in Saudi Arabia, it again became quite a Herculean task to study the impact of social media in such pro-democracy protests in the longer run. The lack of inter-subjective understanding further deepened the gap in understanding these protests that had vertical, horizontal and even lateral mass appeal. Adding to the caveats was the unpredictable and contemporary nature of these protests, in terms of their strength, location and portrayal. But this did shift the study of Arab democracy from initial shades of occultation and prejudice into the limelight and prominence. Scholars such as Hamid Dabashi even argues that the so-called 'Arab Spring' had put an end to post-colonialism and it is now necessary to discover and create new verbatim, definitions and meanings of revolutions, liberation geography and governance.[7] Nevertheless, the highly pertinent question remained: Did the Saudi citizens have the power to create changes? The uprisings certainly had much more revolutionary power in other Arab States than in Saudi Arabia. Undoubtedly, the international community ran out of metaphors to describe the lack of progress of Arab democratisation although it did become pregnant with ideals of empowerment and emancipation.

Neo-Patrimonial System in Saudi Arabia

The main conflict in the case of Saudi Arabia, at a certain level, was the existence of a neo-patrimonial state functioning. What aggravated the lacunae further was the absence of concrete dialectics among the Arab scholars themselves to reveal the strands of conflict within the neo-patrimonial set-up and its survival.

Shmuel Eisenstadt opined that, in neo-patrimonial states, the control rests with the authoritarian ruler as he dominates the administration apparatus and also retains economic and military power by amassing the loyalty of the elites.[8] Very often, the unity of elites is consolidated by actually pitting them against one another, thereby subtly reinforcing the power of the very authoritarian ruler himself. The structuralist analysis of revolutions, starting from Hannah Arendt, predicts a regime change. A change of regime in a neo-patrimonial set-up seems difficult in spite of the fact that such regimes are sensitive to imbalances, especially economic ones. However, culture then started to play its important role in countries such as Saudi Arabia where the authoritarian rule itself was tied to religious denominators that could not be questioned. The traditional tools of development in the Saudi neo-patrimonial state have been controlled and even contained by the accumulation of the authoritarian head and his elites, causing non-uniformity in the very process of industrialisation and active trade with foreign counterparts.

Another essential argument by Jason Brownlee asserts that the Gulf States are not built on ideologies in spite of having religious control and, thus, might easily give way to the mere idea of proto-democratic reforms to confront demonstrations of a political, economic and social nature.[9] Scholars have also stated that democracy has enjoyed a patchy status in the Gulf countries, especially in Bahrain, Qatar and even Saudi Arabia, which are reminders of the process of becoming democratic. Thus, democratisation is not irrelevant in the region, but the process is not only gradual but also reversible.[10]

This swing from authoritarian to democratic and then back to authoritarian regimes is not a new phenomenon. Scholars such as Juan Linz have analysed how, during the period 1949–1979, the revolutions against neo-patrimonial states such as China, Cambodia, Iran, Vietnam and Cuba led to the emergence of either Islamist theocracies or Communist regimes, being eventually pushed back into authoritarianism due to the lack of economic development models.[11] On the other hand, political earthquakes in Georgia, Indonesia, Kyrgyzstan, Haiti, Romania and the Philippines have ended up producing weaker proto-democratic systems of governance.[12]

These references also had an important layer of cultural context and inter-subjective understanding, which perhaps would have rendered the comparison with Saudi Arabia. It should also be noted that such revolutions cannot take place very easily in the oil monarchy due to the strict surveillance and control by the government. The diversity of the impacts of the pro-democracy uprisings also revealed that revolutions cannot be cloned from one Arab Gulf country and transposed to another because of the diversity and lack of homogenous narratives of identity. In fact, for the past 33 years, the Gulf elites have been meeting annually to discuss the issues that feature in the priority lists of their communities. The 2012 meeting in Doha, for example, addressed the issue of the 'Arab Spring' in the Gulf States and how the option of reform might be exercised.[13] Most of the time, the protests are fragmented, leaderless or ambiguous, thereby cementing the Euro-centric notion of 'Arab Street'. Interestingly, however, the conjunctures at which such revolutions take place are similar to those that transformed Europe and the Soviet Union in 1848 and 1989 respectively. These conjunctures include high levels of corruption, lack of employment and the growing ineptitude of the authoritarian elites.

In the case of Saudi Arabia, two concrete case scenarios may predict the breakdown of the neo-patrimonial state system. The first scenario concerns the rupture in the line of succession, set up by Saudi Arabia's new King, Salman, following the death of his half-brother King Abdullah. It is still debatable whether this long-term road map will be sufficiently flawless to face any looming disaster in the coming years. The second perspective deals with the emergence of rifts between the clerics and the royal family. Although Wahhabism is still prominent and the clerics are holding on to power, a few religious dictates are not heeded. Recently, the Kingdom allowed investors to purchase shares in a multibillion dollar public offering for a national bank, in spite of top clerics dictating that buying shares was not allowed on Islamic grounds.[14]

At the same time, it must be understood that embryonic and impulsive analysis cannot predict the future of this rift, especially taking into consideration the longevity of the Saudi model. However, returning to the conjectures on the causes of revolutions, the gravity of mass mobilisation due to oppression in neo-patrimonial states existed in Saudi Arabia in terms of corruption, low standard of living, demographic bulge, low unemployment and unjust powers of control over the masses. What could never have had happened then, and stands little chance now, is the very basic foundation that prevents these issues from becoming prominent role-players. It is important to understand why these conjectures were not consolidated.

Unfortunately, there are several reasons for the failure of these conjectures to be transformed into potential entropy of revolt and conflict in the case of Saudi Arabia. Firstly, as Josef Gugler states, with time, the contemporary nature of revolutions transforms essentially into an urban one.[15] Thus, even after the death of 26-year-old Khalid al-Labad at the hands of the police on 26 September 2012, the protests could not galvanise the Shi'i minority as this group, accounting for 10 per cent of the Kingdom's population, is concentrated in the rural Eastern province, isolated by the Persian Gulf and the vast Arabian desert.[16] The low rate of internet penetration and the fact that the rural population outnumbered their urban counterparts were also major reasons for this failure. There is no mutual dialogue system between the rural and urban areas of Saudi Arabia, which is further fragmented due to sectarianism and tribal diversities.

Secondly, the deepening of divisions between the consensus mobilisation and action mobilisation grew quite treacherous over time. Bert Klandermans, defining these two forms of mobilisation, stresses how the former is a social movement which tries to obtain massive support for its viewpoint of movement strategy, collective good, confrontation and achievement of results.[17] Klandermans and Dirk Omega also described the different stages of mobilisation – general preparedness, specific preparedness and actual participation. These three stages are not uniform, varying from location to culture and, hence, in most of the analysed cases a very minor population that did indulge in general preparedness actually ends up actively participating.[18] In the case of Saudi Arabia, the skirmish protests in the Eastern Province, especially Qatif, were emboldened by the uprisings in the Arab world but the conservative monarchy, in its regular fashion, did not entertain the dissent and blamed it on Iran.[19]

The impact of social movement on Arab uprisings in Saudi Arabia was immediately smothered by the authorities, who cracked down on the dissent and pumped $US130 billion into the economy.[20] Thirdly, and most importantly, these uprisings were eventually engulfed by sectarian and ethnic conflicts within their own set-ups. The analysis of this phenomenon became very contested in the Eastern Province, where the uprisings were contained due to them being perceived as sectarian in spite of the country having a decade-long history of non-sectarian activism, as was the case in Bahrain.[21]

Moreover, the theoretical isolation of Islamic activism, which Quintan Wiktorowicz describes in his study of social movement theory, led to the failure to produce a descriptive analysis based on theoretical paradigms for the Muslim societies.[22] In fact, what eventually did emerge in scholarly debates was the nomenclature of social media by media pundits that, once again, was pregnant with the grotesque claims teeming with Euro-centrism because academic scholars credited the revolutions to Western technology rather than to the power of popular protests in the Arab world. The scholar opines that the viral enthusiasm of uprisings in West Asia seemed to have been caused by Silicon Valley rather than the 'Arab Street'.

The Role of Social Media in Saudi Arabia

Although credible academic work has been undertaken to define the concept of 'social networking sites', the exact meaning of the term 'social media' remains ambiguous, flexible and adaptive. Danah Boyd and Nicole Ellison define 'social networking site' as an online service that permits its users to create and modify their profiles, in both public and semi-private domains, thereby helping them to accumulate and view connections and utilise social media services.[23] Over the years, however, it is the term 'social media' that has become more common, interactive and far more capable of having an impact on political-cultural transformation.[24] Meanwhile, other scholars such as Garrett believe that 'social media' is a generic term that comprises a large number of platforms and technologies that share principal characteristics.[25] Facebook and Twitter were the most used social media platforms in the 2011 uprisings in the Arab world.[26] Factors such as low participation costs, the creation of an idea of community, promotion of consciousness and collective identity, and 24-hour online connectivity helped social media to fill the vacuum left by the information dissemination of the traditional Arab media.

Dick Costolo, the CEO of Twitter, stated in 2012 that Saudi Arabia had the fastest recorded growth in Twitter usage.[27] At the same time, it is still risky to post one's opinion on social media, in spite of the process of catharsis that it involves, due to the strict imposition of laws by the State and the disadvantage of being easily located by the secret police. In order to understand the users of social media in Saudi Arabia, it is essential to know their population and opinions, two important factors that cause political-cultural transformation in any country. As of December 2013, Saudi Arabia had 16,544,322 internet users and 60.5 per cent penetration. Of these, there were 5,852,520 Facebook users (almost the population of Riyadh).[28] Along with a high standard of living, finance, and a technically aware population, there are a few other interesting reasons for this high social media usage in the Kingdom.

John Scarpino and Ali Alshif state that Saudis find social media a cost-effective, convenient and effective way of *building* new connections and fostering existing relations, especially overseas. Such analysis reveals that the internet and globalisation have transformed the concept of space and time, which will affect the political-cultural understanding of an individual.[29] Interestingly, however, social media have also played a pivotal role, especially in Saudi Arabia, in fostering national identity and patriotism. Explaining this phenomenon, Saudi blogger and social media specialist Waleed Samoum states that social media users in the Kingdom are mature.[30] Connecting the understanding of the term 'maturity' with politics and culture, one can recall a very interesting episode that took place in Saudi Arabia on the occasion of National Day when citizens began changing their profile pictures and using nicknames that reflected their love of their country.[31]

The cultural transformation was also taking place among the clerics, who in the 1990s used to issue fatwas or tafseer (Quranic commentary by religious scholars) through audio tapes but now use social media. Jonathan Schanzer and Steven Miller explain how Saudi clerics, who write in both Arabic and English, offer a glimpse of Saudi society and how Wahhabism works.[32] Both religious and corporate authorities are trying to limit dissent on social media, especially Twitter, in Saudi Arabia, as these media have started to act as a civil society, giving people the platform to converse on social, political and cultural issues.[33]

The Arab Social Media Report of 2012 produced by Dubai School of Government's Governance and Innovation Programme conducted a regional online survey in eight Arab countries (Saudi Arabia, Bahrain, UAE, Oman, Lebanon, Kuwait, Jordan and Egypt).[34] It scrutinised the usage and perception of social media and their respective impacts on the societies and cultures of these countries. With 70 per cent of the respondents being aged between 18 and 30 years, the survey included private sector employees, public sector professionals, undergraduate students and even unemployed youth. 4,754 responses were received with an average response rate of 86.4 per cent.

In the context of Saudi Arabia, the report revealed that 32 per cent of the respondents believed that social media played a role in their empowerment. 92 per cent of respondents felt more connected with their society through social media and were growing more tolerant of different points of view.[35] However, Saudi Arabia remained quiet, in terms of dissent and protests, during the time of the Arab uprisings in 2011. Khalid Al-Tawil attributes this to the fact that the internet is highly censored in the Kingdom and the government restricts and blocks politically sensitive material.[36] Additionally, Daniel Drezner states that authoritarian states that have a greater interest in maximising economic growth also need to restrict political sensitive content but without sacrificing commercial possibilities.[37]

Qanta Ahmed has pointed out that the Saudi citizens themselves are quite confident of finding ways to bypass security blocking measures incorporated by the regime, just as they did in 2010 when the Blackberry BBM messaging was blocked.[38] This instance is one of the innumerable examples of the gaps that exist in understanding the role of social media, especially in authoritarian Kingdoms such as Saudi Arabia. However, before delving into this battle of causality, it should be noted that the gap between the roles of social media and democratisation in the Arab world has yet not been filled. Indeed, social media did help in conflating the motivations demanding political actions with the battle of causality. Technology helped people to create instant connections leading to the idea of perpetual connectivity.[39] This led to the creation of the network society, a term coined by Manuel Castells in his Communication Power theory that links the networks of trust with the technology of wireless communication, thereby creating the synergy of networks of resistance that mobilise an attack on the social target.[40] The network society is perceived as more efficient than the hierarchical structure of states involving the military, industrial elites and bureaucracy.

In the context of Saudi Arabia, although it avoided the pro-democracy protests during the 2011 Arab uprisings, there has been a 300 per cent growth in the number of internet users. The recent report, 'State of Social Media in Saudi Arabia', conducted by The Social Clinic in collaboration with The Loft Creative Hub revealed that 93 per cent of residents in the oil monarchy are active on Facebook. Out of the 8.4 million Facebook users, approximately 7.6 million access Facebook through their mobiles. The social network is dominated primarily by users from the 18–35 age group, currently demonstrating a penetration rate of 83 per cent. These primary users reside in the urban areas of Riyadh, Damman and Jeddah. Turning to Twitter, Saudis alone produced 210 million tweets per month from 5.4 million users.[41] In fact, the Twitter penetration in Saudi Arabia is the highest in the world.[42]

In spite of the virtual sphere of Saudi Arabia being pregnant with social media use, its impact has been of limited utility in demanding political transformation. The causal link between social media and the democratisation of the Arab world has become blurred because, after 28 January 2011, when the state had banned their use, the momentum of the protest actually gained in ferocity. In Malcolm Gladwell's term, the Arab world witnessed a 'tipping point' in its social phenomenon.[43] It now became essential to contest the idea of Clay Shirky, who suggested that social media make the process of group formation ridiculously easy.[44] Scholars such as Khaled Hroub believe that it can only be hoped that internet connectivity and social media are the principal agents causing the mobilisation for social and political change; the reality, however, is different.[45] In fact, they act as auxiliary actors rather than the protagonists of change. One of the reasons for such a diagnosis is that electronic communication, although extending our senses, also eventually numbs the perception of the audience by entrapping them into a closed system that is isolated from the real conflict, leading to tensions between connection and isolation.[46] Nevertheless, communication had been integral.

This would suggest that both the regime and the protesters in Saudi Arabia targeted the channels of connectivity. In the case of the state, the

Saudi government also used social media to spread the *Wahhabi* ideology, announce the fatwas and create a mutual dialogue demanding trust and faith in its political legitimacy.[47] On the other hand, the internet penetration rate, being quite minimal in the Eastern Provinces, which included the marginalised Shiʿi protestors, did not produce a platform for the protestors to voice their dissent and mobilise well organised protests through the use of social media. Thus, social media became the means for targeting the very tools of the government by turning into an anti-thesis of the prior means of state-controlled communication.

Eventually, as the crisis continued there was an evident divide among the scholars and media pundits in their analysis of the role of social media. This nascent scrutiny shifted from whether or not the social media played a role in Arab democratisation to whether they were able to escalate or contain it. The decrease in the number of political tweets or Facebook messages reduced the impact that social networking as a platform endowed. Slowly, the analysts enhanced the dichotomous role of social media, including two subgroups: techno-realists and digital evangelists.[48] Techno-realists blatantly refrained from crediting social media with the ability to cause mobilisation, often judging the platforms as fabricated and lacking authenticity. On the other hand, the digital evangelists supported the social media, a little too enthusiastically, for their revolutionary role. As there remained a dearth of empirical research for a very long time after the Arab uprisings had started, it became even more difficult to take sides or even investigate the actual reasons for the emergence of such a dichotomy. Eventually, this dichotomy in itself evolved more prominently than those actual people who had caused the Arab uprisings. The failure of Arab uprisings in Saudi Arabia questioned whether or not the social media in themselves were sufficiently democratic. Other questions further contesting the role of social media were raised by William Carroll and Robert Hackett in attempting to understand the difference between democratisation through media and the democratisation of media.[49]

This analysis reveals that a few cyberspaces are more participatory than the others. For example, although both Twitter and Facebook are open-ended and concentrated, the system of walls and followers limits, respectively, the participation and the fluidity of networking.[50] Thus, the virtual space is unable to reflect the social reality as national politics evolve in such social media platforms. Moreover, the gap between the activists and the common man is not reduced in this virtual sphere because these two distinct entities have their own circles of communication, and in most cases the boundaries are not permeated due to cultural and social factors. For example, the information tweeted or Facebooked is dependent not so much on the content of the actual message but more on the social connections and user profiles.[51] Furthermore, since social media were unable to bridge the gap between the urban and rural social divides, it became even more challenging to portray their homogenous role. In addition, social media did not always guarantee that it was the victim's voice that received online attention and thus, at times, even this form of network society was imbued with the propaganda models of manufacturing a manipulated discourse.

Bridging the Gap: Social Theory of International Politics

Several authors have revealed the gap that still exists between the role of social media and democratisation in the Arab world. This gap exists because of the absence of reflective understanding between the structures and processes, with the former often gaining greater advantage than the latter. It also tests the question of identity and interests due to which it becomes difficult to analyse why the same stimulus causes different reactions. In this case, the stimulus of pro-democracy protests failed in its momentum when applied to Saudi Arabia. However, the study does accept the contemporary and still unfolding nature of the 2011 Arab uprisings as one of the limitations in the study of this phenomenon and the linking of the two subfields of social media and Arab democratisation in Saudi Arabia. Thus, in order to fill this gap, the insight of the social theory of international politics provided by Alexander Wendt is incorporated to further understand the phenomenon and its disparities.[52]

The Social Theory of International Politics gives importance to identity and interests rather than the structure. It questions where the identity and interests come from and how political institutions can change behaviour but cannot influence the former. It demands complex learning in order that re-definition might take place. In this context, the study deals with the role of social media as a process and the Arab democracies as the structure for study. It does not entail the dichotomous privileging of structure over process. In other words, Arab democratisation was more important than the role of social media. The social theory explains how transformation of identity and interests through process can lead to transformation of structure.

In the case of Saudi Arabia, there are several distinct identities divided along the lines of sectarian divides, ethnicity, nationality and ideologies. Since no theoretical paradigm has questioned the very existence and portrayal of these identities and interests, transformation never takes place. Religion and identity have been playing an integral role in conflicts in Saudi Arabia. Furthermore, victims have a different identity, adding to their latent sectarian and ethnic loyalties. The question of interests becomes more vital when studied through the lens of neo-patrimonial state structure. The interests of various identity groups differ, adding to the economic, political, social and cultural divisions. In addition, identity politics play an important role in causing the politics of difference.

The idea of transformed identities is not dealt with in great detail, especially in the context of Arab societies. This is the very reason why the recent uprisings in Saudi Arabia were not understood and were caught up in the dichotomy of sectarianism and ethnic tensions. Thus, the social theory of international politics, when applied to this scenario-building, shares a cognitive and inter-subjective understanding of the concept of process, in which the identities and interests are endogenous to the vital interactions. The focus on process, in this case social media, helps us to look at its role through the lens of learning and knowledge. Hence, it refrains from being a part of the dichotomy of digital evangelists and techno-realists. It is only through interaction that the ambient and ubiquitous role of news can be understood.

The social theory of international politics draws the distinction between structure and process. This explains why the role of social media has encountered different reactions in various different Arab countries. Moreover, the way people act towards an object depends on the meaning the object has for them. However, the study does not objectify social media but simply introduces the strand of thought of utility creating meaning. This explains why the social media did not have utility for the rural class in Saudi Arabia.

The utility of social media was prominent in cities such as Riyadh, Jeddah and Damman, where the need to demand political transformation did not have as much intensity as it did in the Eastern Provinces. The rural areas had limited knowledge of social media and the lack of internet penetration further curtailed the communication process.

The institution of democracy in the Arab world can only be stable when the identities and interests are understood, since any political institution is a relatively stable set of identities and interests. Only when new identities and interests are internalised can the functioning of institutionalisation take place. Thus, distribution of power, with reference to the Arab world, will have meaning for state action only when understandings and expectations constitute institutional identities and interests.

The role of social media as a process became important because the protesters themselves were able to use the platform for the portrayal of their identity and interests by building on social capital. In the very process itself, new identities and interests were explored because not even the protesters initially had any idea about the momentum to which their uprisings might lead. The social media were able to signal, interpret and, hence, respond to the everyday metamorphosis of the uprisings and still continue to do so.

Conclusion

The waves of pro-democracy protests in the Arab world have not been understood through the lens of constructivist theory and have been narrated through Western and Eurocentric perspectives that define 'Arab Streets' but not 'Arab public opinion'. This in itself reflects the continuous neo-orientalist gaze to discern Arab society. The mere idea of democracy itself has been considered incompatible with Arab societies, and the same Western countries that judge are often involved in tacit alliances with the authoritarian regimes. The outbreak of Arab uprisings thus shocked the media pundits and liberal democrats who had never imagined such a political earthquake emerging in the Arab world.

This current study first describes the caveats in how Arab societies are perceived and the very structure of the neo-patrimonial state. It examines the reasons why different neo-patrimonial states vary from one to the next. It then discusses the role of Arab media and their use as a propaganda tool by the states, which helped cause the emergence of social media along with other factors. The theoretical insights of resource mobilisation theory and communication as power are discussed to reveal the lacunae in them. However, strictly categorising the social media either as revolutionary or as having a minimal effect in the Arab uprisings would not do justice to their involvement. At the same time, it is also necessary to avoid being too optimistic about their roles, not because of some latent disadvantage in their existence but because of the manner in which different neo-patrimonial states have controlled the usage of social media in different processes. It is also essential to delve deeper into why the rural communities and regions in most of the countries where these uprisings took place could not consolidate with greater momentum.

Ultimately, the social theory of international politics is used to explore the role of social media. Hence, the current study stresses that the role of social media leads to the creation and acceptance of identities and interests that can cause political and cultural transformation. The other insights into regime change, such as neo-conservative democracy exportation, are criticised on the grounds that they failed because they did not take into account the identity and interests of the protesters. However, as the uprisings still continue to unfold, it is essential to delve deeper into the links between social media and Arab democratisation by further exploring the social theory of international politics.

Notes

1 Khalil Rinnawi, 'Cyber Uprising: Al-Jazeera TV Channel and the Egyptian Uprising', *Language and Intercultural Communication*, 12 (2006), 118–132 <doi: 10.1080/14708477.2012.671607>.

2 Richard Augustus, *The Puzzle of Political Reform in the Middle East* (Oxford: Oxford University Press, 2009).

3 Ibid.

4 Toby Dodge, 'From the Arab Awakening to the Arab Spring: The Post-Colonial State in the Middle East', *LSE Ideas*, 2012, pp. 5–11 <http://www.lse.ac.uk/IDEAS/publications/reports/pdf/SR011/FINAL_LSE_IDEAS__fromTheArabAwakeningToTheArabSpring_Dodge.pdf>.

5 Kapiszewski Andrzej, 'Saudi Arabia: Steps toward Democratization or Reconfiguration of Authoritarianism', *Journal of Asian and African Studies*, 41 (2006), 489–482.

6 Sudipta Kaviraj, 'An Outline of the Revisionist Theory of Modernity', *European Journal of Sociology*, 46 (2005), 497–526 <doi:10.1017/S0003975605000196>.

7 Hamid Dabashi, *The Arab Spring: The End of Post Colonialism* (New York, NY: Zed Books, 2012).

8 Shmuel Eisenstadt, *Traditional Patrimonialism to Modern Patrimonialism* (London: Sage Publications, 1973).

9 Jason Brownlee, 'Low Tide after the Third Wave: Exploring Politics under Authoritarianism', *Comparative Politics*, 34 (2002), 477–498.

10 Augustus.

11 Juan Linz, 'Totalitarian and Authoritarian Regimes', in *Handbook of Political Science*, ed. by Fred Greenstein and Nelson Polsby (Colorado: Lynne Rienner Publications, 2000), p. 143.

12 Jack Goldstone, 'Understanding the Revolutions of 2011: Weakness and Resilience in Middle Eastern Autocracies', *Foreign Affairs*, 2011 <http://www.foreignaffairs.com/articles/67694/jack-a-goldstone/understanding-the-revolutions-of-2011>.

13 Mohammed Al-Rumaihi, 'The Gulf and the Arab Spring', *The Majalla*, April 2012 <http://www.majalla.com/eng/2012/04/article55231198>.

14 Ben Hubbard, 'Saudi Arabia's Succession Line Is Set, but the Nation's Path Remains Uncertain', *The New York Times*, 23 January 2015 <http://www.nytimes.com/2015/01/24/world/middleeast/king-abdullah-saudi-arabia-funeral.html>.

15 Josef Gugler, 'The Urban Character of Contemporary Revolutions', *Studies in Comparative International Politics*, 17 (2002), 60–73.

16 Kevin Sullivan, 'Saudi Arabia's Secret Arab Spring', *The Independent*, 23 October 2012 <http://www.independent.co.uk/news/world/middle-east/saudi-arabias-secret-arab-spring-8223550.html>.

17 Bert Klandermans, 'Mobilisation and Participation: Social and Psychological Expansions of Resource and Mobilization Theory', *American Sociological Review*, 49 (1984), 583–600.

18 Bert Klandermans and Dirk Omega, 'Potentials, Networks, Motivations and Barriers: Steps towards Participation in Social Movements', *American Sociological Review*, 52 (1987), 519–531.

19 Safa Alahmad, 'Reporting Saudi Arabia's Hidden Uprising', *BBC*, 2014 <http://www.bbc.com/news/world-middle-east-27619309>.

20 Erlich Reese, 'In Saudi Arabia, Shiite Muslims Challenge Ban on Protests', *NPR*, 2013 <http://www.npr.org/2013/03/23/175051345/in-saudi-arabia-shiite-muslims-challenge-ban-on-protests>.

21 Toby Matthiesen, *Sectarian Gulf: Bahrain, Saudi Arabia and the Arab Spring That Wasn't* (California: Stanford University Press, 2013).

22 Quintan Wiktorowicz, *Islamic Activism: A Social Movement Theory Approach* (Bloomington: Indiana University Press, 2004).

23 Danah Boyd and Nicole Ellison, 'Social Network Sites: Definition, History, and Scholarship', *Journal of Computer-Mediated Communication*, 13 (2007), 210–230 <doi:10.1111/j.1083-6101.2007.00393.x>.

24 AbdulAziz Aljabre, 'Social Networking, Social Movements, and Saudi Arabia: A Review of Literature', *ARPN Journal of Science and Technology*, 3 (2013), 161–168.

25 Kelly Garrett, 'Protest in an Information Society: A Review of Literature on Social Movements and New ICTs', *Information, Communication and Society*, 9 (2006), 202–224.

26 Aljabre.

27 Jane Kinninmont, 'To What Extent Is Twitter Changing Gulf Societies', *Chatham House*, 2013 <http://www.chathamhouse.org/publications/papers/view/189413>.

28 Internet World Stats, 'Internet World Stats, Usage Population and Statistics', *Miniwatts Marketing Group*, 2014 <www.internetworldstats.com>.

29 John Scarpino and Ali Alshif, 'The Impact of Social Networks on Saudi Residents Living in the United States', *Issues in Information Systems*, 14 (2013), 72–81.

30 Renad Ghanem, 'Social Media Connecting People', *Saudi Gazette*, 2012 <http://www.sauress.com/en/saudigazette/137282>.

31 Mariam Abdallah, 'Saudi Arabia: Boycotting Twitter to Save It', *Al-Akhbar-english*, 31 January 2012 <http://english.al-akhbar.com/node/3783>.

32 Jonathan Schanzer and Steven Miller, *Facebook Fatwa: Saudi Clerics, Wahhabi Islam and Social Media* (Washington, DC: FDD Press, 2012).

33 Khulood Miliany, 'The Impact of the Internet on Saudi Students' Use of Television' (Unpublished doctor's dissertation. University of Leicester, UK, 2013).

34 Fadi Salem and Racha Mourtada, 'Social Media in the Arab World: Influencing Societal and Cultural Change', *Arab Social Media Report*, 2012 <www.arabsocialmediareport.com/userManagement/PDFD/ASMR 4 updated 29 08 12>.

35 Racha Mourtada and Paul Salem, 'Social Media in the Arab World: The Impact on Growth, Women and Social Change', *Arab Social Media Report*, 2012, pp. 269–274 <http://www.iemed.org/observatori-en/arees-danalsi/arxuis-adjuncts/anuari/med.2012/mourtada salem-en>.

36 Khalid Al-Tawil, 'The Internet in Saudi Arabia', *Arab IP Centre*, 2001 <http://www.arabipcentre.com/the-internet-in-saudi-arabia.php>.

37 Daniel Drezner, 'Weighing the Scales: The Internet's Effect on State-Society Relations', *The Brown Journal of World Affairs*, 16 (2010), 31–44.

38 Qanta Ahmed, 'Saudi Arabia's Struggle with Social Media: Twitter Clowns and Facebook Fatwas', *The Blaze*, 2013 <http://www.theblaze.com/contributions/saudi-arabias-struggles-with-social-media-twitter-clowns-and-facebook-fatwas>.

39 Howard Rheingold, *The Virtual Community: Homesteading on the Electronic Trontier* (New York: MIT Press, 2000).

40 Manuel Castells, *Communication Power* (New York, NY: Oxford University Press, 2009).

41 The Social Clinic, 'The State of Social Media in Saudi Arabia', *The Social Clinic*, 2015 <http://www.thesocialclinic.com/the-state-of-social-media-in-saudi-arabia-vol-3/>.

42 *Saudi Gazette*, 'Facebook and Twitter Gain More Users in Saudi Arabia', 2014 <http://english.alarabiya.net/en/media/digital/2014/01/09/Use-of-mobiles-in-social-media-on-the-rise-in-Saudi-Arabia.html>.

43 Malcolm Gladwell, *The Tipping Point: How Little Things Can Make a Big Difference* (Boston: Little, Brown and Company, 2006).

44 Clay Shirky, *Here Comes Everybody: How Change Happens When People Come Together* (London: Penguin Books, 2009).

45 Khaled Hroub, 'Internet Freedom in the Arab World: Its Impact, State Controls, Islamisation and the Overestimation of It All', *Culture and Society*, 2009, 267–271 <http://www.iemed.org/anuari/2009/aarticles/a267.pdf>.

46 Marshall Mcluhan, *Understanding Media: Extensions of Man* (New York, NY: McGraw-Hill, 1964).

47 Some of them such as Abdul Aziz Al-Sheikh, Abdullah Lehaidan, Saleh AlFawzan and Abdullah Al-Sheikh who have their own websites and use social media to provide guidance to people regarding different local issues including not allowing Saudi people to protest against the current government. For example, Sheikh Saleh AlFawzan has 188,000 followers on Twitter. There was an agreement between those scholars to prevent demonstrations in Saudi Arabia, but not in Syria.

48 Francesca Comunello and Anzera Giuseppe, 'Will the Revolution Be Tweeted? A Conceptual Framework for Understanding the Social Media and the Arab Spring', *Islam and Christian–Muslim Relations*, 23 (2012), 453–470.

49 William Caroll and Robert Hackett, 'Democratic Media Activism through the Lens of Social Movement Theory', *Media Culture Society*, 28 (2006), 31–44 <doi:10.1177/0163443706059289>.

50 Miliany.

51 David Weinberger, *Small Pieces, Loosely Joined* (Cambridge: Cambridge University Press, 2002).

52 Alexander Wendt, *Social Theory of International Politics* (Cambridge: Cambridge University Press, 1999).

3

Arab Social Media: From Revolutionary Euphoria to Cyber Realism

Omair Anas

Theoretically,[1] the emergence of the bourgeoisie public sphere was a direct outcome of the unfolding nation-state system in the Post-Westphalian system. Gradual bifurcation of 'public and private' emerged and public opinion became the source of legitimacy for state power. The public sphere hence became a fundamental normative theory towards democratisation. Theoretical contours of the public sphere faced many challenges, with the forces of globalisation unsettling the nation state and counter-publics becoming more active in its unmaking.[2] The 'Arab Public Sphere' was criticised for its incompatibility with its original conception evolved by Jurgen Habermas because the Arab world lacked the fundamentals of a democratic society.[3]

The post-Ottoman system constituted an anti-colonial militant leadership supported by religious authorities to end occupation and colonial rule. Influential Islamic personalities, Islamic movements and Arab nationalist movements emerged to complement rather than compete with one another. The discourse of Arab and Islamic unity prevailed as a powerful tool against colonial and post-colonial challenges. The common Arabic language, shared Islamic beliefs and cultural proximities encouraged pan-Arabism or pan-Islamism more than the territorial identities of nation states.

Arab unity remained the most cherished 'dream' of Arab nationalists and Islamists alike. It was very difficult to differentiate between public and private, and authority has often overlapped between the state and religion. With the stability of the nation states of the modern world, Arab states remained under pressure to create a separation of powers and a separation of religion and the state. Different formats of political and social reforms were suggested and adopted by these states to comply with modern institutions. It is state authorities that have the major say in defining civil society, the public sphere and actions of non-state actors. This chapter examines these matters by looking in depth at how Arab social media have been steered from revolutionary euphoria to cyber realism and how this affects the relationship between citizens, political systems, societies and Arab governments.

For the last three decades, the Arab press has not challenged the Arab system of governance and has been defined as a 'loyal' 'mobilising', 'diverse' or 'transitional' media system.[4] States have controlled licensing, editorial appointments and media production. The only occasion on which a powerful state media apologised to its audience for following state instructions was after Hosni Mubarak had been removed from power following successful protests in Egypt in January 2011.[5] This event marked an aspiration for change in the system and structure of the power controlled by states for decades. Power relations between and among media and political system, society, audiences, political parties, streets, authorities and external forces have started to change. In some countries, this shift is in favour of previously marginalised and banned Islamist groups such as the Muslim Brotherhood and *Ennahda* and also in favour of many secular and nationalist parties and groups in the region.

The nature of civil society started to transform from a state-dependent civil society to an independent civil society. Similarly, trade unions, students and youth groups, women's groups and other professional unions have asserted their aspirations to more power. Tunisia's trade unions' mediation in the political crisis in the country is just one notable example. This change has been accompanied by a discursive transformation in the communication of public as well as private voices. If the state is becoming more and more obsessed with the interests of its people, civil society, political parties and activists are also concerned about citizens' rights without a dominant role for religion in public life.[6]

The role of media in the Arab world or in any authoritarian state is affiliated with the role of the state's ruler. Media are often treated as a vehicle for the leader's public relations; hence, people' expect the same from the media as they expect from the leader himself. Al-Jazeera, for example, has been projected as an icon or brand of social and political change in the Arab world that has 'rattled' authoritarian governments, despite the fact that the media's original role does not allow them to do so.[7] Arab newsrooms were equated with the parliament and audiences were treated as voters, all in the mediated public sphere, far from the reality. Contesting this simplified projection of Arab media's ever increasing power, Kai Hafez argues that the media show varying potential to contribute to political change within various types and phases of transformation. However, in all possible situations, the mass media are not a primary political actor but rather a mediator between the government, the opposition and the people.[8] A negotiated system can only be achieved through pressure from strong opposition groups, parties and movements that have the capacity to engage with an authoritarian regime, establish pacts and alliances within the ranks of the opposition, and force the regime to introduce political change.

In the post-Arab-uprising period, many new TV channels mushroomed across the region which led to new discursive threads contesting with each other and diversifying the public sphere, which had once appeared monotonic. Soon after the military intervention in Egypt to remove the first elected President, Mohammad Morsi, many TV channels sympathetic to the Muslim Brotherhood were closed down and a hysterical media war ensued between pro-military and anti-military camps in Egypt. Tunisia has similarly seen many new channels supporting opposing political views, although they are not owned directly by either side. This is not only about news media; it is also about films, family soaps, documentaries, entertainment and other genres.

Defining Social Media's Role

In the Arab world, the traditional public sphere and the space of communicative action was not sufficiently open for common citizens; hence, the introduction of social media was no less than a 'revolutionary platform' for many Arabs who were always willing to speak. In a very short period of time, social media captured the imagination of Arab streets. Political, sectarian and cultural debates and discussions on art, poetry, films, comedy, music and religion suddenly filled this space. Pithy complaints, images and religious sermons were posted. Followers of religious preachers received messages from them directly with the same sanctity by 'liking' their statuses or commenting on them with good wishes. In the early years, user-generated content was of little commercial interest, and states were more or less observers of these developments. However, the 2011 Arab uprisings have given social media activists a historic opportunity to try this newly arrived tool.

The way in which social media were used during the recent uprisings in Tunisia, Egypt and Syria created a sense of euphoria about these social media platforms. But, gradually, as the situation unfolded from good to bad and bad to worse, social media, too, became victims of the situation and failed to maintain their euphoric status.[9] As one Arab commentator claims, 'the number of users in the Arab world will easily double in the next five years', calling the recent Facebook use just a first wave which will be followed by second, the third and the fourth. Such lofty claims do not appreciate the criticality of social media and their dependence on many factors that may not allow these media to continue in a very desirable way. In Egypt, in the post military intervention period, social media faced hysterically anti-army and anti-Muslim Brotherhood posts, followed by arrests of a number of social media activists from the Muslim Brotherhood. This exposes the limitations of social media and their dependence on certain rules that were not very visible in their early days. A critical analysis of social media may help to locate their real strengths and weaknesses and their transformative power in the Arab public sphere.

Medium is the Message

With the introduction of social media, there is an understanding of the medium as a message.[10] The way in which social media are affecting society, including Arab society, and the way in which they have enabled their users to do many things are also important when studying a new social media theory. Self-expression was not as easy as it has become today 'thanks' to social media. At the same time, authoritarian governments have been trying to trace every hostile user, a tactic not unknown to the users. A game of *hide and seek* is taking place between the authorities and the users, with the help of many proxies and technical tricks.

Not only individuals but also corporate organisations, media groups and state authorities have changed the way they communicate with the people. Prior to the 2011 Arab uprisings, Egypt's state authorities, mainly the army and interior ministry, 'never' tried to communicate with the people. But with the huge amount of viral questions on social media raised against interior minister, the ministry sought to establish its own account to communicate directly with the protesters. Almost all major public institutions in Egypt have their own Facebook pages to communicate with the people. For example, the Egyptian Military's Official Spokesperson Facebook page is followed by 2.2 million people.[11] The language they use for public communication is entirely different from what their opponents accuse them of using. Political parties, eminent personalities and members of civil society have strong presences in social media. This suggests that social media per se have influenced the basic nature of the Egyptian public sphere. Social media themselves are the message along with their contents.

Virtual versus Real Interaction

An important question that is always raised about the long-term impact of using social media and the internet concerns whether users are disconnected from the 'real world' and are more embedded in a 'virtual world'. The virtual world's juxtaposition with the real world is itself a contestable proposition. Tom Boellstorff has developed an interesting theory to identify the interaction between technology and society[12]: 'First *techne*, a person who engages in techne not just as *homo faber* (man the maker) or *homo ludens* (man the player), but above all as *homo cyber*. The human online is the virtual human'. In his use of the term 'techne', Boellstorff argues that, by using intentional creativity, people craft their own life worlds and, hence, the virtual selfhood is predicated in this process. He contests the idea that the virtual world means escapism or is contaminated by capitalism. There are those who think that the virtual and real worlds are two different worlds and that the real world is the actual world in which one should live. Boellstorff also argues that 'science fiction and fantasy literature have been fundamental to imaginings of virtual worlds and throughout human history, technologies – from the wheel to the book and beyond – have shaped forms of selfhood and community'. For example, the telephone represents the first virtual world:

> A phone conversation, for instance, is a unique event taking place "within" telephone technology. With the rise of electronic mass media, the time delay involved in postal correspondence or print media could disappear; in comparison to static technologies like photographs, movies and audio recordings "were able to store … time" (Kittler 1999: 3). The telephone probably represents the first virtual world in the contemporary sense of the term: "cyberspace is the 'place' where a telephone conversation appears to occur. Not inside your actual phone, the plastic device on your desk. Not inside the other person's phone, in some other city".[13]

The extent to which the Arab world is switching from the real to the virtual world is a current debate. This is not to suggest that only a medium makes a virtual or real world. The Arab world represents a slightly different case from other regions where speaking in both the real and virtual worlds has the same consequences. The Arab world lacks basic institutions that facilitate free speech.

Change in Media Grammar

The long-established media grammar has been defined in terms of media, audiences, media systems and the circle of communication, which must have a feedback end. The key players and processes in communication such as sender, receiver, and processes of encoding and decoding are the basic assumptions of understanding conventional mass media. Social media have changed this basic grammar of understanding and introduced a kind of chaotic communication generated, received and reacted to by a huge, geographically dispersed mass. In this system, audiences and their reactions cannot be strictly controlled, as occurred in the case of a documentary on Prophet Muhammad. Political and cultural reactions to these contents do not take place among states; they take place largely between people and the social media companies. In India, many social media companies were summoned to respond to many petitions filed by individuals. In Egypt, when powerful private media were broadcasting extremely anti-Muslim Brotherhood information, the pro-Muslim Brotherhood social medium, Rassd News Network (RNN), proved to be a counter-medium against the hysterical anti-Brotherhood campaign in the aftermath of the military intervention on 3 July 2013. In traditional communication theory, the number of media is very limited and the majority of users are disconnected from one another. In the case of social media, however, the number of content producers is almost equal to the total number of users. Most of the users are able to interact with one another, as was proved by the vehemence of Facebook contents during the period of the anti-Hosni Mubarak protests.[14]

Political Economy of Social Media

The political economy of social media has not yet been thoroughly examined, but over the last decade it can be observed that social media have become an important brand promotion tool, and companies and individuals are spending huge amounts on the promotion of their brands through communication experts. How the increasing commercial use of social media and the profit dynamics of social media companies are affecting common users of social media has yet to be determined. The purchase of 'likes' and followings has become common, thereby increasing the number of bogus users of social media whose profiles are created only to promote certain political, entertainment or commercial brands. Since social media users are both labourers and audiences at the same time, who are producing content without being paid for their work, most of their labour is unpaid and their intellectual properties are unsecured.

Since the arrival of digitised media, active audiences have been involved in producing 'social difference (identities and cultural meaning) in a social and cultural economy, which is then made the object of productive consumption'.[15] There is a pattern of gradual rather rapid commercialisation of social media space, and the marketing ability of the ordinary user for non-commercial purposes is decreasing, particularly in comparison to social media's corporate users. In the recent elections in the United States and India, there were many anti-government protests; social media have emerged as a major business.[16] Since users both generate and read the contents, which are acts of consumption as well as labour, revenue generated by social media and investment in social media have made this sphere increasingly competitive as well as politically and culturally sensitive.[17] A recent social media trend has suggested that 10 per cent of users will become members of the digital buyer audience by 2017. New applications and social media features are designed directly in response to their potential contribution to online shopping, social events and social business. E-commerce sales in the region's media will increase from $9 billion in 2012 to $15 billion in 2015.[18]

With the increasing influence of corporate and big business in social media, manipulation of their space is now an emerging phenomenon around the world. This exposes the fact that technology is not empowering the ordinary user in the same way that a rich corporate entity is empowered. It is unlikely that social media will remain unaffected by intense corporate competition for their space. In the Arab world, too, social media are gradually entering the corporate communication in which big corporations are managing the accounts of certain political parties and leaders and supporting certain social and political campaigns. There has been news about the shifting ownership of a number of social media organisations, most recently WhatsApp, which was taken over by Facebook. Social media's limitations will be decided by the role of corporate ownership and the corporate use of their space which now seems to deeply influence the cyber public sphere. It can be argued that social media's diversity and originality will be reduced as commercial and corporate users make greater use of them.

Social media should be seen in their broadest context in which they are strongly connected with e-commerce and online shopping. A report suggests that worldwide social media revenue is expected to rise to US$34 billion by 2016. In the United States, more than 40 per cent of social media users also have tablets or smartphones which allow them to use social media more frequently.[19] In the Arab world, the use of tablets and smartphones is mainly concentrated in the Gulf countries where e-commerce and social media are also on the rise. According to Nielsen,

> Social media's influence on purchase intent is strong across all regions, but strongest among online consumers in the Asia-Pacific, Latin America and Middle East/Africa markets. Thirty percent of online consumers in the Middle East/Africa region and 29 percent in Asia-Pacific use social media on a daily basis to learn more about brands/products/services, with one-third of respondents in both regions connecting on a weekly basis.[20]

The use of social media is defined by market forces and brand managers who are turning users into potential customers for their products and services. Social media are defined as a tool of social influence, monitoring and reputation management. Those working on social influence also engage in social casting and citizen journalism. For brand managers, it is important to have information on brand sentiment, reach and relevance, interactions of users, activity ratio, conversions and customer satisfaction. According to the Magna Global report, social media revenue in the Arab world will grow by 6.3 per cent in 2014.[21] The basic trigger for the explosion of social media in the Arab world is not political or social. It is the direct implications of social media's ability to empower entrepreneurs through branding and marketing, tapping into wider markets, and fostering an entrepreneurial spirit within the enterprise.[22]

Does this have a direct impact on social media uses? It appears that global and national trends support the claim that locally produced pages, local brands and local celebrities do not have great prominence in the global ranking of social media, although no study has yet compared global brands' popularity in the Arab world and their customer share on social media. A social media monitoring website, known as Social Bakers, has documented Facebook pages of the Arab world according to their categories. In the category of brands, the most liked brands in Saudi Arabia and Egypt are Samsung Mobile, Pepsi, Kitkat, and McDonald's. Their global ranking and Egyptian ranking are similar, although Saudi Arabia's ranking of these brands is relatively different. But this is mainly because in Saudi Arabia all the brands bear Saudi names which are more popular than their global names on Saudi social media. For example, McDonald's and Samsung are closer to their global rankings under their Saudi names but not under their global names.[23] It can be argued that social media's popularity in the Arab

Table 3:1 Social Media Fans of Western Media from Eastern Countries

	CNN		**CNN International**		***The Economist***		***Huffington***		**BBC**	
	Total Fans	**% of total**	**Total Fans**	**% of total**	**Total Fans**	**% of total**	**Total Fans**	**% of total**	**Total Fans**	**% of total**
1	191902	1.50	98859	1.70	85276	2.10	20697	0.70	343789	4.30
2	476761	3.70	177016	3.10	84966	2.10	34029	1.10	334479	4.20
3	741559	5.80	295054	5.20	509003	12.60	146353	4.80	1006420	12.70
4	191422	1.50	84471	1.50	48320	1.20	28537	0.90	104474	1.30
5	106079	0.80	36061	0.60	34969	0.90	12180	0.40	158592	2.00
6	562160	4.40	727996	12.80	72923	1.80	13739	0.40	327644	4.10
7	299540	2.30	186051	3.30	181349	4.50	50889	1.70	409155	5.20
8	923810	7.20	341808	6.00	183673	4.60	66724	2.20	336809	4.20
9	116296	0.90	54680	1.00	21194	0.50			104304	1.30
10	77092	0.60	39997	0.70	24439	0.60	8178	0.30	73598	0.90
Total Fans	**12797258**	**28.70**	**5695703**	**35.90**	**4026685**	**30.90**	**3056449**	**12.50**	**966492**	**40.20**

1. Bangladesh; 2. Egypt; 3. India; 4. Indonesia; 5. Iran; 6. Nigeria; 7. Pakistan; 8. The Philippines; 9. Saudi Arabia; 10. United Arab Emirates.

world in general and in the Gulf countries in particular is directly linked with their users' increasing online purchasing habits.

A typical example of the limitations of social media's globalising capacity is the fact that most of the English channels in the Arab or Asian countries will fail to achieve a fan following from the Western countries. For example, nearly 90 per cent of Facebook followers of Al-Jazeera English come from Arab and Asian countries while only 10 to 12 per cent of followers are from the Western countries. Table 3:1 suggests that five selected Western media Facebook pages were liked by a large number of residents of Asian, African and Arab countries; 28 per cent of the total number of fans of CNN and 40 per cent of the total number of fans of BBC News Facebook pages are from these countries and, similarly, 30 per cent of fans of *The Economist* are from these countries. In contrast, Al-Jazeera English, despite having a large fan following, is perhaps the only medium from the entire range of Arab and Asian countries that has 13 per cent of its fans in five selected Western countries. However, in the case of other popular and important media, NDTV India, for example, has just 2.2 per cent of fans from selected Western countries. This shows that the basic nature of media and the basic relationship between the dominance of capital and consumers has not changed, even after the arrival of social media.

Technological Evolution

Social media are a very technology-specific or technology-dependent space in which the evolution of new software and applications has contributed greatly. With the evolution of technology, the universality of social media may not continue as it is today. China has already evolved its own servers which have restricted the use of many global social media including Facebook. Many Gulf countries have been using highly sophisticated applications to monitor anti-government, pornographic and blasphemous contents. Similarly, social media themselves have been evolving their applications which have different implications for their uses. Differences between users of other social media such as LinkedIn, Twitter and Facebook suggest that the use of social media may not take a linear direction. Along with technological evolution, the priorities of users have changed the future of social media depending on their utility for the desired purposes.

Social media users may not always look for viral; they may prefer a purposeful and considered engagement.

State Control of Social Media

With the gradually increasing social and political implications for social media, states are more concerned about their regulation. Unlike in their early days, these media have become a social and political force that influences political and social opinion in a large section of society. The use of social media has become widespread among politicians and activists. States are worried about the potential threat posed by social media to the state institutions and the effectiveness of the state bodies. The London riots first alerted the state institutions to the fact that social media can also be used to instigate organised violence, while the Egyptian protests informed states that activities organised on social media have direct implications for their stability. These concerns have justified states' interests in regulating social media. The most alarming case is presented by WikiLeaks and former National Security Agency agent Snowden, who has provided a great deal of evidence that the social media have become easiest spying platform for the United States.[24]

Increasing surveillance applications on social media poses a direct threat to individuals' right to privacy as well as their right not to be monitored. Along with secret applications, many states have dragged social media before local courts to explain why they should not be subject to local laws. In India, Pakistan and many other countries, social media have been made parties in many cases of inciting violence, blasphemy and pornography. States' increased surveillance activities over social media may not necessarily discourage their users; however, they will gradually adopt a different language of expression and tactics to counter their opposition or to mislead each other. It is said that the Egyptian military intend it will have direct implications for their self-expression on social media and on using them with more secure options, including the use of proxies. Most of the Arab states have been using advanced software and applications to monitor social media and to track anything that may violate the red lines of their Constitutions. For instance, in the post-military-intervention period, the Egyptian authorities have arrested many pro-Muslim Brotherhood activists for their social media activities.[25]

Ineffective Self-regulation

Unlike the formal media of television and the press, social media lack a self-regulatory mechanism, which has made this a highly vulnerable space where damage control is too late. For example, in many cases of violence in India and other Asian countries, material posted on Facebook has gone viral, inciting public anger against certain communities and prompting the police to ask Facebook to remove that content.[26] Facebook and other social media have no mechanism to address users' reports on an urgent basis, particularly in cases where violence and threat to life is involved. Egypt has seen a war of disinformation following the military intervention.[27]

Pro- and anti-Morsi camps have been using photo-shopped images to misinform public opinion.[28] There are options for reporting a post, image or a video, but actions on these reports are often delayed. Almost all social media experts in the Arab world agree that this has become like a battleground for rival political groups. Many countries, such as Egypt, have found that their use of propaganda and misinformation has made this space more susceptible to disinformation and fabrications, thereby harming its status as a site for rational deliberation. Since they have insufficient applications to discourage the use of social media to spread misinformation, hatred and violence, state authorities are seeking an ever-increasing regulatory role in social media, and new cyber laws are being introduced everywhere in the world. As a result, social media in these countries are changing their behaviours.[29]

Social Media after the Arab Uprising

Among the many conventional assumptions about social media is the notion that it always mobilises opinions on regime change. However, in countries such as Saudi Arabia, where Facebook and Twitter were never banned, although they are under constant surveillance, there is much more non-political use of social media than in Egypt. Saudi Arabia and Kuwait had the highest penetration of Twitter and tweets during 2013. According to the Arab Social Media Report, Arabs produce 10 million tweets every day. Tweets from Saudi Arabia constitute 47 per cent of the total number of tweets made in the Arab world, followed by Egypt (12 per cent) and UAE (11 per cent) although neither of these countries are democratic.[30] So, what are these tweets all about? Another survey indicates that 67 per cent of social media users in the region use them for music and movies, 46 per cent for community issues, 43 per cent for sports, 34 per cent for politics and 14 per cent for religious issues.[31] According to the Pew Research Center's survey of social networking sites in the Arab world, Arab publics are turning to social networks to express various views, including political views.[32] Politics is the most important topic of discussion in Arab media, followed by religion.

The current social media landscape in the Arab world and especially in Egypt is extremely chaotic. Sometimes, it resembles a simple propaganda war between two rival factions; on other occasions, it is more of a public forum for political and religious debate. In the aftermath of the military intervention in Egypt, social media became like a battleground carrying a flood of misinformation and propaganda material. Generator Research estimates that the total number of social media users had reached 1.8 billion by the end of 2013, with a projected 38 per cent increase by 2017. Despite the predictions that the total number of users of social networks and total amount of revenue per user will increase globally, there is also apprehension that social network landscapes are largely 'unpredictable' and 'volatile'.[33] The failure of democratic transitions in Egypt, Libya and Yemen and the civil war in Syria have negatively affected the use of social media and have also negatively impacted on its business as well as the growth in digital and social media purchases.

In terms of political discourse, social media activists and pages are engaged in polarised political discourses against each other. A comparative analysis of posts of *Kulluna Khaled Said* (We are all Khaled Said) and Tamarrod will reveal the extent of the political antagonism which has also created divisions within the admins of these Facebook pages. The famous Facebook campaign page *Kulluna Khaled Said* decided not to continue after 3 July following its persistent anti-Morsi postings. It appeared that many of the team members of *Kulluna Khaled Said* were not convinced by its anti-Morsi position. The English page 'We are All

Table 3:2 Discourse Comparison between Two Facebook Pages

Kulluna Khaled Said[a]	Tamarrod
About the United States, 28 January 2011 The State Department has only urged all parties to exercise restraint, and expressed 'concern' over the Egyptian government's massive blocking of communications in-country. We ask our government to take a firmer line against the Egyptian government's repression, and in support of the democratic aspirations of its people.	**About the United States, 6 July 2013** Posted an image of Barack Obama with a caption: Obama is caretaker of terrorism. There were three other posts similar to this, one carrying an image of Obama with beard and a turban on his head. Leader of Muslim Brotherhood has received phone calls from American and Israeli mediators before his speech at Rab'a Al Adawiya.
Key Issue is only Egypt, 28 January 2013 Please! Special request from the great people on this page. Let us just focus on E G Y P T today. If you want to talk about Iran, 911, Israel, etc. Please avoid this until those who are about to be killed in Egypt survive. Where I am now, what is my religion and what is my race have nothing to do with anything. This page is for E G Y P T not me. Sorry, but I had to say this to the few who distract us.	**External countries are accused, 5 July 2013** Be firm Egyptian army!! Entire Egyptian people are with you. Qatar, America and Israel are under boot of Egypt. **Other main narratives:** Frequent appeals and demand from Egyptian army for intervention. 'Muslim Brotherhood is terrorist' was very frequent reference.
Muslim Brotherhood, 26 January 2013 Egyptian government conveyed to the US government that Muslim Brotherhood is behind all protests. Hey liars! This is made of all Egyptians, Christians, Muslims and Copts. Muslim Brotherhood is just one minority of this majority. You are using Muslim Brotherhood's name only to protect yourself and to make the world afraid.	**Demand to Arrest President Morsi from Republican Guard, 3 July 2013** Tamarrod demands that republican guards arrest President Mohammad Morsi. Bearded cartoons were frequent references for Muslim Brotherhood and clean-shaven cartoons for Egyptian nation. Frequent appeals from interior ministry to provide security at Tahrir square.

[a] Source: Compiled from Facebook Posts of Kulluna Khaled Said (Arabic page) and Tamarrod (Arabic page).

Khaled Said' decided to take a position against military intervention, and it is still posting anti-military contents. The Tamarrod movement, which was considered a grass-roots movement that successfully mobilised Egyptian opinion against the Morsi government, has deleted many provocative contents from its official Facebook page following successful protests.

The example of Egypt also represents strong evidence of social media's impact on the mainstream news agenda. The series of events during the military intervention suggests that the hysterical coverage of the violence and counter-violence between the rival groups had reached the social media, as many of these stories were picked by the social media and many were subsequently proved false. The use of photo-shopping was rampant throughout this period on Egypt's social media. In April 2014, two #hashtags went viral and created deep anger among the supporters of General Abdel Fattah Al Sisi. The two #hashtags on social media were #Elect_the_pimp and #Sinai_out_of_coverage.[34]

Post-military-intervention Egypt has provided a diverse scenario for social media in the Arab world. There was an idealist situation until the resignation of President Hosni Mubarak, a politicised situation during the electoral campaign, and then a hysterical-opposition situation during the anti-Morsi protests and their aftermath. Many newsroom debates demanded a ban on Twitter.[35] There was much excitement about these #hashtags. Perhaps anti-protest laws have made a negative contribution to the worsening social media misuse in Egypt. Mohammad Elmasri argues in one of his articles that the entire rationalisation of military intervention against an elected president is noticeably exclusionary.[36]

This creates two impressions about Egypt's cyber sphere. From the perspective of the first revolution in 2011, the discourse appeared very inclusive and political, with no religious-sectarian prejudices. The *Kulluna Khaled Said* page in the early days following its launch in June 2010 can be seen to have followed certain common values to mobilise greater public opinion. It was based on certain demands of the policemen responsible for the death of Khaled Said. Compared to the Khaled Said campaign on social media, the Tamarrod campaign on social media represents an entirely different picture, although Tamarrod itself gradually sank into

Table 3:3 Popular Facebook Pages of Egyptian Media

Page	Total likes[a]	Local fans [From Egypt]
RNN	6205467	4137993
ENN Egypt News Network	5938588	3209411
Al Youm Al Sabe	5097896	4051283
Al-Jazeera MobasherMisr	4950591	2759578
Al MasriAlyoum	4284619	3593422
CBC	3787974	2926911
Al Shoruq News	2911236	2155712
Al Ahram	2708417	2017763

[a] Source: Compiled from Socialbakers.com on 31 May 2014.

internal strife and many of its prominent faces quit the movement, making serious accusations of complicity with the army.[37] Mohamed Fawzi, Abdel Aziz, Hasan Shahin, Ghada Mohammed Naguib and many other prominent members of Tamarrod either left or had their membership suspended following internal divisions.[38] Post-military-intervention social media became like a warzone between two sides. This was completely different from the very idealistic and principles-based social media campaign of *Kulluna Khaled Said* of 2011, which had been appealing to its supporters to maintain dignity and adopt a peaceful approach.[39] In the post-military-intervention period, the political pages of Facebook have remained highly popular among Egyptians in comparison to pages on music, art or religion. Among the most popular pages are RNN, which is a pro-Muslim Brotherhood online news network followed by 6.1 million users. The page of Al-Jazeera Mubasher Misr is followed by 4.9 million, after which come *Al Ahram* (2.7 million), *Alyoum Al Sabey* (5 million) and *Al Masri Alyoum* (4.2 million) users.

In contrast to Egypt's crisis-obsessed social media, Saudi Arabia has a reputation for being more humane and society-oriented. A paralysed patient pleaded for help on his Twitter account and surprisingly received many visitors in response and obtained their help.[40] Patient Ibrahim sent a message on his Twitter handle @gladd2007: '*I am Ibrahim. I am lying in King Khaled Hospital, wing 21, room 3, bed 3. I had an accident, which left me paralyzed. I need stem cell treatment in Germany to recover.*' Egyptian social media are presumably covering similar humane stories but they have fallen far behind and are neglected in the perpetual chaos.[41]

Conclusion

Will the increased commoditisation, commercialisation and securitisation of social media have direct implications for the diversity of the cyber public sphere and, subsequently, on the public sphere? As Denis McQuil argued, the structure of the media, regardless of their forms and formats, tends towards concentration and contents, and audiences are commoditised; then diversity decreases and, finally, opposition and alternative voices within those media become marginalised.[42] The independence of the cyber public sphere also comes into question where a large section of the public is gradually becoming 'subordinate to private interests'. As Facebook is closely linked to the market, social media space is a commercial space and hence a source of profit. Although social media are a user-generated platform, their contribution or their contents have to face competition from the pages owned by corporations and organisations. The post-Arab-uprising social media have seen that individual users are becoming less powerful and more vulnerable. States' careful surveillance of social media has combined with many counter-tactics to control the damage caused by social media and this is becoming possible both through legislation and through intensive legal and illegal surveillance of users and their contents. Though WikiLeaks and Snowden have had an impact in the Arab world, the number of arrests and legislative efforts suggest that social media are gradually becoming a securitised zone, consistent with the real streets under state policing.

With this nature of social media, a powerful force is now trying to infiltrate the personal lives of social media users, which is attracting resistance and the use of proxies and other tools. In the course of a game between social media and their users, the question of individual rights will always be the concern of states, which will seek protection for their citizens against the misuse of their personal data. With the increasing use of social media, the struggle for a 'justified regulation' of social media is inevitable. Social media in the Arab world are still in their early days and are still taking shape. In the natural course of events, the disappearance of Facebook or many other social media networks is also predicted by some experts, although they seem to have overestimated this. In an interesting study based on the rise and fall of MySpace, John Cannarella and Joshua Spechler state that 'Facebook, the largest online social network in history, is set for a massive fall'.[43]

An important picture emerging from the unfolding social media indicates that they have not broken or challenged the dominance of the West over the rest of the world or the dominance of capital over the consumer. Social media users from non-Western countries are generally treated and targeted as potential consumers by the big corporate marketing companies. Despite the huge expansion of social media, global communication has not yet become two-way traffic on social media, as many indicators of social media uses have shown in this chapter. This pattern may be further traced within specific countries between weaker and richer groups, sects, etc. The concentration of social media uses in the same sphere of political economy has the potential to be a space for fomenting tensions and disharmony, which are very frequent in Egypt, Syria, India and many other countries.

Before concluding, it should be argued that social media are by their nature dynamic, and they will continue to evolve innovative applications to repel breaches from all sides. Since current social media, unlike formal media, have no effective self-regulatory mechanism, and individual privacy and security remains at risk, more innovative social media applications have yet to satisfy their users. In the absence of effective self-regulation of social media, states have excuses to intervene in the use of social media under the pretext of maintaining law and order and protecting individuals' rights, and there are frequent instances of this practice in Arab and many Asian countries. The greatest change brought by social media to the public sphere is speed and diversity of argumentative discourses from all sides between individuals or organised groups, so much so that a purposeful war of perception can be seen in these discourses. However, this may not be a universal case because, unlike other democratic countries, the Arab world, particularly its most populous country Egypt, has insufficient free space for social and political debates; hence, social media may remain the last refuge of all desperate voices. That is also the beauty of the expanding social media in the Arab world where 'Arab exceptionalism' is challenged. The Arab online public sphere represents a more dynamic face than the European or American online public spheres. Last but not least, an era of euphoric social media appears to have come to an end and a competitive and argumentative online public sphere is emerging out of the realist struggle between streets, their representatives and the regimes.

Notes

1 This chapter was originally presented at a workshop organised by Gulf Research Centre at their fourth meeting held on 25–28 August 2014 at the University of Cambridge, UK. The author wishes to thank workshop directors and participants and editors of this volume for their generous comments and suggestions to finalise this draft.

2 Nancy Fraser, 'Transnationalizing the Public Sphere on the Legitimacy and Efficacy of Public Opinion in a Post Westphalian World', *Theory, Culture & Society*, 24 (2007), 7–30 <doi:10.1177/0263276407080090>.

3 Basyouni Hamada, 'Satellite Television and Public Sphere in Egypt: Is There a Link?', *Global Media Journal*, 7 (2008).

4 William Rugh, 'Do National Political Systems Still Influence Arab Media?', *Arab Media & Society*, 2007 <http://www.arabmediasociety.com/?article=225>.

5 Al-Jazeera.net, 'Egypt State Media Changes Sides', 2011 <http://english.aljazeera.net/news/middleeast/2011/02/201121361556414860.html>.

6 Omair Anas, 'Changing Profile of Media in the Arab States', *Global Media Journal*, 2 (2013), 28–46.

7 Mohammed El-Nawawy and Adel Iskander, *Al-Jazeera: How the Free Arab News Network Scooped the World and Changed the Middle East* (US: Westview Press, 2002).

8 Kai Hafez, 'The Role of Media in the Arab World's Transformation Process', in *Bound to Cooperate: Europe and the Middle East II*, ed. by Christian-Peter Hanelt and Almut Möller (Bielefeld: Verlag Bertelsmann Stiftung, Gütersloh, 2008).

9 Abdalhadi Alijla, 'Social Networking Sites: Public or Private Sphere', 2014 <http://www.jadaliyya.com/pages/index/16828/arabicl>.

10 Marshall Mcluhan, *Understanding Media: Extensions of Man* (New York, NY: McGraw-Hill, 1964).

11 Mohammed Samir, 'The Official Page of Egyptain Army on the Facebook', 2012 <https://www.facebook.com/Egy.Army.Spox>.

12 Tom Boellstorff, *Coming of Age in Second Life* (Princeton, NJ: Princeton University Press, 2008).

13 Ibid., p. 36.

14 Anas, 'Changing Profile of Media in the Arab States'; Omair Anas, 'Facebook Campaigns in the Arab Uprisings: The Role of "Kulluna Khaled Said"', in *The Arab World: The Role of Media in the Arab World's Transformation Process*, ed. by Christoph Schmidt (Bonn: DW Akademie: International Media Studies, 2013).

15 Göran Bolin, 'The Labour of Media Use', *Information on Communication & Society*, 15 (2012), 796–814.

16 Voice of America, 'In Egypt, Facebook Serves as Tool for Government, Opponents', *Voice of America*, 2014 <http://www.voanews.com/content/in-Egypt-facebook-a-tool-for-government-and-opponents/1844165.html>.

17 Andreas Wittel, 'Digital Marx: Toward a Political Economy of Distributed Media', *tripleC*, 10 (2012), 313–333.

18 Ema Linaker, 'Top Five 2014 Middle East Social Media Trends', *social.ogilvy*, 2014 <http://social.ogilvy.com/top-five-2014-middle-east-social-media-trends/>.

19 Infocomm Authority of Singapore, 'Social Media: Landscape, Technology Roadmap', 2013 <https://www.ida.gov.sg/~/media/Files/Infocomm Landscape/Technology/TechnologyRoadmap/SocialMedia.pdf>.

20 The Nielsen Company, 'State of the Media – the Social Media Report 2012', *Nielsen*, 2012, pp. 2014–05–23 <http://www.nielsen.com/us/en/insights/reports/2012/state-of-the-media-the-social-media-report-2012.html>.

21 *Gulf Business*, 'Middle East Ad Revenues to Grow by 6.3% in 2014', 2014 <http://gulfbusiness.com/2013/12/middle-east-ad-revenues-to-grow-by-6-3-in-2014/#.U4izbfmSyy4>.

22 Fadi Salem and Racha Mourtada, 'Social Media in the Arab World: Influencing Societal and Cultural Change', *Arab Social Media Report*, 2012 <www.arabsocialmediareport.com/userManagement/PDFD/ASMR 4 updated 29 08 12>.

23 Socialbakers, 'Facebook Brands Stats – Saudi Arabia Fans Only', *Socialbakers*, 2015 <http://www.socialbakers.com/facebook-pages/brands/country/saudi-arabia/>.

24 Tom Burghardt, 'Mind Your Tweets: The CIA Social Networking Surveillance System', *wikileaks.org*, 2014 <https://wikileaks.org/wiki/Mind_Your_Tweets:_The_CIA_Social_Networking_Surveillance_System>.

25 Voice of America.

26 *The Indian Express*, 'Cops Ask FB to Block Violence Video', 2013 <http://www.nielsen.com/us/en/insights/reports/2012/state-of-the-media-the-social-media-report-2012.html>.

27 *BBC*, 'Altered Images: Egypt's Disinformation War', 2013 <http://www.bbc.com/news/blogs-news-from-elsewhere-23469516>.

28 A Facebook page Da Begad especially exposing such photo-shopped photos widely used on Egyptian social media, <https://www.facebook.com/DaBegad?fref=photo>.

29 Freedom House, 'Freedom on the Net: Egypt', 2014 <https://freedomhouse.org/report/freedom-net/2014/egypt>.

30 Fadi Salem, Racha Mourtade and Sara Alshaer, 'Transforming Education in the Arab World: Breaking Barriers in the Age of Social Learning', *Arab Social Media Report*, 2013 <http://www.arabsocialmediareport.com/UserManagement/PDF/ASMR_5_Report_Final.pdf>.

31 Visually Creative Service, 'Social Media Usage in the Middle East, Statistics and Trends', 2013 <http://visual.ly/social-media-usage-middle-east-statistics-and-trends>.

32 Andrew Kohut and others, 'Social Networking Popular Across Globe: Arab Publics Most Likely to Express Political Views Online', *Pew Research Center*, 2012 <http://www.pewresearch.org/daily-number/arab-publics-turning-to-social-networks-to-express-political-views/>.

33 Gary Stringer, 'Social Media Revenue Will Hit $30.1 Billion by 2017', *accuracast.com*, 2013 <http://www.accuracast.com/news/social-media-7471/social-media-revenue-will-hit-2-5-billion-by-2017/>.

34 Mustapha Ajbaili, 'Egypt TV Presenters Tout Twitter Ban over Anti-Sisi Hashtag', *Al-Arabiya TV News*, 2014 <Egypt-TV-presenters-tout-twitter-ban-over-anti-Sisi-hashtag.html>.

35 Al-Jazeera.net, 'Egypt's Twitter Hashtags Declare Defiance', 2014 <http://m.aljazeera.com/story/201448154324428189>; Al-Arabiya TV, 'Egypt TV Presenters Tout Twitter Ban over Anti-Sisi Hashtag', 2014 <http://english.alarabiya.net/en/media/television-and-radio/2014/03/31/Egypt-TV-presenters-tout-twitter-ban-over-anti-Sisi-hashtag.html>.

36 Mohammad Elmasri, 'Egypt's Campaign of Elimination: Pro-June 30 Analysts and the Quantitative Rationalization for Egypt's Coup', *Open Democracy*, 2014.

37 Yasmine Salleh, 'Activists Who Backed Mursi's Fall Turn against Military', *Reuters*, 20 February 2014 <http://www.reuters.com/article/2014/02/20/us-egypt-politics-tamarud-idUSBREA1J1E420140220>.

38 Almonitor, 'Egypt's Tamarod Plagued by Division', 2014 <http://www.al-monitor.com/pulse/originals/2014/03/tamarod-movement-egypt-divisions-elections.html>.

39 Anas, 'Facebook Campaigns in the Arab Uprisings: The Role of "Kulluna Khaled Said"'.

40 Al-Arabiya TV.

41 *Al-Arabiya*, 'Paralyzed Saudi Pleads for Help on Twitter, Receives Attention and Money', 2014 <http://english.alarabiya.net/en/variety/2014/05/12/Paralyzed-Saudi-pleads-for-help-on-Twitter-receives-attention-and-mon>.

42 Denis McQuail, *McQuail's Mass Communication Theory* (London: Sage Publications, 2005).

43 John Cannarella and Joshua Spechler, 'Epidemiological Modeling of Online Social Network Dynamics', *Princeton University*, 2014 <http://arxiv.org/pdf/1401.4208v1.pdf>.

4

Social Media and Unethical P2P Diplomacy in the Bahrain Uprising

Marc Owen Jones

Who are the diplomats? The pertinence of this question became abundantly clear when I, as an appellant at a recent tribunal hearing against the Information Commissioner and the Foreign and Commonwealth Office (FCO), was asked by the barrister, 'Are you a diplomat'? I replied somewhat non-committally, stating, 'not technically'. I was not being facetious; rather, I wished to expose the changing boundaries regarding who or who may not be considered a diplomat. For some time, I have been using social media to draw attention to the human rights crisis in Bahrain and, as such, have been advocating a more ethical foreign policy by the UK government. Social media have allowed me and many other like-minded individuals to interact directly with Bahrainis and highlight that the UK government's policy does not necessarily reflect the popular will of British citizens. Such acts themselves constitute acts of peer-to-peer (P2P) diplomacy and challenge traditional notions of diplomatic processes. This chapter, therefore, looks at how people and government in Bahrain use social media, especially Twitter, to provide news and information about the 2011 Bahrain uprising. The chapter also examines the ethics of P2P diplomacy that are undermined by the intimidation, incarceration and killing of citizens to advocate the promotion of social justice and Global Public Goods.

Given the potential problems posed by social media to diplomacy in authoritarian regimes such as Bahrain, this chapter discusses how the Bahraini government has attempted to utilise social media to influence the nature of public, 'peer-to-peer' (P2P) diplomacy. In so doing, it highlights how social media might be exploited to underpin ethically problematic diplomatic strategies. By exploring a number of the activities of Bahrain's 'unorthodox diplomatic community', this chapter discusses how the government has interfered in the social media scope and militated against ethical P2P diplomacy.

Typically conducted by elite officials behind closed doors, the contours of diplomacy have been altered by social media. Social media and the internet have deprived the government of its monopoly on the diplomatic message, and different actors with radically different aims are now engaging in what might be termed 'diplomatic activity'. Indeed, the 2011 uprising in Bahrain brought 'to the fore an undefined cast of informal actors', forming an 'unorthodox "diplomatic community"'.[1] This community includes all manner of people and institutions, from activists, NGOs and bloggers to students and concerned citizens. Twitter in particular has been useful in generating these transnational networks and unorthodox diplomatic communities, and Twitter users have been vocal in commentating on unfolding events, regardless of where they sit on the political spectrum.

Governments, too, have attempted to adapt to the changes brought on by social media. Matthias Lufkens notes: 'Call it Twiplomacy, Facebook diplomacy, weiplomacy, or simply digital diplomacy, the use of social networks has become an integral part of government communication'.[2] Described by Karl Ritter as a 'Twitter Celebrity' in the Persian Gulf, Bahrain's Foreign Minister, Shaykh Khalid Al Khalifa, has been particularly active on Twitter – his prolific social media use is itself an inadvertent diplomatic strategy, one that attempts to portray Bahrain as a tech-savvy and forward-thinking modern monarchy. In 2011, Khalid Al Khalifa's regular tweeting prompted his Swedish counterpart, Carl Bildt, to contact him via Twitter. Carl Bildt simply stated, 'trying to get in touch with you on an issue'. While this tweet exposed Bahrain's worrying diplomatic silence and intransigence, it also highlighted the relevance of new communication technologies, in both official and unofficial diplomatic circles.

Indeed, just as Carl Bildt uses social media to 'build his brand as a politician', so too does Khalid Al Khalifa. Yet while the use of Twitter by these high-profile officials may be good fodder for news-gathering organisations, some countries are claiming to take social media seriously. Diplomatic bodies such as the FCO state that they are using social media to 'crowd source' (FCO Website) information to 'assist in the consultation process'.[3] Although it is not always clear how this is being done, certain strategies are being used to at least give the impression that the FCO is taking social media seriously. On 8 April 2013, former Foreign Office Minister Alistair Burt answered questions about Bahrain live on Twitter.[4] Designed to cause as little offence as possible to all parties, Burt's responses to questions were unsurprisingly diplomatic and did not deviate from a carefully selected script. However, such diplomatic tact appeared notably callous in an era where images and knowledge of human rights abuses in Bahrain were widely disseminated and documented on social media. Bahrainis were not alone in feeling betrayed by the seeming callousness of Britain's self-serving tact. Coupled with an increasingly prevalent global language of human rights, the openness of such diplomatic exchanges has exposed them to further ethical scrutiny.

Social media have been a key platform in exposing this issue of ethics. Technological devolution has not only forced traditional diplomats to adopt new means of communication but has also brought other challenges. It is not enough, as Matthias Lufkens argues, simply to say that social media have allowed governments to bring 'citizens closer to their leaders'.[5] Such arguments may carry more weight in democratic societies where leaders are obliged to listen to their citizens, but in so-called liberal autocracies such as Bahrain, diplomatic efforts tend to reflect the agenda of the Saudi-backed Al Khalifa regime and are less amenable to public influence.

Towards Ethical P2P Diplomacy

Of particular relevance to social media is the idea of public diplomacy. According to Juyan Zhang, public diplomacy falls under three definitions: 'image cultivation' or the branding of a nation; diplomacy aimed at improving mutual understanding between nations; and diplomacy aimed at promoting ideas that facilitate the execution of a nation's foreign policy.[6]

However, Zhang expands the existing definition of public diplomacy to include the promotion of Global Public Goods (GPG). This shift represents 'a way of understanding certain transborder and global problems' as well as the need for diplomatic efforts that promote 'global environment, international financial stability,... market efficiency, health, knowledge, peace and security, and humanitarian rights'. Of particular relevance here are the GPGs of peace, security and humanitarian rights, which have corollary implications for promoting social justice.

Despite Zhang's expansion of the term public diplomacy, his argument still implies that the government retains a monopoly on diplomatic engagement. Yet engagement of non-governmental actors and citizens in Bahrain's social media-scope has resulted in what Shay Attias calls 'peer-to-peer' (P2P) diplomacy, 'wherein civilians – by virtue of social media – are not only consumers of government information, but also information producers, with the potential to bypass existing official government bodies'.[7] Attias views this as an overwhelmingly positive force, arguing that social media are allowing citizens to both carry and shape the message. This, Attias continues, overcomes the biggest problem of traditional public diplomacy, which might easily be perceived as government propaganda. On the other side of the coin, however, P2P technologies and the unorthodox communities that they have helped foster pose significant challenges for traditional public diplomacy in a number of ways. Firstly, the government may lose its relative monopoly over the regulation of information directed at foreign audiences. Secondly, this loss of monopoly makes it harder for the government to remain on message.

If we take the traditional definition of public diplomacy as 'communication with foreign publics for the purpose of achieving a foreign policy objective', the Bahraini government's desire to attract foreign direct investment means that a lot of public diplomatic efforts have been limited to improving Bahrain's image or reputation among potential investors, tourists and global publics.[8] However, this rose-tinted image has been challenged by diverging sensibilities between different political actors following the government's harsh repression of the past four years – repression that has resulted in the polarisation of society, with some supporting the government and many opposing it. As such, there has been a corollary polarisation on Twitter, with some citizens attempting to promote an image of

Bahrain as a country with a repressive, autocratic government and others saying that Bahrain is an 'oasis of peace and tolerance'.[9] Since image is vital when it comes to attracting investment, the regime and its supporters have attempted to cultivate an image of Bahrain as a playground for global capital. Political protest, dissent and repression undermine this image, and official diplomatic efforts in Bahrain have attempted to hide the country's history of brutal repression. The suppression of dissent and promotion of a 'privatised urban infrastructure' are all designed 'to sustain a façade of stability; of Bahrain as a business-friendly tourist hub'.[10]

Ethical Diplomacy versus Public Diplomacy and PR

Nevertheless, with some of these unorthodox online groups attempting to raise issues of social justice and others actively trying to ignore them, an ethical distinction must be made between these different diplomatic acts. If 'anti-diplomacy represents acts undertaken by people who are 'bothered by what their state is doing', then diplomacy is surely those acts undertaken with the approval of the government. Although implied, this definition of 'anti-diplomacy' is devoid of axiological connotations and refers only to the act of disapproval as opposed to the reasons for that disapproval.[11] However, were Zhang's new conception of public diplomacy to be combined with the notion of P2P diplomacy, it might be argued that ethical P2P diplomacy is a process of diplomacy whereby citizen diplomats advocate the preservation, distribution and creation of those GPGs that relate to social justice. Hence, rather than anti-diplomacy, ethical P2P diplomacy may be a better definition *for* those who are concerned about when their state acts in a way inimical to the spreading of social justice.

There are large obstacles to the spread of ethical P2P diplomacy in Bahrain, however. Given Bahrain's small size and historic subordination to larger powers, both government and non-governmental actors have found it necessary to appeal to global publics in order to lobby for their respective causes, which are often in direct conflict, often between pro-democracy activists and human rights organisations on the one hand and the government and the security services on the other.[12] Social media have brought this tension to the surface, making it an increasingly public diplomatic spectacle. Yet Bahrain's lack of sovereignty has meant that its foreign policy has traditionally been subsumed within the interests of external actors such as Saudi Arabia, the UK and the US. As such, Bahrain's capacity to pursue autonomous foreign policy objectives is constrained by the interests of other actors, whose geostrategic interests are often not conducive to the spread of GPG. As a result, Bahrain's public diplomacy is often designed to make the Bahrain-Western alliance more palatable to a global audience. Crucial to the government arsenal are the numerous, mainly British and American PR companies, who have been paid at least $US32.5 million since 2011 to cultivate Bahrain's image.[13] In addition to hiring public relations (PR) companies, Bahrain has reacted to negative publicity by expanding public diplomacy methods through traditional means such as creating news outlets, placing 'media consuls' overseas, and organising youth delegations to meet with people on Capitol Hill.[14]

In addition to these more traditional methods of public diplomacy, the government has not been oblivious to the role of social media and non-state actors. As Shay Attias states, 'there is still a role for governments to play in P2P diplomacy. Governments that can harness the communication potential of their citizens will be the ones to conduct effective public diplomacy offensives'. Indeed, the Bahrain government has capitalised on P2P diplomacy in order to ensure that public diplomacy from Bahrain is not really about GPG but about cultivating the image of a business-friendly Bahrain, one in which human rights violations do not take centre stage. This, coupled with the intimidation of the informal, ethical diplomatic community by the Bahraini authorities or pro-government cyber-vigilantes, has made it easier for 'on message' citizens to perpetuate an image that marginalises suffering and promotes national branding. The hegemonic order's techniques for thwarting the spread of GPG on social media include reputation management companies such as Olton,[15] spyware such as FinFisher, IP spying,[16] and draconian media legislation. These broad processes of surveillance and censorship have been supplemented by intimidation, enacted via techniques such as trolling and naming and shaming.[17]

Influential figures, such as the Foreign Minister Khalid Al Khalifa, also have a moderating effect on social media and have attempted to stymie ethical P2P diplomacy. On one occasion, he relied on the social media equivalent of the 'hue and cry' and tweeted vociferously in criticism of the Al-Jazeera documentary *Shouting in the Dark*, a film extremely critical of the Bahraini government.[18] Khalid Al Khalifa tweeted: 'It's clear that in Qatar there are those who don't want anything good for Bahrain. And this film on Al-Jazeera English is the best example of this inexplicable hostility'.[19] For Bahrain's informal P2P diplomats, the government's line was clear; the documentary ought to be condemned. The ensuing attention generated rumours that Bahrain was to sever ties with Qatar, although Khalid Al Khalifa assured people that this was not the case. The controversy did not end there, and Khalid Al Khalifa called for people to vote against the movie in an online poll for the UK Bafta Awards. The impact was dramatic as, Vanessa Thorpe wrote in the *Guardian*:

> The fight for the top spot in an innocuous British magazine poll first became part of an international public relations war last weekend, soon after Khalid al-Khalifa, Bahrain's foreign minister and a member of the ruling family, tweeted a call for his 80,000 Twitter followers to cast a vote for any one of the other nominees in the *Radio Times* poll... 'I invite everyone to stand with Bahrain and vote against the harmful al-Jazeera film,' he wrote. The tweet caused a Twitter storm of support from the Middle East for the Sri Lankan film. One user called Jaguar wrote: 'Oh noble people of the Gulf, vote for Sri Lanka and prevent the Shia infidels from defaming Bahrain'.[20]

While Khalid Al Khalifa's hue and cry prompted thousands of tweets from Bahrain and the Gulf's informal P2P diplomats, all eager to protect brand Bahrain, he has been notably lax on generating condemnation of illegal behaviour on social media by those working to support government repression. He did not, for example, condemn the pro-government 7areghum Twitter account for engaging in acts that contravened both national and international law. The Bahrain Independent Commission of Inquiry (BICI) report stated:

> The GoB uses firewalls to block certain social media and other websites. However, the GoB has not permanently shut down Twitter feeds such as Harghum [sic] even though they produced material that international law requires to be prohibited and which is in fact prohibited under Bahrain law.[21]

Although the government announced media reforms following the release of the BICI Report, this was little more than an attempt to appease international allies while continuing with censorship. As stated above, new media laws appear to legitimise even tighter state control over the media. The creation of an independent regulator, the Supreme Council for Media and Communication (SCMC), following recommendations in the BICI Report, is questionable considering that all members are essentially appointed by the King.[22] Indeed, the government and its loyalists have attempted to use P2P diplomacy to promote an image that purposely tries to hide or limit the visibility of anything designed to harm Bahrain's reputation.

Social Media Awards

Although social media have the added benefit of appearing to be crowd-sourced, and thus removed from accusations of government propaganda, the GoB have attempted to moderate the social media-scope by offering guidance to those attempting to navigate the information deluge that is social media.[23] The Information Affairs Authority's (IAA)[24] decision to give out Social Media Awards a week before the anniversary of the 14 February uprising of 2011, highlights this.[25] The awards ceremony 'pre-empted the Ministry of the Interior's warning a week later, which read, "Public urged not 2 believe everything on all TV stations or soc media. Get info from official sources"'.[26] Very much aware that social media posed a challenge to the regime's ability to control its image, both at home and abroad, the government used the Social Media Awards in an attempt to confer legitimacy and credibility on certain news sources on Twitter and Facebook.

Unsurprisingly, those who won awards included the Foreign Minister, the Ministry of the Interior, the Bahrain News Agency (itself part of the IAA) and two very pro-government newspapers (*Al-Ayam* and *Al-Watan*). There was even an award for 'most-distinguished-expat', which was awarded to someone who said that Bahrain human rights activist Nabil Rajab sent thugs to cut off an Englishman's fingers.[27] Unsurprisingly, Bahrain's most distinguished expat did not appear at the ceremony, which did little to mitigate people's concerns about who was actually operating such accounts. However, the ceremony and awards attempted to bestow legitimacy on accounts perceived to be 'on message' and thus represented governmental informational intervention in the sphere of P2P diplomacy. This was particularly important with respect to expatriates, for expatriates are often used as diplomatic pawns, a way of demonstrating to the international community that foreigners are content with the current system. Giving the impression that foreigners are content may remove embassies' incentive to lobby in defence of their citizens. In an international community such as Bahrain, these expatriate social media diplomats might then send a positive message to other foreigners considering working in Bahrain.

The Twelve-Point Flag

In order to justify to the outside world that the government was reacting in a reasonable fashion to an exogenous, Iran-inspired plot, Bahrain's public diplomacy efforts involved stigmatising the fringes of popular political movements.[28] Social media provided a fertile breeding ground for this evidence, and such grass-roots conspiracies were appropriated by the government to fit its diplomatic strategy. This was demonstrated by the Twelve-Point Flag Conspiracy. According to the NGO Bahrain Watch,

> 'In a live Al-Jazeera TV broadcast, official salesperson for Bahrain Samira Rajab (an upper house legislator at the time before being promoted to Minister of State for Information Affairs a couple of months later) holds up a photo asserting it shows a Bahraini flag with 12 points rather than the official five, at a pro-democracy demonstration. Her claim is part of a myth that anti-government protesters wanted to convert Bahrain into a Shia Islamic republic with the backing of Iran, including changing the national flag so that it represents the twelve Shia Imams. In fact, the flag in the photo only contains 10 points (two standard 5-point flags joined together)'.[29]

This conspiracy started via a YouTube video which was circulated on Twitter and Facebook. It quickly received 18,400 views (not including mirrors) and was legitimised when a number of online commentators, including one studying for a PhD in Law at Leeds University, confirmed without proof that loyalist students at the University of Bahrain were being bullied into taking down the official Bahraini flag and replacing it with one with twelve points.[30] Another Bahraini, a former professor of international relations, stated on Twitter: 'Do you know what's the story behind the 12 edged flag? Well, all I can say is that majority of Shia in #Bahrain are Twelvism Shia. Research it'.[31] Despite the ludicrous nature of the claims, the conspiracy represents an act of unethical P2P diplomacy, one that was appropriated (if not started) by the state. Yet, because it appeared to have had its roots in social media, it legitimised government claims of outside involvement by implying that there was popular consent for this theory. Amidst a climate of fear and legitimised by credible members of the online community and the government, the conspiracy's impact was perhaps surprising given its entirely erroneous nature. However, the video, spawned from P2P interactions, was enough to increase diplomatic tensions with Iran.

The Twelve-Point Flag Conspiracy even found its way into the Arabic version of the BICI Report, a document written by a group of international legal experts on the causes and occurrences of the 2011 unrest. Due to these dubious insertions in the Arabic translation, it was quickly withdrawn. Samira Rajab's loyalty was duly rewarded, and she was appointed Minister of State for Information Affairs. The fact that the post was created especially for Samira Rajab is particularly galling, not least because she is, as the parody account for Bahrain's Prime Minister states, 'Miss Information'. Populating the government with people whose penchant for truth-telling is subservient to the national interest could potentially lead to defectiveness in foreign policy decision-making.

#UniteBH

The collective effervescence on the ground in the early days of the 2011 uprising, coupled with the relative goodwill between different factions of protesters, led to a Twitter campaign that utilised the hashtag #UniteBH (Short for Unite Bahrain). In many ways, despite the government's killing of protesters in mid-February, the #UniteBH campaign was indicative of a certain sense of hope and unity in the country. The aesthetic impact of the #UniteBH slogan portrayed the origins of the campaign, which had its roots in the Zeitgeist of the time – social media. Initially, social media users were invited to tweet messages of unity to highlight what all Bahrainis had in common, irrespective of their sectarian or political allegiance.

These tweets ranged from the serious, such as that from @baderkamal, 'The best way to stop sectarianism is to stop using the words Shia, Sunni, Sectarianism',[32] to the comical, such as that from @Redbelt, 'Sunnis and shia both pirate satellite channels through Dreamboxes. #bahrain #unitebh'. The #UniteBH phenomenon evolved into efforts of creative solidarity involving a number of different Bahrainis. Saleh Nass, a Bahraini film-maker, asked people to send in clips of themselves saying what #UniteBH meant to them. One interviewee stated, 'We never used to have people saying: He is Shii, he is Sunni, he is Persian, he is Banyan. All of us are brothers and sisters'.[33] Whether or not one agrees with the particular comments of the participants, the sentiments expressed were overwhelmingly a display of unity and bonhomie. A song called 'Bahraini Unite' even emerged. The lyrics include the lines 'Let's stop this fight, unite…no Sunni no Shi'a, let's hold tight, like red and white'.

However, any society that has to pay attention to issues of division and unity, even prior to further polarisation, is a society self-conscious of those cleavages. The reason for #UniteBH's potency lay in its fundamental opposition to the Bahraini regime's divide-and-rule tactics. Shows of peaceful unity, demonstrated by the slogan 'no Sunni, no Shi'a, Just Bahraini', rankled with the authorities, who reacted harshly to these displays of cross-sect and cross-group co-operation. The creator of the #UniteBH movement was arrested and interrogated overnight in connection with his involvement.[34] In another instance, some guards at a checkpoint ridiculed a driver for wearing a t-shirt saying 'No Sunni, No Shi'a, Just Bahraini'.[35] In addition to this intimidation, the government sought to co-opt and monitor the #UniteBH campaign to ensure that it did not get out of the hand and to give the impression that it (the government) was the sponsor of any unity-based phenomenon.

The Ministry of Social Development endorsed the campaign, and it soon became a vehicle for promoting Bahrain's economy and depicting the regime as tolerant and inclusive. #UniteBH events began to be held at symbolically strategic locations chosen to project Bahrain's façade of neoliberal modernity. These included the Formula One motor racing circuit and modern shopping malls. At this stage, it was obvious that the campaign had been co-opted and appropriated by counter-revolutionary actors and was now being used to brand Bahrain as a stable country with a relatively harmonious society. Even the Foreign Minister, Khalid Al Khalifa, tweeted; '#UniteBH made my day. Meant a lot to me as a Bahraini'.[36] If it had not been doomed before, it certainly was now.

Yet, in either its original or co-opted form, the #UniteBH campaign was criticised as being an endeavour created by mainly middle-class Bahrainis, the so-called 'Nidoer'[37] or 'Chicken Nugget'[38] generations. Run by technologically savvy and, usually, good English speakers, the campaign seemed to be directed more at projecting an image of normalcy and unity to the rest of the world, rather than representing the demands of the marginalised segments of Bahrain's populace. The fact that most of the campaign's output was in English tended to highlight the diplomatic, outward-looking intent of those participating in it. Yet, as a facet of public diplomacy, and despite its shortcomings, #UniteBH was very much a crowd-sourced, bottom-up attempt at ethical P2P diplomacy, one that was soon co-opted into an exercise in unethical P2P diplomacy.

#UniF1ed

The following year, activists, human rights associations and journalists were using social media as a form of ethical P2P diplomacy in attempts to have the Formula One Grand Prix motor race cancelled. Their argument was mainly twofold: Holding the F1 a) resulted 'in an increase in human rights violations and b) attempted to whitewash human rights abuses by projecting a veneer of normalcy in Bahrain'.[39] However, the government, its PR agencies, and informal P2P diplomats were attempting to whitewash Bahrain's political stalemate by initiating a social media campaign under the hashtag #UniF1ed. The phrase, a play on the word unified, was an attempt at public diplomacy designed to illustrate a united front and brand Bahrain to the international community as a safe and welcoming place to thousands of potential tourists. Undoubtedly, the slogan itself evolved from the UniteBH campaign and exploited the grass-roots credentials of the previous effort to lend it some legitimacy.

The hashtag #UniF1ed became synonymous with the main slogan, 'Unif1ed, One Nation in Celebration', and government institutions such as the IAA adopted it for their social media campaign,[40] giving it the illusion of modernity and suggesting that it had popular consent. Many people on Twitter and Facebook changed their profile pictures to include the Twibbon *#UniF1ed*, transforming their personal social media accounts into marketing efforts on behalf of the Bahraini regime. Those accounts with the UniF1ed Twibbon marked themselves as being legitimate conveyors of the pro-regime message or a form of inadvertent filtering that demarcated those who could be seen as the Bahrain government's legitimate ambassadors on Twitter. In many ways, these Twibbons were tantamount to wearing Bahrain-branded clothing. By initiating such a scheme, various Tweeps became inadvertent P2P diplomats.

Hence, while the conflict over whether to stage the F1 was tearing up Bahrain, the government maintained that sport brought people together.[41] However, the success of the marketing campaign was partly due to the need to aggressively combat the negative press on Bahrain and partly due to the desire of many loyalist Bahrainis to secure a victory against human rights activists. Ultimately, however, the result was a rather callous exercise in P2P diplomatic branding. To the lay person, social media enforced the idea that the #UniF1ed campaign was a grass-roots campaign. If the Twelve-point Flag Conspiracy was a genuine bottom-up attempt at P2P propaganda diplomacy, then #UniF1ed was a public diplomacy campaign dressed up as a grass-roots initiative. Although in 2011 negative coverage of Bahrain drowned out the positive,[42] harming Bahrain's brand, it is unclear whether subsequent campaigns (after the government had had time to repress dissent and improve its PR/diplomatic strategy) were more successful.

Celebrities

Other examples of the government trying to use social media for public diplomacy include the exploitation of the visits of influential figures to further cultivate a positive image of Bahrain. In March 2014, it was announced that Joe Calzaghe, the retired boxing world champion, was heading to Bahrain's Diplomat Radisson Blu hotel to share anecdotes about his long and successful career.[43] Although Calzaghe withdrew for undisclosed reasons, former England international football player Stuart Pearce took his place.[44] Pearce is one of many celebrities to visit the Kingdom. Other visitors since the outbreak of the unrest in 2011 include milkshake purveyor and socialite Kim Kardashian, opera singer Placido Domingo, Arab pop star Nancy Ajram, British DJ Calvin Harris and, most recently, veteran blues musician Eric Clapton. In addition, various Formula One drivers descend on Bahrain during the annual grand prix, an event also used to increase Bahrain's international profile and project a veneer of civility and modernity. This 'celebrity diplomacy' incenses human rights activists, as it works to normalise a regime accused of widespread human rights abuses.

While this is not a critique of celebrity diplomacy, it begins from the standpoint that celebrities can provide a mediating function between foreign publics and governments and, if exploited, can serve to introduce ideologically weighted sentiments to audiences who would not necessarily describe themselves as political. Of course, a distinction can be made between those celebrities who go to Bahrain with the simple purpose of self-promotion and money-making, and those who actively spout propaganda supporting the current regime on social media. Nancy Ajram, a famous Lebanese singer, was certainly guilty of the latter. Soon after being met by a delegation from the 'Kingdom', she went on Twitter to describe Bahrain as a 'lovely country that is walking on the path of success and prosperity year after year'.[45]

These unusually prosaic words mimicked the lines of the government PR agencies, prompting both praise and condemnation from Twitter users. Kim Kardashian was a little more circumspect, stating that she wanted to 'set the record straight' on Bahrain. She then tweeted: 'I just got to Bahrain! OMG can I move here please? Prettiest place on earth!' Yet Kardashian's tweet glossed 'over any sign of the political repression suffered by many Bahrainis'.[46] At the time, Kim Kardashian was the tenth most followed Twitter user in the world, with 17 million followers.[47] The message was retweeted over 2,200 times. Even Bahrain's premier diplomat, Khalid Al Khalifa, thanked Kim Kardashian on Twitter for her tweet.[48] In another video, Kardashian espoused the merits of Bahrain, telling the gathered crowds that her family and 'everyone in the states' must come to Bahrain.[49]

This video was viewed 166,890 times, not including mirrored copies. Unfortunately for ethical P2P diplomacy,

> Both Kardashian and Ajram's tweets and videos indicate a 'marginalisation of suffering', one where Bahrain's political crisis is either ignored or made to appear absent. As Perlmutter and Wagner state, such rhetoric serves to show not what is actually happening, but to 'direct public gaze' to an interpretation of reality as desired by the dominant power. In this case, the power in question is the Bahraini government, and their desired reality is 'all is well in Bahrain'. So rather than being diplomatic, celebrities are attempting to influence public perceptions of a country's image. In other words – it's blatant PR, a form of voluntary 'ambush-marketing' in which Bahrain builds up its brand by piggybacking on reputation of celebrities.[50]

The government's efforts also present problems for the notion of celebrity activism. While Mark Wheeler and Iian Kapoor argue that 'celebrity activism represents a democratisation of foreign policy processes in which the traditional, closed forms of diplomatic practice have been replaced by more open forms of public diplomacy', this is not necessarily conducive to the idea of diplomacy as ethically motivated global action.[51] Indeed, within a framework that sees the ethical act as one that promotes social justice, the aforementioned celebrity diplomacy is unethical, supporting a status quo obstructive to the emergence of social justice. However, at least when celebrities take to social media platforms to make visible their endorsements of countries, their attempts at branding can be visibly interrogated by these unorthodox diplomatic communities. This was certainly the case with Kim Kardashian, whose comment that Bahrain was the 'prettiest place on earth' was used as a sort of anti-diplomatic detournement, with hundreds posting 'ironic tweets'[52] scorning the celebrity's ignorance. One such example simply read, 'you must be new here'.[53]

A worrying aspect of the use of celebrities is that, by exploiting their popularity, governments are also increasing the likelihood of 'virality', which has the effect of overcoming the informational deluge. In other words, it allows government authorities to pass the noise while keeping the signal. However, this does not mean, as Matthew Wallin states, 'that the message is accomplishing its intended purpose with the target audience'.[54] The Kim Kardashian episode demonstrated this, and it was not long before she deleted her tweet about Bahrain being the prettiest place on earth. Indeed, diplomacy can never guarantee a ubiquitous and homogeneous reception among its audience, yet Kardashian's information intervention can still be utilised as an excuse for foreign audiences to justify an impression of Bahrain as an oasis of tranquillity and security. It inserts complexity into the good-versus-bad binary and allows any singular discourse, ethical or otherwise, to become dominant. The fact that Kim Kardashian also declined an invitation to meet with representatives of the Bahrain Center for Human Rights demonstrated to her fans where her allegiances lay.[55]

In addition to celebrities, the government has contacted power brokers who are on message to extend their attempts to paint the Bahrain authorities as a progressive force fighting an encroaching Shi'i theocratic threat. Ed Husain, a former Islamist activist and now an author and senior fellow at America's 'establishment' foreign policy think tank, the Council on Foreign Relations, was invited to Bahrain, where he proceeded to tweet many of his thoughts. His obsequious praise of the ruling Al Khalifa and his often scathing remarks about the opposition prompted a 'fuss on Twitter'.[56] He described Bahrain's Foreign Minister as 'thoughtful, caveated, and visionary', and dismissed many of Bahrain's activists as 'thugs on streets'. The stir caused by Ed Husain was demonstrated by the sudden creation of a parody account (@FakeEdHusain), the author of which tweeted, among other things 'I know you're supposed to wait at least 3 days, but I called His Excellency today. Just to hear his voice again. To engage'.[57] Despite the criticism and ensuing Twitter reaction, which highlighted the existence of this unorthodox diplomatic community, the social media saga ultimately generated much more interest in Husain's ensuing *New York Times* Op-Ed, which painted the Bahrain regime as progressive and forward-thinking – and thus deserving of Western support.[58] Most troubling of all is the fact that Ed Husain was using Twitter to narrate very traditional diplomatic procedures rather than engaging with the Bahraini activists and opposition on Twitter. Husain's approach seems to reflect an inertia among the establishment in coming to terms with P2P diplomacy. Indeed, it is not the number of followers, or volume of interactions, but the quality and nature of those interactions.

Conclusion

Attempts at ethical P2P diplomacy have been undermined by the intimidation, incarceration, and killing of those citizens more likely to advocate the promotion of social justice and GPG. The GoB's attempts at image cultivation 'through propaganda, psychological operations, information intervention, and strategic public diplomacy' pose problems for the ethical act of diplomacy, which involves the encouragement and upholding of GPG.[59] Despite the rise of social media and the opportunities for ethical P2P diplomacy, the Bahraini authorities and those representing the hegemonic order have been able to engage in a form of P2P diplomacy that remains focused on cultivating Bahrain's image as a modern, liberal, finance-friendly Middle Eastern hub.

Foreign audiences, whether directly or indirectly, can absorb this propaganda, which poses a challenge for news-gathering individuals and organisations.[60] Of course, this does not mean that ethical P2P activism is not effective. Far from it. However, the purpose of this chapter was simply to highlight the challenges it has faced in Bahrain, while also demonstrating how government information intervention on social media platforms might complement citizen-led efforts at public diplomacy as 'branding'. Furthermore, it addresses the issue raised by Shally Attias in discussing the limitations of P2P diplomacy, as governments cannot simply 'impose an image that is desired by the state and not the actual picture'.[61] Indeed, the government's strategy is that of damage limitation and image salvage, one facilitated by simultaneous attempts to silence oppositional voices.

The notion of P2P diplomacy also raises questions about the ethical problems of co-opting citizens to perpetuate a pro-regime message, often achieved by diluting messages from those advocating the need for social justice. For Bahrain, whose small size and lack of true sovereignty has made it amenable to outside influence, the efforts of P2P diplomats in attempting to paint Bahrain as a neoliberal haven, worthy of investment, are increasingly important in a country that is tied economically and politically to conservative Saudi Arabia. P2P diplomats must pick up the fallout of hard-line security measures against reform and convince the outside world that this modern 'oasis of democracy' is more than just a facade.

Furthermore, in a state whose government is widely perceived by many inhabitants as illegitimate, diplomatic efforts undertaken by the state bring with them their own questions of legitimacy. If the country's unelected ministries, dominated by members of the ruling family, cannot be said to have a mandate to conduct international relations on behalf of a willing population, then the actual line between unofficial and official acts of diplomacy becomes increasingly blurred. However, the government has a disproportionate amount of resources compared to those forces typically advocating social justice, and this allows it to distort the information continuum in its favour through the use of PR, P2P diplomacy and reputation management strategies.

Given Bahrain's inability to be entirely autonomous in its foreign policy, policy objectives are subordinated to the ambitions of powers such as the US, whose relationship with the conservative Saudi regime stymies the emergence of democracy in the region. As John Horne states, the GoB works hard to 'control the "field of representability" through which it [is] encountered, a framing buttressed by Western states' keenness to keep democratic challenges to a strategic ally away from their public's gaze'.[62] Much of this has been played out on social media, thus demonstrating another front to P2P diplomacy. However, unless there is meaningful pressure from outside powers such as the US with regard to the exchange of GPG, Bahrain will have little incentive to radically alter its diplomatic strategy.

Notes

1 Clerc Louis, 'Concerned Citizens and Secret Operatives?', *New Diplomatic History*, 2012 <http://newdiplomatichistory.org/concerned-citizens-and-secret-operatives/>.

2 Matthias Lufken, 'Tweet Me to Your Leader: How the World's Big Shots Use Social Media', *The Atlantic*, 2012 <doi:2015-03-22>.

3 Foreign Commonweath Office, 'FCO Social Media Policy', *Foreign Commonweath Office* <http://blogs.fco.gov.uk/digitaldiplomacy/social-media-policy/>.

4 Foreign Commonwealth Office, 'Alistair Burt Twitter Q&A on Bahrain. Storify', 2013 <alistair-burt-twitter-q-and-a-on-bahrain>.

5 Lufken.

6 Juyan Zhang, 'Public Diplomacy to Promote Global Public Goods (GPG): Conceptual Expansion, Ethical Grounds, and Rhetoric', *Public Relations Review*, 35 (2009), 382–387.

7 Shay Attias, 'Israel's New Peer-to-Peer Diplomacy', *The Hague Journal of Diplomacy*, 7 (2012), 473–482.

8 Matthew Wallin, 'The Challenges of the Internet and Social Media in Public Diplomacy', *American Security Project*, 2013 <http://americansecurityproject.org/ASP Reports/Ref 0112 – Challenges of the Internet and Social Media in PD>.

9 *Gulf Daily News*, 'Kingdom "an Oasis of Peace and Tolerance"', 8 May 2014 <http://www.gulf-daily-news.com/NewsDetails.aspx?storyid=376527>.

10 Amal Khalaf, 'The Many Afterlives of Lulu: The Story of Bahrain's Pearl Roundabout", *Ibraaz*, 2013 <http://www.ibraaz.org/essays/56>.

11 Christopher Smith, Andrew Cooper and Douglas Kellner, 'The Effectiveness and Value of Celebrity Diplomacy: An Edited Transcript of a Panel Discussion at the USC Annenberg School for Communication and Journalism', *The Norman Lear Center*, 2009 <http://www.learcenter.org/pdf/celebritydiplomacy.pdf>.

12 As early as the 1920s, oppressed communities in Bahrain frequently went to the British agency to demand protection. In some instances, and perhaps what might be a primitive form of trolling, anonymous messages were attached to stones and thrown through the windows of the British-run police station.

13 Bahrain govt hires 18 Western companies to improve image after unrest new project to track Govt Spin Campaign Shows Over $32M Spent on PR, *Bahrain Watch*, [press release], 23 August 2012, https://bahrainwatch.org/press/press-release-8.php.

14 Justin Elliott, 'Bahraini "Reformers" in Washington, Courtesy of American Spinmeisters', *ProPublica*, 2012 <http://www.propublica.org/article/bahraini-youth-in-washington-courtesy-of-american-spinmeisters>.

15 Marc Owen Jones, 'Social Media, Surveillance, and Social Control in the Bahrain Uprising', *Westminster Papers of Communication and Culture*, 9 (2013), 69–92.

16 William Marczak and Morgan Marquis-Boire, 'From Bahrain with Love: FinFisher's Spy Kit Exposed?', *Citizenlab*, 2012 <https://citizenlab.org/2012/07/from-bahrain-with-love-finfishers-spy-kit-exposed/>.

17 Jones, 'Social Media, Surveillance, and Social Control in the Bahrain Uprising.'

18 Al-Jazeera English, '*Shouting in the Dark*. Television Programme', *Youtube*, 2011 <http://www.youtube.com/watch?v=xaTKDMYOBOU>.

19 Al-Jazeera, 'The Stream-Bahrain Foreign Minister Criticises Al-Jazeera Documentary on Twitter', *Youtube*, 2011 <https://www.youtube.com/watch?v=6HnvaiUweGc>.

20 Vanessa Thorpe, 'Radio Times Poll Provokes Online Battle for Baftas', *Guardian*, 2012 <http://www.theguardian.com/tv-and-radio/2012/may/06/television-baftas-bahrain>.

21 Information Affairs Authority, *Bahrain Independent Commission of Inquiry – BICI* (Manama, 2012).

22 Marc Owen Jones, 'Social Media, Surveillance, and Spying in the Bahrain Uprising', in *The Bahrain uprising*, ed. by Marc Owen Jones and A. Shehabi (London, UK: Zed Books, 2015).

23 Fadi Salem, Racha Mourtade and Sara Alshaer, 'The Arab World Online (2014): Trends in Internet and Mobile Usage in the Arab Region', *Arab Social Media Report* (Dubai, 2014) <http://www.mbrsg.ae/getattachment/ff70c2c5-0fce-405d-b23f-93c198d4ca44/The-Arab-World-Online-2014-Trends-in-Internet-and.aspx>.

24 The IAA is the government body in charge of the affairs of internal and external formal media

25 'Bic All Set for "unifled" Gulf Air Bahrain Grand Prix, BIC, [press release]', *bahraingp*, 2012 <http://www.bahraingp.com/News/National/Circuit/Pages/FEB2012Feb19_A.aspx>.

26 Marc Owen Jones, 'Putting a Price Tag on Repression', *Your Middle East*, 2012 <http://www.yourmiddleeast.com/opinion/marc-owen-jones-putting-a-price-tag-on-repression_14547>.

27 Ibid.

28 Scott Lucas, 'Bahrain Propaganda 101: Bringing the "Right" Youth Delegation to Washington', *Enduring America*, 2012 <http://www.enduringamerica.com/home/2012/3/4/bahrain-propaganda-101-bringing-the-right-youth-delegation-t.html>.

29 Many UOB students were bullied to take off the official Bahraini flag (with 5 points) and replace it with the, [Tweet by @Kalfadhel], 12 March 2011, https://twitter.com/KAlFadhel/status/46576218627248128.

30 Al-Qassim, Faisal, 'The Opposite Direction Programme: the Revolution in Bahrain 2011', *Youtube*, 2011 <https://www.youtube.com/watch?v=y5VGyM6-tWU&feature=youtu.be&t=8m46s#_blank>.

31 Fahad Desmukh, 'Myths and Lies in the Bahrain Infowars', *blogspot*, 2011 <http://revolutionbahrain2.blogspot.se/2011/04/myths-and-lies-in-bahrain-infowars.html>.

32 Ruth McAvinia, 'Bahrainis Get Together in #UniteBH', *Storyful*, 2011 <http://storyful.com/stories/1665-bahrainis-get-together-in-unitebh>.

33 Alementz Imaging Film, '1st #UniteBH Video-Original, [online Video]', *YouTube*, 2011 <https://www.youtube.com/watch?v=V28KpoJkDno>.

34 'Today is the anniversary of my detainment. Just because someone posted my picture on Facebook. Also because I started #UniteBH', [Tweet by @Redbelt], 29 March 2012.

35 Leena Al Olaimy, '"Just Bahraini' Not Welcome at Checkpoints', *Mahmood's Den*, 2011 <http://mahmood.tv/2011/03/19/just-bahraini-not-welcome-at-checkpoints//>.

36 Cited from Twitter page '@Redbelt listen, #UniteBH made my day … Meant a lot to me as a Bahraini …whatever I said about it on BTV was an understatement', [Tweet by @khalidakhalifa], 21 February 2011, https://twitter.com/khalidalkhalifa/status/39810264064991232.

37 Named after the milk powder, the term Nido is used to describe a modern generation of Bahrainis who were typically said to have eschewed breast milk in favour of the convenient Nido powdered milk. The term was soon used to describe a generation of Bahrainis who were arguably Westernised, uncomfortable with Arabic, materialistic, wealthy, and at odds with the traditional generation that preceded them. 'Boobs vs. Nido Milk', *Nido: A Blog for and about the Nido Generation*, [web blog], 2007, https://nidomilk.wordpress.com/2007/01/16/boobs-vs-nido-milk/.

38 The term of 'Chicken Nugget', like 'Nidoer', is a term used to describe a modern, English-speaking class of Arabs who are often Western-educated and more unfamiliar with the traditional Arab culture of their homeworks. Hasan Tariq Al Hasan used the term to mean 'brown on the outside, white on the inside', although this is objectionable for obvious reasons (Al Hasan, 2013).

39 Jones, 'Putting a Price Tag on Repression.'

40 Information Affairs Authority, 'Bahrain Grand Prix 2012 #UniF1ed', *YouTube*, 2012 <https://www.youtube.com/watch?v=mj17QOYiXos>.

41 Information Affairs Authority, 'Bahrain Grand Prix 2012 #UniF1ed.'

42 Robert Govers, 'Brand Dubai and Its Competitors in the Middle East: An Image and Reputation Analysis', *Place Branding and Public Diplomacy*, 8 (2012), 48–57.

43 Gulf Daily News, 'World Boxing Legend to Visit Bahrain', *Gulf Daily News*, 2014 <http://www.gulf-daily-news.com/NewsDetails.aspx?storyid=372194>.

44 Rob Garratt, 'Joe Calzaghe Cancels Bahrain Appearance', *Time Out Bahrain*, 2014 <http://www.timeoutbahrain.com/knowledge/news/50616-joe-calzaghe-cancels-bahrain-appearance>.

45 'Good Morning #Bahrain, This Lovely Country That Is Walking on the Path of Success and Prosperity Year after Year…' [Tweet by @NancyAjram]', 2013 <https://twitter.com/NancyAjram/status/299782369408339968>.

46 Marc Owen Jones, 'Bahrain's Celebrity Anti-Diplomacy', *Your Middle East*, 2014 <http://www.yourmiddleeast.com/opinion/bahrains-celebrity-antidiplomacy_22383>.

47 Max Fisher, 'Why Is Kim Kardashian Going to Bahrain?', *Uncut: Index on Censorship*, 2012 <http://uncut.indexoncensorship.org/2012/12/kim-kardashian-bahrain/>.

48 Thank you:) "@KimKardashian: I just got to Bahrain! OMG can I move here please? Prettiest place on earth!" [Tweet by @khalidalkhalifa], 1 December 2012, <https://twitter.com/khalidalkhalifa/status/274826133239910400>.
49 'Kim Kardashian Loved by the People of Bahrain at the Launch of Millions of Milkshakes!!', *YouTube*, 2012 <https://www.youtube.com/watch?v=aE36X2lV85o>.
50 Marc Owen Jones, 'Bahrain's PR Machine Threatens Free Speech', *Index on Censorship Uncut*, 2012.
51 Mark Wheeler and Ilan Kapoor, 'Should Celebrities Promote Charities?', *New Internationalist*, 2012 <http://newint.org/sections/argument/2012/09/01/should-celebrities-promote-charities/>.
52 Many ironic tweets over @KimKardashian coment on arriving in Bahrain (one of world's most oppressive regimes) as "prettiest place on earth", [Tweet by @NPSusa], 1 December 2012, <https://twitter.com/NPSusa/status/274892147449274368>.
53 You must be new here RT "@KimKardashian: I just got to Bahrain. OMG can I move here please? Prettiest place on earth!", [Tweet by @Droodkin], 1 December 2012, <https://twitter.com/Droodkin/status/274810383414468609>.
54 Wallin.
55 Fisher.
56 Issandr El Amrani, 'What's up with CFR's Ed Husain and Bahrain, [web blog]', *The Arabist*, 2012 <http://arabist.net/blog/2012/4/17/whats-up-with-cfrs-ed-husain-and-bahrain.html>.
57 'I know you're supposed to wait at least 3 days, but I called His Excellency today. Just to hear his voice again. To engage' [Tweet by @FakeEdHusain], 19 April 2012, <https://twitter.com/FakeEdHusain/status/193025367806722049>.
58 Ed Husain, 'The Prince and the Ayatollah', *The New York Times*, 1 May 2012 <http://www.nytimes.com/2012/05/02/opinion/the-prince-and-the-ayatollah.html?pagewanted=all>.
59 Vian Bakir, *Sousveillance, Media and Strategic Political Communication: Iraq, USA, UK* (London: Continuum, 2010).
60 The BBC has also been affected by the insidious influence of PR of late. In 2012, the World Service show 'World Have Your Say', which speaks to experts and residents on particular countries or topics, broadcast a show about the media war in Bahrain. By using Twitter to source guests, the BBC found a particularly eager volunteer who just happened to be the managing director of a company who receives money from the government to do PR. Another guest on the show was also suggested to the BBC by a PR company connected to the royal family, though the BBC was quick to emphasise that she was not representing the royal family.

61 Attias.

62 John Horne, 'Tn Tn Ttn and Torture in Bahrain: Puncturing the Spectacle of the "Arab Spring"', in *The Bahrain Uprising*, ed. by Marc Owen Jones and A. Shehabi (London: Zed Books, 2015).

5

Mobile Phone and Internet Usage in the GCC Region: University Students' Perspectives

Abdul-Karim Ziani and Mokhtar Elareshi

Mobile phones are widely used across the Arab world, and young people have emerged as among the most enthusiastic adopters of this technology.[1] As in other parts of the world, mobile phones are used in the region for a wide range of communications, information and entertainment purposes.[2] The latest high-tech mobile phones not only transmit voice communications but also offer interactive interface, voice, text, video, music and graphics functions. Smartphones using 3G, 4G and/or Wi-Fi technology are equipped with a microphone, camera and high-speed internet connection and have triggered high demand.[3] It has been observed that young Arabs regularly use their mobile phones to seek various kinds of information.[4] There is further evidence that mobile phones are also changing the consumption of local, national and international news in the Arab world.[5]

Despite its near universal use as a crucial part of everyday life, there remains much to be learned about how the mobile phone fits into people's lives.[6] Mobile phones have been found to bring a host of social and economic benefits to people's lives, especially in the developing world.[7] The mobile phone has emerged as a principal interface for engaging with the internet in countries that previously lacked fully developed wired telecommunication networks.[8] It is not surprising, then, that mobile phones have been rapidly adopted in the Arab world, not only for their voice telephony functionality, but also to accelerate the uptake of the internet and its many information and transactional applications.

This chapter aims to examine how Gulf university students obtain local news and information about their communities using their mobile devices and online services. It focuses on reported use of new technologies both in a broad sense and in relation to local news consumption. In so doing, it aims to answer questions about emerging patterns of use of news sources in these countries, which have arisen following the rapid growth in the use of mobile devices as a new platform in the Arab world.[9] This chapter attempts to analyse the use of mobile phones in the Gulf region.

Background

The seeds of mobile telephony were sown in the mid-twentieth century with the development of local Citizens Band radio communications in the United States. Initially the technology was used only by the military, emergency services and enthusiasts.[10] During the 1970s and 1980s, these closed communications systems were opened up with early mobile phone experiments in countries such as Japan and the US, and the technology was regarded mainly as a business tool.[11] The early devices were large and cumbersome and had to be carried around in a briefcase. As computer technology advanced, the technology both reduced in size and became more powerful and versatile. By the final decade of the twentieth century, the mobile phone emerged as a truly mass applications technology. Later, mobile phone networks quickly spread to mass user markets in developed countries and then also to developing nations where they enabled general populations to become linked to telecommunications networks for the first time.[12]

Today, mobile phones represent the most prevalent piece of information and communication technology development in the world, according to a report by Portio Research.[13] The report estimated that 1.2 billion people were using mobile applications at the end of 2012, with predictions that this figure would grow by 29.8 per cent each year to reach 4.4 billion users by the end of 2017. In the Arab regions, 410 million users subscribed to mobile phones, with a coverage of 109.9 per cent per

100 people. In 2014, the International Telecommunication Union (ITU) reported that access to information and communication technologies continues to grow at high speed and, more importantly, the gap separating the developing and the underdeveloped countries has decreased in terms of mobile use.[14]

Initial research into the use of early mobile phones focused on the use of the technology as an interpersonal communications device and how it became integrated into people's domestic lives.[15] Later, as the technology evolved and began to offer a much wider range of functions, including the ability to interface with the internet,[16] research questions broadened to include interest in the use of the mobile phone as an organisational hub in people's lives, a factor that emerges during childhood.[17] For example, studies have examined the opportunity for internet access via mobile devices, which greatly enhances the gratification sought from mobiles by transforming the traditional limits of one-to-one communication afforded by the telephone.[18] Sonia Livingstone and her colleagues found that the most common location of internet use by children aged 9 to 16 was the home, followed by school. They found that 33 per cent accessed the internet via their mobile phones.[19] Thus, the increase in the practice of accessing the internet through mobile phones is seen as the main recent change, along with the early age at which usage now begins.

From a theoretical perspective, media functionalists argue that the media (e.g., mobile devices) serve a variety of needs such as communication, cohesion, social control and cultural continuity in a society.[20] However, the media also fulfil the audience's needs for surveillance, personal guidance, personal relationships and diversion.[21] Other studies[22] have examined how mobiles have come to define personal identity, redefining the distinction between the individual's private and public lives,[23] and restructuring users' concept of time by enabling social arrangements to be changed on the move.[24] For instance, J.P. Roos found that Finnish users identified work-related and social uses as their main reasons for using mobile phones.[25] Robbie Blinkoff[26] and Rich Ling[27] found that social networking and peers, family and security were the motivation for young Norwegian adults to use mobile phones. This emerges as evidence of the increasing access to and use of the internet from different mobile devices.[28]

Mobile Phones and Media Reception

In the early days, mobile phones were used for making calls and receiving messages but they soon emerged as a multimedia platform for communicating and receiving news, information and entertainment; they have recently been used for viewing TV programmes, listening to radio, reading the press and linking to social media.[29] From a media perspective, mobile devices are already being used by Pan-Arab news and other media suppliers (e.g., Al-Jazeera TV and Al-Arabiya TV) to keep their wide audiences up to date with news and information and to reach others, especially young adults.[30] They have engaged viewers, listeners and readers, who are able to follow and contribute content through mobile devices, and they are increasingly able to make content available for mobile devices.[31] For example, Al-Jazeera's coverage and accessibility has increased since 2006 when its mobile service and website were launched.

Mobiles enable consumers to subscribe to SMS-based news updates and feature a platform for interactive engagement with the channel.[32] Users have established the mobile as a key way of staying informed about the news and other information. The same is true for TV programmes such as *Super Star*, with viewers using their mobile phones to vote for their favourite characters.[33] In 2005, for example, the Lebanese channel LBC broadcast the *Star Academy* programme, an Arab talent show. During its transmission, young Arab viewers voted by sending more than 15 million SMSs.[34] This shows the popularity of using SMS for entertainment rather than as a voice telephone service and for emails.[35]

Furthermore, in countries in which the main news media are tightly controlled by the government, there is an additional incentive for people to go online though their mobile devices for their news and information if they believe they can access more uncensored information in that setting. Evidence has emerged that young people are increasingly expressing their individuality through their ownership of mobile phones, personal computers and iPods, and by going online. These devices allow them to express their own identity and gradually escape the control of their parents[36] or their governments.[37] As a result, mobile devices are an environment in which users can gain access to multimedia content and engage in interpersonal transactions. Obtaining news, information and entertainment are just some of the activities that can be pursued using this environment. The use of social media sites is also a subcomponent of mobile phone user behaviour and has multiple purposes including gaining access to different news.[38]

Mobile Phone Use in the Arab World

In the early 1990s the Arab people began to use mobile services, but only to communicate with one another (phone calls). The earliest mobile phone subscriptions began in the region in 1987, in Egypt, Morocco and Tunisia, followed by Mauritania and Algeria in 1990.[39] In those days, the first and second mobile phone generations were very expensive pieces of technology.[40] Businesses, elites and rich people, however, were likely to have a greater diffusion of mobile communication devices.[41] Moreover, in most Arab countries, mobile services were run and controlled by government bodies or allied companies that operated, monitored and provided the services to the public before mobile services were privatised and become more affordable to the public.[42]

Recently, the Arab world has witnessed a rapid diffusion of mobile phone usage, especially among young Arabs.[43] The mobile ownership percentage rates range from 3 per cent (Sudan) to 85 per cent (UAE). Most mobile subscribers (80 per cent) use prepaid phones rather than fixed-term contracts. This is because prepaid services are more likely to be used by those with lower incomes and of lower educational levels,[44] and also by those who prefer to communicate via the sending and receiving of SMSs.[45] Mobile phones are also used in places where landlines are not available. Thus, young adults use mobiles just to receive calls from their parents.[46]

Recent evidence has shown that Africa has experienced the highest mobile phone growth rate globally.[47] In terms of business, for example, mobile phones have a positive impact, increasing business profits in North Africa,[48] and they have become a vital tool for businesses in the region.[49] They also help to reduce travel costs.[50] In many Arab regions, mobiles have been increasingly adopted as a social media platform and have played a role, for example, in the recent 2011 Arab uprisings by mobilising mass protests and giving voice to demands that have been heard globally.[51] Culturally, the mobile phone has become something of a status symbol for many Arabs. Many young Arabs show off with their mobile devices, and their social status is enhanced by the unique ringtones they use and the quality of the messages they store on their devices. Young Arabs use mobile phones to sustain and enhance their communications and keep in touch with their social networks.[52]

Arab people, like many others, use mobile phones not only for personal communication but also as multifunctional personal devices. Features such as internet access, cameras, videos and MP3 players via mobiles have become very popular, particularly among young Arab adults. In 2014, it has been found that around 20 per cent of Arab users gain access to the internet via their mobile devices.[53] This has risen by 8 per cent since 2013, and 42 per cent of them have smartphones. The Arab Advisory Group also found that young Arabs use SMSs for receiving notifications, chatting, voting in contests or participating in TV entertainment show polls.[54]

Mobiles have received great attention in the Arab world because this technology aids social and economic developments in the Arab regions.[55] Besides, mobile phones can reach anywhere in the Arab world without the need for an expensive landline infrastructure.[56] Mobile phones have been seen as unique in creating opportunities for sending and receiving information anywhere and everywhere that is covered by the network.[57] To use a mobile phone, generally speaking, one does not require as high a level of education and literacy as one might need with other technologies such as computers or iPads, although mobile phones are most popular among young adults and teenagers.[58] This makes mobiles accessible to a vast number of young people as well as adults.[59] In the mid-2000s, WiMax and Wi-Fi carriers offered a variety of mobile content services, including news, weather, sports scores, stock updates, games, music, email and the internet. Free Wi-Fi has been considered a great success in some Arab regions, especially in the Gulf region, where users can easily gain access to news, information and entertainment in public areas such as universities, hospitals, cafés and restaurants.[60] Against this background, the current research addressed a number of questions concerning the use and importance of local news among well-educated news consumers in the Middle East. The key questions examined here were as follows:

RQ1: Are young Arab mobile phone users interested in news information?
RQ2: How do young mobile phone users use and access local news and information?
RQ3: How do young mobile phone users describe their internet access and speed?
RQ4: Do young mobile phone users consume their local news?
RQ5: Are there any correlations between mobile phone use and online activities?
RQ6: Do young mobile phone users engage interactively with news online?

Methodology

A self-completion questionnaire survey was carried out in January 2014 with a random sample of 1,221 students from universities in Bahrain, Kuwait, Saudi Arabia, UAE and Oman, with the assistance of media lecturers at these universities. The sample comprised 331 respondents from University of Bahrain, 141 from University of Kuwait, 274 from the Universities of Jazan and Dammam (Saudi Arabia), 190 from University of Ajman (UAE) and 285 from Muscat University (Oman). Of 1,221 responses, 12 were discarded as these respondents stated that they did not possess a mobile phone; hence, the sample for analysis consisted entirely of mobile phone users. This survey mainly targeted media and communication departments in these universities to collect the data. In each department, a random sample was selected from different year levels. Students from each year level were asked to fill in the survey questionnaire voluntarily, having read and signed a consent form.

The pre-structured questionnaire included questions about local news consumption habits, general news interests, local news issues, opinions about place of residence, online activities, mobile phone, computer use and personal details. This chapter will only present findings for reported mobile phone and internet usage-linked local news habits. Survey questions were obtained with permission from the Pew Research Center and some rewording was deployed, where relevant, to reflect local news market circumstances.

The local news consumption questions asked respondents about the frequency with which they kept up with news in general. They were also asked about their mobile ownership, use and online access. Further questions asked about how respondents gained internet access at home and how they described the internet speed in their place or region. A second set of questions asked respondents about mobile local news consumption. Respondents were asked about their use of mobile phones and laptops to seek local news information, whether they had ever received SMSs or emails regarding their local community news, and whether they used their mobiles to check news and information about their local communities and sports activities.

A third set of questions asked respondents to indicate their regular online activities and whether they had ever engaged in any of the following activities online: Contributing to an online discussion or message board about their local community; customising their homepage to include their favourite local information or news sources or issues; emailing a link to a local news story or local news video to someone they know; contributing their own article, opinion piece, picture or video about their local community to an online news site; commenting on a local news story or local blog they read online; and posting news or information about their local community on a social networking site such as Facebook or Twitter. These activities were measured on a three-point scale: 'yes', 'no' and 'don't know'.

A further set of questions asked about local community interest and engagement. Finally, respondents were invited to indicate details of their gender, their family's monthly income and their place of residence. In all, 58.1 per cent of the final sample was female and 41.9 per cent was male. 80.5 per cent of the sample lived in families earning more than $US1001 a month, 17.4 per cent lived in middle-income families earning between $US501 and $US1000 a month, while only 2 per cent lived in families earning less than $US500 a month. With regard to the descriptions of place of residence, 70 per cent of respondents described their community as a large city, while around 16.7 per cent said they lived in a small city or town, or a suburb near a large city (11.5 per cent). Only 2.2 per cent said they lived in a rural area.

Findings

Basic descriptive results for mobile phone uses, internet access and mobile local news consumption habits are presented below and are supplemented by statistical tests designed to reveal significant differences in mobile local news consumption profiles of respondents from different GGC nations and between specific demographic groups.

General news interest

Local news information can now be received via a number of different platforms in the Arab world. Within the past decade, television and the internet have been the news sources most frequently used by young people in both the Western world and Arab world.[61]

In this survey (RQ1), around half of all mobile users (52 per cent) said they enjoyed keeping up with the news in general, 31 per cent said 'some', 16 per cent 'not much' and only 1.3 per cent 'don't follow'. Male users (84 per cent) were more likely than females (29 per cent) to say that they enjoyed keeping up with the news 'a lot'. While 43 per cent of female users said they had 'some' interest, only 14.5 per cent of males said as much. Around three fifths of Bahraini (63.7 per cent) and KSA (61.3 per cent) mobile users said they enjoyed keeping up with the news 'a lot', compared with 47 per cent of Omani, 46 per cent of UAE and only 25 per cent of Kuwaiti users. Less than a quarter (23 per cent Oman, 18 per cent Kuwait, 17 per cent UAE, 14 per cent KSA, 10 per cent Bahrain) said they did not much enjoy doing so. Other studies in the Arab world have confirmed that young Arab adults are keen on keeping up with news and information.[62]

When asked about local news, around three fifths (60.1 per cent) of all users indicated that they followed local news closely when something important was happening, while 40 per cent of them did so most of the time, or when something important was happening. Male users (83.2 per cent) were more likely than females (43.4 per cent) to follow local news closely only when something important was happening, while females (56.3 per cent) were more likely than males (16.8 per cent) to follow local news closely most of the time. Bahraini users (81.7 per cent) were more interested in following local news closely only when something important was happening, compared with 59 per cent of KSA, 56 per cent of Omani, 46.1 per cent of Kuwaiti and 42.6 per cent of UAE users. However, following local news most of the time, regardless of whether something important was happening, was reported by more UAE (57.4 per cent) and Kuwaiti (54 per cent) users than others (Omanis 44.2 per cent, KSA 40.5 per cent and Bahrainis 18.3 per cent).

Regarding national news, more than four fifths (85.3 per cent) of males reported following national news closely only when something important was happening, compared with 35.2 per cent of females. However, 62.5 per cent of females followed national news closely most of the time regardless of whether something important was happening, compared with only 15 per cent of males. Kuwaiti users (92.2 per cent) were most likely to follow national news closely only when something important was happening, compared with the others (Bahrainis 55 per cent, Omanis 52.3 per cent, KSA 50.4 per cent and UAE 47 per cent). Following news closely most of the time regardless of whether or not something important was happening was claimed by around half of respondents across all countries (53 per cent UAE, 50 per cent KSA, 48 per cent Omanis and 41 per cent Bahrainis). The lowest level of national news interest was found in Kuwait (7.8 per cent).

Around half of all users (52 per cent) indicated that they followed international news closely regardless of what was happening (76 per cent Kuwaitis, 62.4 per cent Bahrainis, 49 per cent UAE, 40 per cent KSA and Omanis). More males (80.6 per cent) than females (30.2 per cent) followed international news closely when something important was happening, while 70 per cent of females were more likely to follow international news closely most of the time, regardless of whether or not something important was happening, compared with only 19.4 per cent of males.

Mobile phone usage

In these oil-rich countries, it is not surprising that all the users were the most technologically *plugged in* (RQ2). The results are summarised in Table 5:1. Respondents were most likely to have a smartphone (99 per cent) such as a Blackberry or iPhone, a modern-technology computer such as a laptop or

Table 5:1 Mobile Ownership, Use and Online Access

Mobile Ownership	No.	%
Smartphone (e.g., Blackberry or iPhone)	1209	99.0
Modern technology (e.g., laptop, tablet computer)	1057	86.6
Touch PC	1036	84.8
Mobile Use		
For other things (e.g., emails)	937	76.7
Only to make calls	284	23.3
Online Access		
Phones	654	53.0
Home	229	19.0
University	194	16.0
Café net	144	12.0

tablet computer (86.6 per cent) and a touch PC (84.8 per cent). Male users (98.4 per cent) were more likely than females (78 per cent) to have laptops or tablet computers and were also more likely to have a touch PC (90.2 per cent vs. 81 per cent respectively).

By country, no significant differences were found among users who had smartphones, while significant differences emerged among those with laptops or tablet computers and Touch PCs. Omani users (54 per cent) fell behind the others in terms of laptop or tablet computer ownership (Kuwaitis 100 per cent, Bahrainis 98.5 per cent, UAE 97.4 per cent, KSA 92 per cent). Omani users (73.4 per cent) also fell behind Kuwaitis (99.3 per cent), UAE users (98.4 per cent) and Bahrainis (90.3 per cent) but were slightly ahead of KSA users (73.3 per cent) in terms of high-tech gadget ownership.

With regard to new mobile technology, users indicated that they used their mobile phones or devices to make calls and also obtained news and information about their communities. Around three quarters of respondents (77 per cent) used mobile phones for other things (e.g., emails). Significantly, female users (85 per cent) were more likely than males (74 per cent) to use their phone devices for other things.

By country, most of the users indicated that they used their mobile devices for other things (in decreasing order, Bahrainis 98.5 per cent, UAE users 94 per cent, KSA users 87.6 per cent, Kuwaitis 84 per cent and Omanis 26 per cent). Omani users (74 per cent) were the only participants to report that they used their mobile devices mainly for making calls.

When asked about their use of the internet to search for and view material and send or receive emails, the results indicated that all users (99 per cent) reported similarly high levels of interest in internet use in general. Moreover, similarly high percentages of both male and female users in the five countries reported using the internet.

The majority of users (53 per cent) reported that they accessed the internet via their mobile devices most of the time. Less than a fifth of all users (19 per cent) accessed the internet at home, university (16 per cent) or café net (12 per cent). While female users (65.6 per cent) were more likely than male users (37 per cent) to access the internet via their mobile phones at home (30 per cent vs. 13 per cent respectively), male users (16.4 per cent) were slightly more likely than females (15.5 per cent) to do so at university and café net (17.6 per cent vs. 3.7 per cent respectively).

UAE users (94 per cent) were more likely than the others (Kuwaitis 84.4 per cent, Bahrainis 63 per cent, Omanis 36 per cent and KSA users 17 per cent) to access the internet via mobile phones. Omani users (32 per cent) were more likely to access the internet at home than were the others (Bahrainis 27 per cent, KSA users 10.2 per cent, Kuwaitis 8.5 per cent and UAE users 5 per cent), and also at universities (31.2 per cent) compared with the others (KSA users 23.4 per cent, Bahrainis 9 per cent, Kuwaitis 6.4 per cent and UAE users 1.6 per cent).

When asked how they accessed the internet at home (RQ3), 72 per cent of all users indicated they did so via their mobile devices, followed by 25.1 per cent via dial-up landline and only 2.9 per cent via wireless connection (Table 5:2). Female users (90 per cent) were more likely than males (47.2 per cent) to access the internet at home through mobile devices. Females (4 per cent) were also more likely than males (1.6 per cent) to use wireless connection, while males (51.3 per cent) were more likely than females to use a dial-up landline system.

Kuwaiti (96.5 per cent) and UAE (93.2 per cent) users were the most likely to use their mobile devices at home to access the internet (KSA 71

Table 5:2 Reported Home Internet and Speed Access

Internet Access	N	%
Mobile phone	879	72.0
Dial-up landline	307	25.1
Wireless	35	2.9
Internet Speed		
High speed	1042	85.3
Good speed	141	11.5
Moderate	30	2.5
Slow	8	0.7

per cent, followed by Bahrainis and Omanis both 60.4 per cent). Dial-up landlines were used more by Bahraini users (38.7 per cent) than the others (Omanis 35.4 per cent, KSA users 22.3 per cent, UAE users 6.3 per cent and Kuwaitis 3.5 per cent). Wireless systems received less usage by most of the users.

Most of the users described their internet connection as high-speed (85.3 per cent). Male users (93.3 per cent) were more likely than females (79.6 per cent) to have high-speed internet access. UAE (98.9 per cent), Kuwaiti (96.5 per cent) and Bahraini (90.9 per cent) users were more likely to have high-speed access to the internet compared with Omani (76.8 per cent) and KSA users (72.3 per cent).

Mobile local news consumption

The surveyed respondents were also asked about their use of local news alerts (RQ4). They indicated that they received news alerts about their local community via their mobile devices, texts or emails (80 per cent), while 20 per cent said 'no'. Female users (84.8 per cent) were more targeted than males (74 per cent) to receive news alerts about their local community through their mobile devices. More than nine in ten Bahraini (98.5 per cent), UAE (94.2 per cent) and Omani (94 per cent) users received news alerts about their local community, compared with 65 per cent of KSA and 21 per cent of Kuwaiti users. This is a clear indication that people in the

GCC region are in touch with their local communities and are using new technologies to do so.

Use of mobile devices to gather news or information online about local communities, local sports scores or local sports updates and the like were very common among most of the users. Overall, male users (98.4 per cent) were more likely than females (89.7 per cent) to use a mobile phone or tablet computer to obtain local news or information online and were most likely to check local sports scores or obtain local sports updates (9.6 per cent vs. 71.4 per cent respectively). A great majority of users in all these countries (UAE 96.3 per cent, Bahrain 95.5 per cent, KSA 94.9 per cent, Kuwait 93.6 per cent and Oman 87.4 per cent) used their mobile devices to search for information and news about their local communities. As for checking local sports scores or receiving local sports updates, Bahraini users (62.5 per cent) were less likely to do so than the others (Kuwaitis 98.6 per cent, KSA users 97.4 per cent, UAE users 90 per cent and Omanis 81.4 per cent).

Relationships between mobile phone use and online activities

Mobile technology is emerging as an important online interface technology. As reported earlier, the majority of users indicated that they used their mobile devices to access the internet and receive local news alerts. It was found, as presented previously, that respondents with more devices tend to enjoy following the news more.

Here, the Pearson *r* correlations were computed to explore the relationships between using a mobile phone and various online activities (RQ5). The results are summarised in Table 5:3. Using a mobile phone was positively associated with posting news or information about the local community via social media sites (*r*=.58), going online for information about the local community (*r*=.37), contributing to an online discussion or topics about the local community (*r*=.30) and using Facebook (*r*=.28) and Twitter (*r*=.27). These correlations indicate that, regardless of the device used, users tend to carry out different activities with their mobile phones and, more importantly, receive news from online sources via their mobiles.

Table 5:3 Correlations between Mobile Phone Use and Online Activities

Correlations	*r*
Post news or information about your community on social media	.584**
Go online for information or news about your local community	.374**
Contribute to an online discussion or topics about your local community	.305**
Use of Facebook	.279**
Use of Twitter	.272**

** Correlation is significant at the 0.01 level (2-tailed). Pearson *r* Correlation. All *Ps<0.01* (N=1209).

Local community interest and engagement

Respondents were also asked to indicate their regular online activities and whether they went online to engage in certain activities (RQ6). Respondents stated that they went online sometimes, for example for social media activities such as Twitter (39 per cent), emails (83.2 per cent) and Facebook (80.8 per cent). MySpace (28.3 per cent), Google Maps (21.4 per cent) and LinkedIn (14.7 per cent) were less frequently utilised by the respondents.

There were several significant differences regarding online activities. Male users (99.6 per cent) were more likely than females (88.2 per cent) to say that they tweeted, emailed (94.7 per cent vs. 74.9 per cent respectively), facebooked (98.4 per cent vs. 68.2 per cent respectively), used MySpace (62.2 per cent vs. 3.8 per cent respectively), used LinkedIn (34.4 per cent vs. 0.6 per cent respectively) and searched on Google Maps (47 per cent vs. 3.0 per cent respectively).

The majority of users reported (Table 5:4) that they engaged in several online activities, such as posting news or information about their local community on Twitter (98 per cent), contributing to online discussions or topics about their local community (90 per cent), emailing local stories to others (78 per cent), commenting on a local news story they had read online (67 per cent), customizing their homepage to include their favourite local information (66 per cent), contributing their own articles and opinions about their local community (63 per cent) and posting news about their community on Facebook (62 per cent).

Respondents distinguished between the use of Twitter and Facebook. This result, in particular, confirmed several recent studies undertaken in the Arab world indicating that Twitter is a more popular platform in GCC countries than Facebook.[63]

On most of the individual items measured here, male users were more likely to say they engaged in these activities than were females. Males were slightly more likely than females to post news about their local community on Twitter (99 per cent vs. 96 per cent respectively), contribute to an online discussion (99 per cent vs. 84 per cent respectively), email a local news story to others (96 per cent vs. 64 per cent respectively), customise their homepage to include their favourite local news (96 per cent vs. 44 per cent respectively), contribute their own articles and opinions (96 per cent vs. 39 per cent respectively), post news about their community on Facebook (96 per cent vs. 38 per cent respectively) and comment on a local news stories (74 per cent vs. 62 per cent respectively).

Bahraini users were more likely than the others to post news about their community on Twitter (99 per cent vs. 98 per cent KSA users, 97 per cent Omanis, 95 per cent both Kuwaitis and UAE users), contribute to an online discussion (99 per cent vs. 98 per cent Kuwaitis, 93 per cent UAE users, 86 per cent Omanis, 78 per cent KSA users), email a news story link (97 per cent vs. 78 per cent Kuwaitis, 73 per cent both Omanis and KSA users, 52 per cent UAE), comment on a local news story (99 per cent vs. 88 per cent UAE users, 75 per cent KSA users, 67 per cent Kuwaitis and 8 per cent Omanis) and customise their homepage (82 per cent vs. 76 per cent Kuwaitis, 68 per cent KSA users, 65 per cent UAE users and 40 per cent Omanis). Kuwaiti users (79 per cent) were more likely than the others (71 per cent KSA users, 65 per cent Bahrainis, 56 per cent UAE users and 45 per cent Omanis) to post local news via Facebook. KSA (95 per cent) and Kuwaiti (94 per cent) users were more likely than the others (84 per cent UAE users, 36 per cent Bahrainis and 34 per cent Omanis) to contribute their own articles and opinion pieces about their local community.

Table 5:4 Reported Online News-Related Activities

Items	N	%
Post news or information about your community (e.g., Twitter)	1192	97.6
Contribute to an online discussion or topics about your local community	1103	90.3
Email a link to a local news story/video to someone you know	950	77.8
Comment on a local news story or local blog you read online	820	67.2
Customise your homepage to include your favourite local information	801	65.6
Contribute your own article/opinion/picture about your local community	769	63.0
Post news or information about your community (e.g., Facebook)	756	61.9

Discussion and Conclusion

The objective of this study was to investigate how university students use mobile phones to obtain local news and information in different GCC countries. It also aims to address the question from a student perspective. Those students were asked to state their opinions regarding their use of mobile phones and online services to obtain their local community news. In general, the use of mobile phones for news or as a source of news and entertainment seems common, especially among young Arabs.[64] Most users, for example, indicated that they enjoyed keeping up with news and information, including local, national and international news. This is an indication that young adults still retain an appetite for consuming news and using their mobiles to do so. It is also an indication that they use everything a mobile phone offers, from news to entertainment. Consistent with previous research studies[65] the findings of this study support those who found that young Arabs are keen on news and information and that they use their new communication technologies to obtain local and non-local news.[66]

Users also indicated that they were the most technologically plugged-in. Most of them have smartphones, modern technology and touch PCs. More importantly, they use their mobile devices not only for making calls but also for doing other things such as sending/receiving emails, engaging in social networks and accessing internet content. These findings are consistent with several previous studies that have found that mobile devices are used for multiple purposes including gaining access to news.[67] Similarly, Fadi and his colleagues found that 36 per cent of Arab users access the internet through a smartphone and 25 per cent through a mobile phone.[68]

In most of these oil-rich regions, mobiles were used most of the time to access the internet.[69] Some indicated that they also used dial-up landline systems to access the internet. In a similar vein, previous research has found that mobile and dial-up landline systems are the most popular platforms for accessing internet content.[70] There is, however, a tendency for users to engage with local news, especially in an interactive way in which they contribute their own content; this is more likely to occur among respondents who use dial-up to access the internet rather than their mobile phones. Thus, people find it more comfortable to contribute interactively using a computer interface with a keyboard that is easier to use and a bigger screen that makes working online easier. It is, therefore, too early to suggest that having a mobile phone makes such activities more likely.

Consistent with other studies, Dennis and his colleagues found that the most common form of internet access in most GCC regions was broadband (73 per cent), with only 21 per cent using mobile broadband to access the internet. Moreover, these oil-rich countries have paid great attention to providing high-speed connection to the internet.[71] This may be due to the fact that, in these countries, new technologies and mobile devices have a positive impact, increasing business profits,[72] reducing travelling costs[73] and, more importantly, acting as a social media platform, especially during the recent 2011 Arab uprisings.[74]

The use of mobile devices to gather news or information online about local communities, local sports scores or local sports updates and the like was very common among most of the users. Respondents were found to receive local news alerts and up-to-date information about their communities. This may help to keep local citizens up to date with their communities' activities, especially when news and information are not easy to access in some parts of the GCC region due to the sheer size of the country, such as in Saudi Arabia.[75] Mobile phones are useful in the region. This was clearly found in the relationship between the use of mobile phones and other online activities, going online for local community news and information and contributing to online discussions. Further evidence on this point comes from several Arab media studies that reported the importance of mobile devices for accessing the internet and receiving news on local communities in the region.[76]

Regular online activities were reported by most of the users. For them, tweeting, emailing and using Facebook were the most popular online activities pursued in their free time. Since the recent Arab uprisings, Twitter and Facebook have become the preferred places for Arab users to place their postings, discussions and updates.[77] These sites emerged as dominant platforms because they were the most versatile in allowing users to share posts easily on the internet and discussing ideas and material.[78] This is an indication that respondents engaged in several online activities. Respondents look for news and information about their local communities as well as different types of entertainment via their mobile devices and other new technologies. In a similar vein, Arab people have been found to access and engage with their news through social media sites (mainly Facebook and Twitter) as they are simply not receiving enough information and news on current events. They were also found to receive community news that inspired them to take action.[79]

Mobile phones in the Arab world, like tablet computers, laptops and desktop computers, have become an important platform for accessing internet content, including news and information about local communities and businesses. Using the mobile internet in the Arab world has facilitated increased communication, the sharing of ideas and the convergence of people. These new technologies enable users to reach large audiences (Al-Jazeera TV and Al-Arabiya TV in the 2011 Arab uprisings) rapidly. This allows them not only to view information but also to contribute to it.[80]

Finally, in interpreting the findings of this study, one must pay attention to several limitations. First, in the model parsimonious, the proposed research model focused on the use of mobile phones and the internet only for obtaining local news, not national and international news. Second, the survey respondents were all university students. The study mainly represents student users of online social networks. Nevertheless, this research has raised several interesting questions. It is believed that the current research will trigger additional theorising on and empirical investigation of intentional mobile phone use in social networks. In this context, it is important that such countries implement mobile phone policies that allow them to successfully address the needs of local citizens. Lastly, the findings on this subject must be handled with great caution as far as mobility in the Arab world is concerned.

Notes

1 Fadi Salem, Racha Mourtade and Sara Alshaer, 'The Arab World Online (2014): Trends in Internet and Mobile Usage in the Arab Region', *Arab Social Media Report* (Dubai, 2014) <http://www.mbrsg.ae/getattachment/ff70c2c5-0fce-405d-b23f-93c198d4ca44/The-Arab-World-Online-2014-Trends-in-Internet-and.aspx>; Ran Wei, 'Motivations for Using the Mobile Phone for Mass Communications and Entertainment', *Telematics and Informatics*, 25 (2008), 36–46 <doi:10.1016/j.tele.2006.03.001>; Manuel Castells and others, *Mobile Communication and Society: A Global Perspective* (Boston, MA: MIT Press, 2007).

2 Nicole Ellison, Charles Steinfield and Cliff Lampe, 'The Benefits of Facebook "Friends": Social Capital and College Students' Use of Online Social Network Sites', *Journal of Computer-Mediated Communication*, 12 (2007), 1143–1168 <doi:10.1111/j.1083-6101.2007.00367.x>; Shopie Mohsen, 'The Role of New Information and Communication Technologies and Social Media during the Arab Spring' (Unpublished master's dissertation, University of Ottawa, Canada, 2013); Katrin Verclas and Patricia Mechael, 'A Mobile Voice: The Use of Mobile Phones in Citizen Media', 2008 <www.mobileactive.org>.

3 Wei; Yusuf Ozcan and Abdullah Kocak, 'Research Note: A Need or a Status Symbol? Use of Cellular Telephones in Turkey', *European Journal of Communication*, 2003, 241–254 <doi:10.1177/0267323103018002004>.

4 Khulood Miliany, 'The Impact of the Internet on Saudi Students' Use of Television' (Unpublished doctor's dissertation. University of Leicester, UK, 2013); Wael Ghonim, *Revolution 2.0: The Power of the People is Greater than the People in Power: A Memoir* (New York: Houghton Mifflin Harcount, 2012).

5 Ghonim; Jeffrey Ghannam, *Social Media in the Arab World: Leading up to the Uprisings of 2011* (Washington, DC: Center for International Media Assistance, 2011).

6 Mirca Madianou and Daniel Miller, *Migration and New Media: Transnational Families and Polymedia* (London, UK: Routledge, 2012); Ghannam, *Social Media in the Arab World.*

7 Claus J. Tully, 'Growing up in Technological Worlds: How Modern Technologies Shape the Everyday Lives of Young People', *Bulletion of Science, Technology and Society*, 23 (2003), 444–456 <doi:10.1177/0270467603260812>; Madianou and Miller.

8 Abi Jagun, Richard Heeks and Jason Whalley, 'The Impact of Mobile Telephony on Developing Country Micro-Enterprise: A Nigerian Case Study', *Information Technologies and International Development*, 4 (2008), 47–63.

9 Everette Dennis, Justin Martin and Robb Wood, 'Media Use in the Middle East: An Eight-Nation Survey', 2013 <http://menamediasurvey.northwestern.edu/>; Jeffrey Ghannam, *Digital Media in the Arab World One Year after the Revolutions* (Washington, DC: Center for International Media Assistance, 2012); Ghonim.

10 Lee Rainie and Barry Wellman, *Networked: The New Social Operating System* (Cambridge, MA: MIT Press, 2012).

11 Kumiko Aoki and Edward. J Downes, 'An Analysis of Young People's Use of and Attitudes toward Cell Phones', *Telematics and Informatics*, 20 (2003), 349–364 <doi:10.1016/S0736-5853(03)00018-2>.

12 Khulood Al-Qaisi, 'Mobile-Phone Subscriber's Motivations for Using Mobile System in Jordon' (Unpublished master's dissertation, Jordon University, Jordon, 2000); Castells and others.

13 Portio Research, 'Latest Mobile Stats', *Mobile Thinking*, 2013 <http://mobithinking.com/mobile-marketing-tools/latest-mobile-stats/e#lotsofapps>.

14 ITU, 'World Telecommunication/ICT Development Report 2014: Measuring ICT for Social and Economic Development', 2014 <http://www.itu.int/ITU-D/ict/publications/wtdr_06/index.html>.

15 Roger Silverstone and Eric Hirsch, *Consuming Technologies: Media and Information in Domestic Spaces* (London, UK: Routledge, 1992); Leslie Haddon, *Information and Communication Technologies in Everyday Life: A Concise Introduction and Research Guide* (Oxford, UK: Berg, 2004); John Dimmick, Jaspreet Sikand and Scott Patterson, 'The Gratification of the Household Telephone', *Communication Research*, 21 (1994), 643–663 <doi:10.1177/009365094021005005>; Robert LaRose, 'Understanding Personal Telephone Behavior', 2001 <htt://info.tc.msu.edu/faculty/larose/html/fonbehav.html>.

16 Salem, Mourtade and Alshaer, 'The Arab World Online (2014): Trends in Internet and Mobile Usage in the Arab Region'; Ozcan and Kocak; Thomas E. Ruggiero, 'Uses and Gratifications Theory in the 21st Century', *Mass Communication and Society*, 3 (2000), 3–37.

17 Sonia Livingstone and others, 'Risks and Safety on the Internet: The Perspective of European Children', *EU Kids Online*, 2011 <www.eukidsonline.net>; Mary Madden and others, 'Teens and Technology 2013', *Pew Internet & American Life Project*, 2013 <www.pewinternet.org/Reports/2013Teens-andTech.aspx>; Andrew Kohut and others, 'Key News Audiences Now Blend Online and

Traditional Sources: Audience Segments in a Changing News Environment', 2008, 43.

18 LaRose; Mohammad Ibahrine, 'Mobile Communication and Sociopolitical Change in the Arab World', in *Handbook of Mobile Communication Studies*, ed. by James E. Katz (London: Massachusetts Institute of Technology, 2008), pp. 257–272; Robbie Blinkoff, 'The Mobiles: Social Evolution in a Wireless Society: Context-Based Research Group', 2001 <http://www.contextresearch.com/context/z.study.cfm>; Ozcan and Kocak.

19 Livingstone and others.

20 Charles Wright, *Mass Communication: A Sociological Perspective*, 3rd edn (New York: Random House, 1986).

21 Jay Blumler, 'The Role of Theory in Uses and Gratifications Studies', *Communication Research*, 6 (1979), 9–36; David L. Swanson, 'Gratification Seeking, Media Exposure, and Audience Interpretations: Some Directions for Research', *Journal of Broadcasting & Electronic Media*, 31 (1987), 237–254.

22 For example, Leopoldina Fortunati, 'The Mobile Phone: An Identity on the Move', *Personal and Ubiquitous Computing*, 5 (2001), 85–98 <doi:10.1007/PL00000017>; Diana Gant and Sara Kiesler, 'Blurring the Boundaries: Cell Phones, Mobility and the Line between Work and Personal Life', in *Wireless World: Social and Interactional Aspects of the Mobile Age*, ed. by Barry Brown, Nicola Harper, and Richard Green, 2001, pp. 121–131.

23 Emma Bond, 'Managing Mobile Relationships: Children's Perceptions of the Impact of the Mobile Phone on Relationships in Their Everyday Lives', *Childhood*, 17 (2010), 514–529 <doi:10.1177/0907568210364421>.

24 Eva Thulin and Bertil Vilhelmson, 'Mobiles Everywhere: Youth, the Mobile Phone and Changes in Everyday Practice', *Young: Nordic Journal of Youth Research*, 15 (2007), 235–253 <doi:10.1177/110330880701500302>.

25 J.P. Roos, 'Sociology of Cellular Telephone: The Nordic Model (300,000 Yuppies? Mobile Phone in Finland)', *Telecommunications Policy*, 17 (1993), 446–456.

26 Blinkoff.

27 Rich Ling, 'We Will Be Reached: The Use of Mobile Telephony among Norwegian Youth', *Information Technology and People*, 13 (2000), 102–120 <doi:10.1108/09593840010339844>.

28 Livingstone and others.

29 Bond; Thulin and Vilhelmson.

30 Jordan Cook, 'Social Media, American Interests, and the Arab Spring', *Dalhousie Journal of Interdisciplinary Management*, 9 (2013) <doi:10.5931/djim.v9i1.3354>; Yangyang Yuan and Gerald Kosicki, 'Citizen Use of Internet and Traditional News Media Sources: What's New about New Media?', in *Paper presented at the annual meeting of the International Communication Association, Marriott Hotel* (San Diego, CA , 2003).

31 Deloitte, 'Arab States Mobile Observatory 2013', 2013 <http://www.gsma.com/spectrum/arab-states-mobile-observatory-2013/>.
32 Verclas and Mechael; Ghannam, *Social Media in the Arab World.*
33 Marwan Kraidy, 'Reality Television and Politics in the Arab World: Preliminary Observations. Annenberg School for Communication', 2006 <http://repository.upenn.edu/asc.papers/303>.
34 *The Economist*, 'Arab Satellite Television: The World through Their Eyes', 2005 <http://www.economist.com/PrinterFriendly.cfm?Story_ID=3690442>.
35 Ibahrine; Ghannam, *Social Media in the Arab World.*
36 J. Powell, *33 Million People in the Room: How to Create, Influence, and Run a Successful Business with Social Networking* (New Jersey: FT Press, 2009); Teresa Correa, Amber Hinsley and Homero de Zuniga, 'Who Interacts on the Web? The Intersection of Users' Personality and Social Media Use', *Computers in Human Behavior*, 26 (2010), 247–253 <doi:10.1016/j.chb.2009.09.003>; Kuan Yu Lin and Hsi Peng Lu, 'Why People Use Social Networking Sites: An Empirical Study Integrating Network Externalities and Motivation Theory', *Computers in Human Behavior*, 27 (2011), 1152–1161 <doi:10.1016/j.chb.2010.12.009>.
37 Ghannam, *Digital Media in the Arab World One Year after the Revolutions*; Dennis, Martin and Wood.
38 Tiffany Pempek, Yevdokiya Yermolayeva and Sandra Calvert, 'College Students' Social Networking Experiences on Facebook', *Journal of Applied Developmental Psychology*, 30 (2009), 227–238 <doi:10.1016/j.appdev.2008.12.010>.
39 Castells and others.
40 Ibahrine; Ghannam, *Social Media in the Arab World.*
41 Castells and others.
42 Ghannam, *Social Media in the Arab World.*
43 Ibahrine; Salem, Mourtade and Alshaer, 'The Arab World Online (2014): Trends in Internet and Mobile Usage in the Arab Region'; Ghannam, *Social Media in the Arab World: Leading up to the Uprisings of 2011.*
44 Livingstone and others; Ghannam, *Social Media in the Arab World*; ITU.
45 Ozcan and Kocak.
46 ITU; Wei.
47 ITU; Ghannam, *Social Media in the Arab World.*
48 (BBC, 2005).
49 ITU; Ghannam, *Social Media in the Arab World.*
50 Jagun, Heeks and Whalley.
51 Ghannam, *Digital Media in the Arab World One Year after the Revolutions*; Ghannam, *Social Media in the Arab World.*
52 Salem, Mourtade and Alshaer, 'The Arab World Online (2014): Trends in Internet and Mobile Usage in the Arab Region'; Ghannam, *Social Media in the Arab World.*

53 Salem, Mourtade and Alshaer, 'The Arab World Online (2014): Trends in Internet and Mobile Usage in the Arab Region'.

54 Arab Advisors Group, 'Reports on the Arab World's Communications and Media Markets', 2005 <http://www.arabadvisors.com>.

55 Dennis, Martin and Wood; Ghannam, *Social Media in the Arab World.*

56 Jagun, Heeks and Whalley.

57 Eric Zuehlke, 'In Arab Countries, Mobile Internet and Social Media are Dominant, but Disparities in Access Remain', 2012 <http://www.prb.org/Publications/Articles/2012/arab-region-internet-use.aspx>; Jagun, Heeks and Whalley.

58 Salem, Mourtade and Alshaer, 'The Arab World Online (2014): Trends in Internet and Mobile Usage in the Arab Region'; Madden and others; Bond.

59 Peter Kyem and Peter LeMaire, 'Transforming Recent Gains in the Digital Divide into Digital Opportunities: Africa and the Boom in Mobile Phone Subscription', *The Electronic Journal on Information System in Developing Countries*, 28 (2006), 1–16.

60 Ghannam, *Social Media in the Arab World*; Castells and others.

61 Rabie Barakat, *New Media in the Arab World: A Tool for Redesigning Geopolitical Realities* (Lebanon: Lebanese American University, 2011); Mokhtar Elareshi and Barrie Gunter, 'News Consumption among Young Libyan Adults: Are New Satellite TV News Services Displacing Local TV News', *Arab Media & Society*, 2010.

62 Elareshi and Gunter; Ghannam, *Digital Media in the Arab World One Year after the Revolutions.*

63 Ghonim; Mohammed T. Simsim, 'Internet Usage and User Preferences in Saudi Arabia', *Journal of King Saud University: Engineering Sciences*, 2011, 101–107; Fadi Salem and Racha Mourtada, 'Social Media in the Arab World: Influencing Societal and Cultural Change', *Arab Social Media Report*, 2012 <www.arabsocialmediareport.com/userManagement/PDFD/ASMR 4 updated 29 08 12>; Ghannam, *Social Media in the Arab World.*

64 Ibahrine; Salem, Mourtade and Alshaer, 'The Arab World Online (2014): Trends in Internet and Mobile Usage in the Arab Region'; John R. Nield, 'Orbits of Influence: A Special Report on Telecoms', *MEED*, 2004 <http://www.meed.com/orbits-of-influence/347516.article>.

65 Dennis, Martin and Wood; Miliany; Salem and Mourtada; Salem, Mourtade and Alshaer, 'The Arab World Online (2014): Trends in Internet and Mobile Usage in the Arab Region.'

66 Fadi Salem, Racha Mourtade and Sara Alshaer, 'Transforming Education in the Arab World: Breaking Barriers in the Age of Social Learning', *Arab Social Media Report*, 2013 <http://www.arabsocialmediareport.com/UserManagement/PDF/ASMR_5_Report_Final.pdf>; Elareshi and Gunter.

67 Pempek, Yermolayeva and Calvert; Salem, Mourtade and Alshaer, 'The Arab World Online (2014): Trends in Internet and Mobile Usage in the Arab Region'; Salem, Mourtade and Alshaer, 'Transforming Education in the Arab World: Breaking Barriers in the Age of Social Learning.'
68 Salem, Mourtade and Alshaer, 'Transforming Education in the Arab World'.
69 Salem, Mourtade and Alshaer, 'Transforming Education in the Arab World'; Dennis, Martin and Wood.
70 Salem, Mourtade and Alshaer, 'The Arab World Online (2014): Trends in Internet and Mobile Usage in the Arab Region'; Deloitte; Salem, Mourtade and Alshaer, 'Transforming Education in the Arab World'; Dennis, Martin and Wood.
71 Dennis, Martin and Wood.
72 (BBC, 2005; Dennis et al., 2013)
73 ITU; Ibahrine; Jagun, Heeks and Whalley.
74 Ghannam, *Digital Media in the Arab World One Year after the Revolutions*; Ibahrine; Dennis, Martin and Wood.
75 ITU; Wei; Deloitte; Jagun, Heeks and Whalley.
76 Fadi Salem and Racha Mourtade, *Arab Social Media Report (July, 2012), Arab Social Media Report* (Dubai, 2012) <www.dsg.ae/en/imagees/ASMR4finaltopost.pdf>; Salem, Mourtade and Alshaer, 'Transforming Education in the Arab World'; Salem, Mourtade and Alshaer, 'The Arab World Online (2014): Trends in Internet and Mobile Usage in the Arab Region'; Dennis, Martin and Wood; Deloitte.
77 Cook.
78 Marie Gillespie, 'BBC Arabic, Social Media and Citizen Production: An Experiment in Digital Democracy before the Arab Spring', *Theory, Culture & Society*, 2013, 1–39; Pempek, Yermolayeva and Calvert; Cook; Gadi Wolfsfeld, Elad Segev and Tamir Sheafer, 'Social Media and the Arab Spring: Politics Comes First', *The International Journal of Press/Politics*, 18 (2013), 115–137 <doi:10.1177/1940161212471716>.
79 Cook; Omair Anas, 'Changing Profile of Media in the Arab States', *Global Media Journal*, 2 (2013), 28–46.
80 Cook; Anas; Wolfsfeld, Segev and Sheafer.

6

Social Media Usage and the Changing Context in the United Arab Emirates

David W. Bulla and James Buie

Mobile telephones are a significant personal apparatus – and a major part of everyday reality – in the United Arab Emirates (UAE). Emiratis and the large expatriate labour force that live in the nation are major consumers of smartphone technology, especially those made by Apple and Samsung. A high percentage of those who live in the UAE own multiple smartphones with multiple accounts from one of the two national carriers. In other words, the UAE as a nation is one of the most advanced in the world in terms of the adoption of cellular telephones. By 2016, the penetration rate is expected to exceed 70 per cent. This has occurred despite the fact that the nation is only 42 years old and has no major research and development in the area of telecommunications. The nation offers a good case-study of what is happening with social media in the Arabian Gulf region, an area of the globe with substantial wealth largely due to the existence of petroleum production and distribution.

Sheikhs, citizens and ex-pat labourers alike share in the broad use of twenty-first-century social media and the hardware and software that make those media platforms possible. Two of the nation's leaders, Mohammed bin Zayed, the ruler of Abu Dhabi, and Mohammed bin Rashid, the ruler of Dubai, have a strong presence on social media. They use these platforms as a means of communicating directly with

Emiratis, nationally and internationally. Ordinary citizens certainly use social media to share their news and information with one another, but they also stay in touch with the leaders of the country by following their Twitter and Facebook accounts. This provides a stronger connection between the monarchical rulers and their citizens, and young adults claim that it make them feel closer to the nation's leaders, to whom they look for a sense of guidance and optimism about their fairly small nation on the Western edge of Asia and the south-eastern part of the Arabian Gulf. Meanwhile, professional communications personnel, in both journalism and public relations, consider social media a means of disseminating their self-produced messages and keeping their fingers on the pulse of the nation. For example, journalists use Twitter and Facebook as a platform to let friends, family and the public know about their more recently published (on the internet) work.

This study was designed to examine the use of social media by political dissidents, bloggers, satirists and videographer bystanders to crime, and the serious legal problems they have encountered, including imprisonment, as well as a social media usage policy proposed by the federal government. This chapter, therefore, examines the UAE's broad cyber-crime law, as well as the broad definition of defamation, and how these laws have been applied in specific cases.

The emphasis in this study is on how three key stakeholders perceive the function of social media in UAE society: government leaders view them as a public relations (PR) tool to reduce the distance between them and their citizens and to quickly and clearly disseminate important information; journalists consider the social media as tools for promoting content, generating traffic to their websites, and helping them report on the issues of the day; and students believe that social media are not only a way to share mainly trivial information with one another, their families and friends, but also a way to get closer to their leaders, cutting out the public relations middlemen associated with traditional media. Young people, in particular, are quick to use new technology in ways that increasingly shape the boundaries between online and offline activities.[1] Facebook is among the most popular social networking sites in the Arab region, followed by Twitter. Therefore, most Arab studies have explored the use of Facebook. Hence, this chapter examines how the three different groups see social media in terms of their potential and overall usefulness as they negotiate their lives in Emirati society.

One of the aims of this chapter is to examine the social media policy in the region, including a somewhat clumsy law that makes it illegal to tag photographs of Emiratis on Facebook without their permission, as well as a federal law that limits commentary on social media on work-related topics by federal employees, including teachers and professors.[2] Therefore, this study provides a snapshot of how social media are being used by various groups in the UAE, in the middle of the second decade of the twenty-first century. The chapter also explores both the 'top-down' and 'bottom-up' approaches to social media in the seven Emirates of the UAE.

Literature Review

Youth in the UAE face several potential perils when they use social media.[3] For example, Martin Underwood, a reporter for *The National* newspaper, reported that some Facebook users in the UAE share their blackberry pins, and this includes cases of men attempting to rendezvous with girls. Meanwhile, the Dubai Police Department has reported that blackmail via social media sites has increased. Such blackmail often involves girls or young women who have posted photographs of themselves on various internet sites.[4] Seventy-three such blackmail cases were reported in the UAE in 2103.[5] Mobile phones are easily accessible in the UAE, and a high percentage of Emirati teens and young adults possess multiple mobile phones.[6] The primary use of mobile telephones among young people in the country is to engage in social media.[7] Indeed, the high mobile telephone penetration rate and the presence of such vast numbers of mobiles increase the opportunity for misuse of social media. Therefore, the authorities in Dubai have encouraged parents to be more vigilant about the potential harm that might arise from social media usage. Martin Underwood also reported that, by 2013, there were 45 million Facebook users in the Arab world.[8] As a percentage of its population, the UAE had the highest usage.[9]

A study by Badreya Al Jenaibi looked at possible definitions and categories of social media use by United Arab Emirates users.[10] Al Jenaibi concluded that social media could be broken down into categories: Blog; micro-blog; video-sharing; social network services (e.g., Facebook);

image-sharing (e.g., Instagram); social bookmarking; and opinion-sharing websites for the posting of different perspectives on various topics and issues of the day. Al Jenaibi pointed to the fact that social media penetration is strong in the Arab world because they help in the 'crafting of strong bonds'. She also found that a large majority (80 per cent) of Emiratis using social media were on Twitter; only about half that number was on Facebook (9–10). Al Jenaibi also stated that social media have the potential to facilitate political dialogue.

Fatima Al-Sayegh noted that social media usage has become very prevalent in the United Arab Emirates, but the study indicates that there are tensions in its rapid adoption rate.[11] In a web-based document from the nation's Centre for Research, Al-Sayegh indicated that 'the new forms of social media have put many of our conventional modes of communication in danger', as the former have become the favourite of the young generation and have a huge capacity to communicate at a faster rate and free of charge. Al-Sayegh also noted that there is concern that such media 'threaten' the older, face-to-face and oral-based culture of the nation. However, the study found that it was difficult to stem the tide of modern technology and social media: 'Many families in the UAE face the pressures of modern life, the responsibility of educating and raising children. Most of them use mobile phones, e-mails and social networking sites to keep in touch with their children'. Frequently, parents and elders, as well as family domestics, do not fully understand how social media work. This means that a communication revolution has taken place in the UAE, one that includes a major generation gap.

Muhammad Ayish studied 20 UAE organisations, exploring how they used the internet as a public relations tool. In his study, Ayish compared news updates, press releases, search engines, institutional or corporate profiles, photographic galleries and feedback. The study found evidence that these Emirati organisations were well aware of the importance of public relations through digital and online platforms.[12]

In terms of public relations, the leadership of the nation puts an emphasis on peace, prosperity and security, and it must constantly communicate its competency at maintaining these societal goals. Trust and legitimacy are, therefore, key issues for the UAE government, and social media offer a platform for establishing and maintaining both. In *Public Relations and*

Social Theory, Ihlen and his colleagues examine how to gain favourable media coverage.[13] They point to Irving Goffman, the founder of framing theory, as a key figure in the development of impressionistic PR theory – also known as impression management – where the emphasis is on relationships and image construction.

The government of Abu Dhabi encourages citizens and residents of the Emirate to connect with the government via its Facebook and web pages. The government calls this 'a convenient option for the fans of the popular social networking website to reach their favourite e-Government platform, avail themselves of its variety of services and information and have their say on their usefulness and efficiency'. The site says the intent is to strengthen the bonds between users of the site and government through 'personal communication'. Included in the content of the Gateway are news and government publications. The website encourages feedback.[14]

In a study conducted by undergraduate students at Zayed University in Abu Dhabi, ten participants in a focus group were asked about their use of social media in following members of the royal family.[15] Al Dhaheri and her colleagues found that the royal family's use of social media personalised their relationship with the citizens of the nation, especially when it became clear that one member of the royal family was himself actually transmitting on social media. The respondents said that while they followed the UAE royal family, the leaders 'were not effective both in the UAE and internationally as far as the usage of social media is concerned'.

Jeffrey Ghannam noted in an article entitled 'Social Media in the Arab World' that some leaders in the Middle East initially viewed social media with scepticism, but most have come to see the value of these platforms for 'promoting their agendas'.[16] Those who have refused to join the twenty-first century are said to be 'analogue ministers'. Ghannam also indicated that interaction was fairly limited and concluded that 'to be sure, blogging and social networking alone cannot be expected to bring about immediate political change. It is the long-term impact, the development of new political and civil society engagement and individual and institutional competencies on which analysts are focusing'.

In *A History of the Arab Peoples*, Albert Hourani calls social media a 'catalyst for change' in the Arab world. Hourani terms the social media platform '"horizontal" communication between networks of individuals'.[17]

Referring to the ideas of British journalist Paul Mason, Hourani says that Twitter can 'be deployed for group activity by facilitating "real-time" organization and news dissemination, bypassing the cumbersome "news-gathering" operations of the mainstream media'.[18] Hourani adds that in the Arab world there is little depth to the kind of civil society infrastructure that would render any democratic dialogue of sufficient strength to take hold in the wake of the so-called 'Arab Spring'. Rather, Islamist movements tended to have greater success in the aftermath of the social media-aided popular revolts of 2011. Citizens of the UEA seem to have been little affected by the sentiment of the 'Arab Spring'. Under the UAE constitution, criticism of the royal family is forbidden, as is defaming Arabs, their civilisation and heritage.[19]

Marshall Sponder noted that fans of social media are being studied. Media scholars are analysing items such as loyalty and recommendations.[20] Such research focuses on content analysis of keywords in blogs and forums, and also looks at available website metrics. Emirati royalty, national celebrities, and the tourism industry might certainly benefit from such analysis.

Methodology

This study employs qualitative and quantitative approaches. Several journalists, public relations professionals, students and university faculty members in the UEA were interviewed. They were asked about their use of social media and their purposes of using such platforms. A pre-structured questionnaire email included questions about time spent on social media, sharing information, socialising, communicating with family and 'stalking', and how often they use social media, including how often they post photographic images on platforms such as Instagram and WhatsApp, and where they go for news and information. They were also asked about their opinion on the impact of social media on their lives and the way they use social media.

The survey was conducted to find out about young people's use of social media in the UEA, as this group makes the most use of social media in the nation, with several studies suggesting that the percentage of young Emiratis' use of social media is greater than 80 per cent – and as high as 94 per cent among teenagers, according to the Arab Social Media Report.[21]

Indeed, media scholars in the UEA have found that the penetration of social media nears 100 per cent for teenagers in schools.

A survey email was sent to 256 users in the UEA. They were aged between 18 and 32, and all were Emirati. The majority of the respondents were female. One hundred and sixty-five responded, giving a response rate of 64.4 per cent, which is considered well above average for an email survey. The study credited the very decent response rate to the fact that young Emiratis are highly interested in social media.

Findings

In a survey of more than 160 young people in the UAE, the study found that the great majority (more than 75 per cent) use social media at least 21 hours per week. Some individuals reported spending as many as 35 hours a week on social media. In the case of students in schools or universities, this meant that they spent more time on social media than in the classroom and doing homework. In a similar vein, Metzger and her colleagues found that college students rely heavily on the internet for studying, news information and entertainment, and that this usage is expected to develop over time.[22] Predictably, students drew attention to the rising importance of the internet and social media, especially among young people, as a source of information and as a job-seeking tool.[23]

Socialising with friends was by far the main reason for using social media among respondents. While communicating with family was the second most significant reason for using social media, respondents said there were often multiple reasons for using social media. A typical response was as follows: 'social media give me insight on my friends' and family's life.' 'It informs me on any up-to-dates in their lives, since I do not get to see them every day.' In other words, there is a sort of surveillance of the individual social media user's environment. Similarly, one noted that respondents used social media for 'up-to-dates about fashion, politics and news in general through reading tweets or checking Instagram. Also, they use it for shopping because there are a lot of online shops on Instagram'. Not surprisingly, Sopher found that television remains young people's primary source of local news, with the internet considered equally important for national and international news.[24] Young people in the Arab world are spending an increasingly large proportion of their free time online.[25]

Quite a few respondents said that their first action of each day was to participate in social media. For example, one young person wrote:

> *I use social media daily. When I wake up, the first thing I do is open my phone and see who will chat with me! Then I take a look on Instagram for what others have posted.*

Another poster worried that dependency on social media unintentionally increased the distance between people. The respondent wrote:

> *I think using social media heavily will affect people's social interaction negatively by pushing them away from face-to-face interaction.*

Nearly 84 per cent of the respondents said that they posted a photograph on a social media or content-sharing website at least once a week. All but 18.70 per cent reported that they posted an image at least once a month. Some 83 per cent said they viewed social media usage as positive, with the vast majority of those respondents considering it extremely positive (74 per cent). Sharing content was one of the major reasons for participating in social media. One respondent commented:

> *I use social media to share my daily life, my thoughts and happy moments. I also use it to learn the news about the world.*

Another poll found that a majority of UAE students used social media for educational purposes, including talking about the school environment, various lessons and units, and even practising specific skills (such as using social media to help with research projects). One respondent in the current survey reported: *I specifically use blogging for educational reasons.* Several students said teachers/professors asked them to use social media to disseminate information. For example, one professor routinely asks students to publish items they have learned to 'show off' their knowledge and share the information with their digital peers.

In the current survey, respondents were asked about how they received news and current events. The internet is a platform on which news users can gain access to multiple news sources, including news provided by offline media such as major newspapers, news magazines, radio and even TV news stations. While newspapers exist in the UAE, very few young people read print editions or visit news websites. They are much more likely to get their news through social media, email or interpersonal communication. In this regard, newspapers were used to a lesser extent by respondents, and this may affect the way in which respondents used newspapers as a source of news. When asked which social media platforms were used to obtain daily news, the majority (56 per cent) said that they received news and different information from a combination of Twitter (18 per cent), Instagram (13 per cent) and texting (21 per cent). Some considered blogging as part of social media. One respondent followed food blogs to get new recipes and health blogs to help maintain a healthy lifestyle. This is also an indication that usage of local newspapers by respondents was low compared to other media platforms such as the internet.

These findings are consistent with several pieces of earlier research that revealed that college students are less likely to read newspapers.[26] For instance, Leo Bogart found that only 8 per cent of those aged 18 to 24 are frequent newspaper readers.[27] A 2008 Pew survey found that 15 per cent of young people aged 18 to 24 reported reading newspapers the day before the research was undertaken.[28] The study's findings, which reveal that newspapers are consumed by relatively few respondents, are somewhat expected, given the rise of the use of social media and the internet.

One clear indication in such a relationship is that 'several offline media have been quick to move their content online to capture internet users'.[29] For example, Lee and Kuo studied the relationship between internet use and television viewing, newspaper reading, radio listening, sports and physical exercise, interaction with family and socialising with friends.[30] They found that internet use is positively associated with an increase in newspaper reading and radio listening. They indicated that readers and listeners benefited from the internet.

Indeed, Twitter is a popular place to obtain news for young Emiratis. Thus, journalists in the UAE are learning that crowd-sourcing is best done on Twitter – and Instagram – among the available social media platforms. Very few young Emiratis are active in a daily manner on Facebook. Obtaining news was cited by several respondents as one of the primary uses of social media. For example, one respondent said they used social media to 'know about the world'. Another cited social media as a place 'to get the news'. Another respondent said that 'sharing and exchanging ideas and thoughts with random people around the world' was a primary activity on social media. Yet another said they used social media for 'texting, reading news and sharing pictures'. And yet another said they liked to 'act as a reporter, giving her/his opinion about restaurants and food products'.

In addition to their strong desire to maintain the nuclear and extended family, Emiratis also highly value their privacy. Where the Emiratis were interviewed, several respondents discussed concerns about the public nature of the digital world, including social media. Indeed, because of the structure of Emirati families – usually including a large number of children who are supervised by maids or nannies, living in large villas or houses – there is a real concern about isolation. Therefore, young people may be left in vulnerable situations with regard to social media. A study of 127 families in Abu Dhabi found that children were in fact isolated from real-world activity in human interaction because of the amount of time they spent on social media, the internet in general and video games. Such isolation gave rise to situations where they were interacting with strangers on social media. Perhaps the biggest problem raised in this study was the publication of 'selfies', other photographs of themselves and friends, and videos that are contrary to Emirati custom.[31]

In the open-ended section of the survey, respondents provided interesting anecdotes about their social media usage. For example, one respondent said that they like 'Instagram and Tumblr because they feed my artist's eyes'. 'I find ideas and inspiration there'. 'I think social networks can be positive when you surround yourself (follow) with the right people'. Another said that social media offered 'a platform for sharing "feelings" with others'. Yet another said that news was an important reason for using social media. The respondents learned about and shared business, education and sports news via social media. Another respondent said that sharing 'news pictures from around the world' was an important part of her daily social media routine.

Distance was a key issue for several of the respondents. One wrote that social media were valuable because they helped maintain communication with relatives and friends living abroad. Others said that they used platforms such as YouTube and MySpace to listen to music. The emergence of the internet was associated with concerns about what young people do with media. The internet has been considered a popular tool among young Arab people for downloading music or obtaining information about movies, books and other leisure activities.[32] Young people often use the internet to send emails, listen to music, chat with friends and play games, with online entertainment and communication activities comprising around 75 per cent of young people's internet time.[33]

Social media were also a vehicle for making consumer purchases, such as music, tickets to concerts, games, etc. One respondent stated: 'When it comes to fashion, I like using social media because you can see in a picture how a dress looks'. It was found that young Saudi people are becoming the primary users of media because of the opportunities for using different media in their daily lives. They divided their time among many mediated activities such as social networking, viewing videos, watching TV, exchanging Instant Messages, listening to music, playing games and searching for information.[34] Several respondents had different reasons for using the internet and social media. For example, they used video telephonic platforms such as Skype and Face Time to connect with family or friends in faraway places. One respondent noted: 'I just use Skype to connect with my cousin, who is studying in the UK'.

Another important aspect of social media usage among young Emiratis is the opportunity to meet new people and share ideas with those outside one's circle of friends. Several statements about the important of social media were given, such as '#I use SM to meet new people', 'finding new people is easy via social media' and 'I have made and met many people nationally and globally'. Moreover, several respondents like the immediacy of social media. For example, some indicated that they 'share instant moments by capturing them and sharing with others', 'many of my Instagram followers actually enjoy my photo stream and constantly check for updates' and 'this instant communication reaches such a wide range of individuals, and that is how I like to use social media'.

Dependency on social media emerged as a theme from the survey. One respondent wrote: 'I cannot imagine my life without social media'. Several respondents noted that they were concerned about over-use of social media, even seeing it as a potentially harmful addiction. One respondent wrote: 'I use it in my free time because I am really attracted to it, and I think it is a disease sometimes. For example, I tweet every single thing in my life, which means my phone never leaves my hands'. Another respondent said they used Twitter 'to vent, talk to myself and support myself by tweeting stuff like "You can do it"'. Indeed, time management and balancing social media with the rest of one's life were key issues for some of the respondents. As some respondents indicated, 'It is all about having a balance when using social media'.

Yet others put this balancing act in the following way: 'Sometimes social media is positive – such as sharing information with your family and friends. Also, you are sharing laughs and fun, but sometimes social media is very bad – such as when you are wasting your time in social media instead of caring for your studies and your work'. Some also indicated that Emiratis should not misuse social media, noting: 'It will affect others, and you might send messages and people get in the wrong way, so we have to be very careful about what we publish'. The same sample was concerned about rumour and innuendo, adding: 'We also should not believe everything we read'.

Escapism is another dimension of social media, according to several of the survey respondents. One commented that social media usage is a tactic for withdrawing from tense social situations. Instead of continuing a contentious dialogue or facing an embarrassing situation, the respondent withdraws from the real world via her mobile phone into the world of social media. Some indicated that they used social media when they are bored. Likewise, respondents reported using social media for entertainment purposes. Some shared music and jokes. Others followed celebrities. In addition to music, humour, and following celebrities, SM users also used these platforms for recreation:

> *I am a gamer and social media for gaming community is very essential. We can hook up with different people from different countries through them. We also plan strategies and timings, and form groups through social media. We also share in-game info requests and items through social media.*

Approximately 19 per cent said that social media are negative. One of the major concerns about social media is their ability to encourage behaviour proscribed by law, tradition and religion – including the breaking of the gender segregation barrier. The posting of a teenager's or young woman's photograph is a major issue in Emirati society. It is frowned upon by most of these females' parents and brothers.

Respondents also reported an activity they termed 'stalking' – which they defined as watching what others posted on social media with the intention of sharing 'private' information about those being watched with the respondents' friends. Some admitted that 'stalking' was not necessarily a positive activity and had a certain level of *schadenfreude* to it. A negative activity potentially related to 'stalking' is cyber bullying, in which a social media participant willingly and deliberately uses the technology and software as a platform to publish false, hostile, or embarrassing information about another person. Cyber bullying in the UAE is done through message boards, instant messaging, and other social networking sites, as well as email.

Another key to social media usage in the United Arab Emirates is change. Emiratis are so wired that they keep up to date not only with the latest technology but also with most of the newest social media platforms. One respondent observed that

> *In the few past years my usage has become totally different. It was all about socializing with friends and tweeting useless things, but now it is totally different. It's a gateway for me to share thoughts through Twitter and different apps. I read the news daily through social media and get involved in many volunteering events or activities that I explore through social media.*

In other words, this person's use of social media shows growth, progressing from selfish to unselfish reasons. One of the respondents said that she/he used social media in her/his volunteer work. On the other hand, another respondent said that social media were a 'waste of time'. Some of the respondents were clearly drawn to the open nature of social media, despite the existence of privacy controls. They view social media as an avenue for open and free expression. For example, one respondent stated that

> *I can be very honest on social media, and especially when I'm tweeting because I'm really basically talking to no one and everyone. And people don't have to agree on an issue, and so on.*

Finally, some respondents said that the value of social media depended on how they were used. One commented that

> *It depends on how people use social media. If you are negative, you more likely will get a bad experience from it. If you're positive, it will help boost your lifestyle.*

Discussion

While the current study provides a fair indication of how young Emiratis take advantage of social media, mainly through their dependency on mobile phone technology, it is not generalisable. It emerged that the majority of respondents use social media for entertainment purposes. For example, they use the internet to watch music programmes and videos. Indeed, neither younger nor older Emiratis were questioned in this survey. Because they are young, many are not yet employed. Furthermore, the in-depth interviews with communication professionals do not paint a very broad picture of what is happening in the country.

The current study recommends the undertaking of a comprehensive survey of a representative sample of the country's population, including non-Emiratis, who after all make up nearly 90 per cent of the population – and who generally do not have the same discretionary income as Emiratis. The United Arab Emirates, a nation of approximately 13 million people located in western Asia on the Gulf of Arabia, has a remarkably high use of digital platform technology for a nation that is only 42 years old. Citizens and expatriate workers are both strongly connected to the world by their mobile phones and other web-based technologies, including laptops and tablets. In this context, the UEA has one of the world's highest penetrations of smartphone use, standing at 62 per cent in 2013 and projected to reach 71 per cent or 3.75 million by 2016, according to a survey by Google.

The study also acknowledges that follow-up surveys of other major groups in the UAE may not yield nearly as high a response rate. Clearly, young people in the Emirates are highly wired, often own multiple mobile phones, and are very active on social media and the internet in general. Many Emiratis own multiple smartphones and are consistent users of BlackBerry Messenger, WhatsApp, Instagram, Twitter, Keek, and other forms of social communication exchange. The UAE has one of the world's largest participation rates in social media, with more than 3.5 million Facebook users, 69 per cent male and 31 per cent female, as of mid-2013. Among young people, Instagram and WhatsApp are the preferred social media. In view of the hundreds of thousands of followers on Facebook and Twitter, government leaders have taken an aggressive approach to the use of social media, holding regular social media symposia for government agencies and launching campaigns to make government more interactive and responsive to UAE residents. At the same time, hundreds of UAE citizens and residents have launched charitable and volunteer campaigns using social media with tangible results, which we will document.

The third and fourth questions in the survey[35] should have had follow-up questions to give the subjects the opportunity to tell us more about how they obtained news. The survey allowed multiple answers, and to these questions such answers were given. For example, in Question No. 3, the study should have asked a follow-up question about how the respondents document their lives and, since 'Other' had a 33 per cent response rate, another follow-up question might have asked them to describe those other experiences with social media.

Conclusion

It has been found that young Emiratis are both heavy and savvy users of social media and the internet. These subjects are worth studying because they use social media for a variety of reasons: keeping up with friends and family, collecting and sharing news, deliberating on consumer choices, making vanity postings, etc. Indeed, many young Emiratis spend more time on social media that on any other activity in their lives. In this context, it is clear that Emiratis spend time on different social media sites in various ways.[36] Regardless of whether they are using them to kill time[37] or as a social instrument,[38] each platform has its own effects and purposes.

It is worth saying that, ultimately, it is the users who make the decision to use the social media by placing value on them. The uses and gratifications model can be applied here to understand and provide a background for a better understanding of why and how different social media users become more or less actively involved[39] and what outcomes users feel they have gained from the usage.[40] The approach is simply concerned with measuring very broad-based notions about reasons and how they relate to the use of specific platforms, such as television versus radio versus newspaper versus the internet. It is a very blunt way of measuring behaviour. Building on these assessments, media scholars have attempted to develop other theories that assist our understanding of the relationship between media exposure and consumers' behaviour; one of these theories was the theory of the niche.

Furthermore, the findings of this study should give parents and those in charge some sense of foreboding. Ought these young people to be so addicted to their mobile phones and social media? And what are the cultural and regional reasons for such an addiction? The authors, as communication academics, fully admit that these questions are more the preserve of psychology than traditional communication research fields. This study, therefore, encourages a cross-disciplinary approach to better understand what exactly is occurring with social media practice in the United Arab Emirates.

Furthermore, focused research should be conducted on social media and cultural change. Media scholars should look at how intense social media usage is affecting traditional cultural activities, societal laws and rules, and personal behaviour. The tension between the material wealth from the petroleum industry that creates the rather large discretionary incomes enjoyed by most Emiratis and the traditional mores of an Arab and Islamic society that only a generation ago conducted almost all of its communication face to face and orally is an area of concern and worthy of in-depth analysis. How, for example, can many young people routinely participate in digital 'stalking' when Emiratis believe in the ethic of treating the other with respect? Additionally, how can such a privacy-oriented society square itself with the public nature of posting visual images on websites such as Instagram, YouTube and Keek? These and other critical questions deserve further examination by scholars of communication, sociology and psychology.

Notes

1 Khulood Miliany, 'The Impact of the Internet on Saudi Students' Use of Television' (Unpublished doctor's dissertation. University of Leicester, UK, 2013).

2 Publications and publishing law. (1980). Abu Dhabi, UAE: Federal Government of the United Arab Emirates. <URL: http://nmc.gov.ae/en/pages/MediaLawsAndRegulation.aspx>. Retrieved: 26 May 2014.

3 Martin Underwood, 'UAE and Social Media: Dangers out in the Open', *The National*, 2013 <http://www.thenational.ae/news/uae-news/uae-and-social-media-dangers-out-in-the-open>.

4 Freedom House, 'Freedom in the World 2013', 2013 <http://freedomhouse.org/report/freedom-world/freedom-world-2013#.U0uSdfm-1cY>.

5 Nader Ibrahim, 'Does Social Media Carry out Change in the Gulf?', 2013 <http://www.bbc.co.uk/arabic/middleeast/2013/12/131230_gulf_social_media.shtml>.

6 Underwood.

7 Mokhtar Elareshi, Abdul-Karim Ziani and Barrie Gunter, 'The Use of Mobile Phone and Internet in Getting Local News in GCC Regions: A University Student Study', *Journal of Media and Communication Studies*, 3 (2015), 001–010.

8 Underwood.

9 Everette Dennis, Justin Martin and Robb Wood, 'Media Use in the Middle East: An Eight-Nation Survey', 2013 <http://menamediasurvey.northwestern.edu/>.

10 Badreya Al Jenaibi, 'Use of Social Media in the United Arab Emirates: An Initial Study', *Global Media Journal-Arabian Edition*, 1 (2012), 3–27.

11 Fatima Al-Sayegh, 'The Impact of Social Media on UAE Society', *The Emirates Center for Strategic Studies and Research*, 2013 <http://www.ecssr.ac.ae/ECSSR/print/ft.jsp?lang=en&ftId=/FeatureTopic/Fatma-AlSayegh/FeatureTopic_1698.xml>.

12 Muhammad Ayish, 'Virtual Public Relations in the United Arab Emirates', *Public Relations Review*, 2005, 381–388.

13 Oyvind Ihlen, Betteke Ruler and Magnus Fredriksson, *Public Relations and Social Theory: Key Figures and Concepts* (New York, NY: Routledge, 2009).

14 Abu Dhabi E-Government Gateway, 'Official Facebook Page to Engage Users with Abu Dhabi E-Government Gateway', 2014 <https://www.abudhabi.ae/portal/faces/en/abu_dhabi_emirate/government/news/news_detail?docName=ADEGP_DF_299606_EN&_adf.ctrl-state=12n65ndr0f_4&_afrLoop=1981937430112760>.

15 M.S. Al Dhaheri and others, 'Public Image in the UAE' (Abu Dubai, 2014).

16 Jeffrey Ghannam, *Social Media in the Arab World: Leading up to the Uprisings of 2011* (Washington, DC: Center for International Media Assistance, 2011).

17 Albert Hourani, *A History of the Arab Peoples* (London, UK: Faber and Faber, 2013). p. 498.

18 Ibid.

19 Ibid.

20 Marshall Sponder, *Social Media Analytics: Effective Tools for Building, Interpreting, and Using Metrics* (New York: McGraw-Hill, 2012).

21 Fadi Salem, Racha Mourtade and Sara Alshaer, 'The Arab World Online (2014): Trends in Internet and Mobile Usage in the Arab Region', *Arab Social Media Report* (Dubai, 2014) <http://www.mbrsg.ae/getattachment/ff70c2c5-0fce-405d-b23f-93c198d4ca44/The-Arab-World-Online-2014-Trends-in-Internet-and.aspx>.

22 Miriam J. Metzger, Andrew J. Flanagin and Lara Zwarun, 'College Student Web Use, Perceptions of Information Credibility, and Verification Behavior', *Computer and Education*, 41 (2003), 271–290 <doi:10.1016/S0360-1315(03)00049-6>.

23 Deborah Chung and Chan Yoo, 'Audience Motivations for Using Interactive Features: Distinguishing Use of Different Types of Interactivity on an Online Newspaper', *Mass Communication and Society*, 11 (2008), 375–397.

24 Christopher K. Sopher, 'Younger Thinking: An Evaluation of Young America and the Future of News Media and Civic Life', 2010 <http://youngerthinking.com/upload/ResearchPaper-reduced.pdf>.

25 Imad Karam, 'Satellite Television: A Breathing Space for Arab Youth?', in *Arab Media and Political Renewal: Community, Legitimacy and Public Life*, ed. by Naomi Sakr (London: I.B.Tauris & Co. Ltd, 2007), pp. 80–95.

26 Leo Bogart, *Press and Public: Who Reads What, When, Where, and Why in American Newspapers* (Hillsdale, New Jersey: Lawrence Erlbaum Associates, 1989); George Thurlow and Katherine Milo, 'Newspaper Readership: Can the Bleeding Be Stopped, or Do We Have the Wrong Patient?', *Newspaper Research Journal*, 14 (1993), 34–44.

27 Ibid.

28 The Pew Research Center, 'News Media Consumption Survey', *The Pew Research Center for The People & The Press*, 2008.

29 Lars Willnat, 'The Impact of Internet News Consumption on Mass Media Use', in *Paper presented at the annual meeting of the International Communication Association* (Dresden, Germany, 2006) <http://www.allacademic.com/meta/p90915_index.html>, p. 1.

30 Waipeng Lee and Eddie C. Y. Kuo, 'Internet and Displacement Effect: Children's Media Use and Activities in Singapore', *Journal of Computer-Mediated Communication*, 7 (2002), 0 <doi:10.1111/j.1083–6101.2002.tb00143.x>

31 Mohamed El Khouli, 'The Most Important Negative Aspects of Suing Social Networking Affecting the Family Stability in Abu Dhabi: A Pilot Study', *International Journal of Engineering and Technology*, 5 (2013), 85–90.

32 Lee Rainie and Andrew Kohut, 'Tracking Online Life: How Women Use the Internet to Cultivate Relationships with Family and Friends', *The Pew Internet Project*, 2000 <http://www.pewinternet.org/reports/pdfs/Report1.pdf.>.

33 Tshepo Batane, 'Internet Access and Use among Young People in Botswana', *International Journal of Information and Education Technology*, 3 (2013), 117–119 <doi:10.7763/IJIET.2013.V3.246>; Aine Dunne, Margaret-Anne Lawlor and Jennifer Rowley, 'Young People's Use of Online Social Networking

Sites: A Uses and Gratifications Perspective', *Journal of Research in Interactive Marketing*, 4 (2010), 46–58.

34 Miliany.

35 The question words was 'Q3. What is the main purpose of social media for you?' The fourth question words was 'Where do you get your daily news from?'

36 Alan B. Albarran and Arrese Angel Reca, *Time and Media Markets* (Mahwah, NJ: Lawrence Erlbaum Associates, 2003).

37 Elihu Katz, Jay Blumler and Michael Gurevitch, 'Uses and Gratifications Research', *The Public Opinion Quarterly*, 37 (1973), 509–523; David Tewksbury, 'Differences in How We Watch the News: The Impact of Processing Goals and Expertise on Evaluations of Political Actors', *Communication Research*, 26 (1999), 4–29 <http://crx.sagepub.com/cgi/reprint/26/1/4>.

38 Philip Auter, Mohamed Arafa and Khalid Al-Jaber, 'Identifying with Arabic Journalists: How Al-Jazeera Tapped Parasocial Interaction Gratifications in the Arab World', *International Communication Gazette*, 67 (2005), 189–204; Alan Rubin, 'Media Uses and Effects: A Uses and Gratifications Perspective', in *Media effects: Advances in theory and research*, ed. by J. Bryant and D. Zillman (NJ: Erlbaum, 1994), pp. 417–436.

39 Kimberly Massey, 'Analysing the Uses and Gratifications Concept of Audience Activity with a Qualitative Approach: Media Encounters during the 1989 Loma Prieta Earthquake Disaster', *Journal of Broadcasting and Electronic Media*, 39 (1995), 349; David L. Swanson, 'Gratification Seeking, Media Exposure, and Audience Interpretations: Some Directions for Research', *Journal of Broadcasting & Electronic Media*, 31 (1987), 237–254.

40 Philip Palmgreen and J.D. Rayburn II, 'Uses and Gratifications and Exposure to Public Television: A Discrepancy Approach', *Communication Research*, 6 (1979), 155–180; Swanson.

7

Women and Online Political Participation in Kuwait

Fatima AlSalem

In light of the activist movements that took place in Kuwait in 2012, the opposition coalition called for an overnight occupation of *Alirada* Square the day before the National Assembly opened in December of 2012 as an act of opposition, together with a boycott of that Assembly. The call for the occupation was posted on social media and invited everyone to occupy the square. However, a massive reaction occurred in the country, from activists, feminists, religious leaders and within the opposition group itself. Interestingly, unlike other Assemblies, women were invited, which raises the question of the role of Kuwaiti women. Recently, Kuwaiti women have played a vital role in politics and their involvement in the activist movement in 2012 cannot be overlooked.

This chapter examines Kuwait's political system and the appropriation of social media by female online users by looking at the influence of the technological revolution on Kuwait's political and social structures. The chapter also explores the backdrop of active political life in Kuwait in order to investigate the dynamic of social media effects, especially Twitter. There is, however, a dearth of data on the relation between social media use and women's political participation in Kuwait, online and offline, the factors that influence women's online political participation, the effect of social and political systems on the ways in which social media are used in the Gulf region, especially the effects on marginalised groups such as women and young people, and the roles of social media in such events. This chapter is designed to shed new light on these matters.

Literature Review

Although Kuwait has seen several political activist movements and overnight occupation events, such as the one that took place in 2006, women had never before been invited to join in such events if they involved overnight stays. Lately, Kuwait has witnessed activist movements and protests that were organised on social media and many observers believe that women have had a more significant role in these movements than in previous political events.[1] Women's involvement in political affairs has traditionally been minimal, and only in the last few years have they begun to contribute effectively to political and social movements.

Kuwaiti women used various social media platforms to participate in various political movements, such as sharing pictures and information. As a result, more women had been participating in protests and in different political events, and they had become an essential part of the 2012 *Karamat Watan* (nation's dignity) movement in Kuwait.

On the other hand, women's participation in overnight events was not acceptable to much of society; those opposed to it included religious leaders, conservative and liberal activists, and, most importantly, many women themselves. As soon as the *Karamat Watan* movement sent out an invitation via Twitter to take part in the overnight occupation, a strongly negative reaction occurred, with critics accusing the movement of degrading and not respecting women, and asserting that the notion of women sleeping overnight on the square with men was simply not acceptable for religious reasons. Some female activists (who remained anonymous on social media) tried to protect their rights by claiming that they knew the difference between right and wrong and that they should be granted equal rights to those of men. In reaction to these objections, the movement sent out another Twitter message calling for the event to be restricted to men only and announcing that women would only be present in the square until late evening.

What does this tell us about the role of social media and the role of social norms and cultural restrictions in women's political involvement? In a culture such as Kuwait's, it is very important to look at the social and cultural factors in play in order to understand the relationship between the internet and political participation. Although research in developed democracies has found that there is a positive relationship between the internet and political participation, it is important to examine that relationship in other political systems in which culture, traditional values and norms must be considered as significant as the power of the internet.

Kuwait

Kuwait is one of the smallest countries in the Middle East, located in the northwest corner of the Arabian Gulf. Kuwait is a hereditary Emirate and the political system is a constitutional monarchy consisting of legislative, executive and judiciary branches.[2] The legislative branch is made up of 50 members who are democratically elected every four years by Kuwaiti men and women aged 21 years and older. Several factors – socio-cultural, political and economic – have influenced Kuwaiti citizens and the government to become more politically active compared to many other Arab nations.[3]

First, there were the socio-cultural factors related to the country's original organisation, which was based on tribal and Bedouin families.[4] Second, certain political factors played a pivotal role in advancing the process of political participation in Kuwaiti society to protect the country from external threats such as that from Iraq.[5] However, in the last few years, Kuwait has witnessed considerable political activism by groups opposed to the government. This political conflict and activism is mostly due to the repeated clashes between the executive and legislative branches, which have led to the parliament being dissolved many times.[6] Since 2006, the National Assembly has been dissolved three times and early elections have been called due to the impasse between the legislature and the government.[7] Furthermore, the constitutional court has dissolved the National Assembly twice since 2006 by nullifying the results of elections on the grounds of flawed procedure.

This repeated conflict between the executive and the legislative branches has led to an increase in political activism movements in the country. In sum, political life in Kuwait resembles to some extent that of many other countries with a reasonably democratic and open political system.[8] The country has had some degree of participatory governance since its early establishment, and the public shared in decision-making with the government in the early 1920s and 1930s.

Women and Politics

Kuwaiti women have struggled and fought a fierce battle for four decades to gain their political rights and to participate in decision-making and the development of Kuwait's social and political life. Women's movements against marginalisation and inequality have often been faced with many traditional, tribal, religious and social challenges.[9] The women's rights battle persisted over decades, including women's movements, demonstrations and the occupation of the public gallery in the parliament.[10]

In May 1999, the late Amir, Sheikh Jaber Al Ahmad Al Sabah, issued a decree that granted women the right to vote and to be nominated for the National Assembly.[11] However, the Amir's decree was overruled by the parliament, which argued that the majority of women are not interested in women's rights and that the women's movement is elitist.[12] After a long and persistent campaign by the women's movement, the conservative and Islamist members acquiesced and the parliament passed a bill granting women the right to vote and to be nominated for the National Assembly on 16 May 2005.[13] The historic session in which the Women's Rights Bill was passed was described by observers as one of the most challenging in the history of the National Assembly. Since then, women have been fighting to gain their full rights in the areas of leadership positions and social equality.[14]

Statistically, women constitute 50.3 per cent of the total population of Kuwait[15] and constituted 53.4 per cent of the total number of registered voters in Kuwait compared to only 46.5 per cent among men. Nevertheless, there is a persistent gender gap in nominations for the parliament. Only eight women ran in the July 2013 election campaign, compared with 418 male candidates; i.e. only 1.9 per cent of the candidates were women.[16] While women's rights in Kuwait have been won, there are still some serious reservations about women's full political participation and representation.

Women in Kuwait face many obstacles that prevent their full political inclusion, such as traditions, culture and male domination.[17] The 'Arab Spring' and the active political scene in Kuwait in the past few years have influenced women's social and political activist movements. More Kuwaiti women have started to voice their opinions and organise social movements in several fields, including human rights and equality.

Internet and Political Participation

Scholars have been asking whether social media will have an impact on democracy by enhancing political participation. However, there is no direct answer to this question, due to the various assumptions that one might make about the character of democracy.[18] Scholars are sceptical about the impact of the internet on people's political participation, and these concerns have grown over time as internet penetration has increased.[19] Others have argued that new communication technologies have changed the way people participate in politics.[20] Social scientists are trying to determine the potential positive or negative impact of social media on political participation, as the exact effect remains largely unexplored.[21]

Scholars have obtained mixed findings about the role of social media in people's political behaviour and participation.[22] The main effects can be categorised into three main schools of thought. Although some scholars argue that most research has categorised social media's effects as either optimistic or pessimistic, there is a third line of thought in the literature that argues that social media have a normalising effect.[23] An optimistic view sees social media providing the resources needed for online participation such as access to information and electronic participation opportunities.[24] Meanwhile, pessimistic scholars believe that social media have a potentially negative effect on social engagement. Many scholars believe that the use of the internet weakens social cohesion and causes people to abandon their social environment.[25] Studies have shown that the internet reinforces existing social and political structures.[26] This third group of scholars presents a normalisation hypothesis that states that the internet has barely affected the levels of participation.[27]

The technological revolution and social networks have clearly changed election advertising campaigns in Kuwait. Given the social habits of the

Kuwaiti culture and the increased level of family visits and social clubs, many candidates use social media such as Twitter, YouTube and blogs to advertise their campaigns and communicate with voters.[28] The active social media sphere has influenced political campaigning and provided a space for young people and the elderly to obtain information about politics. The Arab uprisings in 2011 and the active political sphere in Kuwait provide good examples of how social media have been used as a tool for participation and organisation.[29] The significance of the use of social media by women cannot be neglected and its effect in mobilising women to play a greater political role in Kuwait and the Arab region has become a reality.

To sum up, studies have found that the use of the internet for participating in politics has a small but significant effect on the extent of women's offline participation.[30] The literature on Kuwait sheds interesting light on how technology is providing women with opportunities for political inclusion and activism. However, empirical research is needed to examine the effect of social media use on women's political participation and the factors that influence it. Below are the research questions that were addressed in this study.

RQ1: What factors influence women's online political participation?
RQ2: What is the relation between social media use and women's political participation online and offline?

Online Anonymity and Empowerment

Studies have shown that Kuwaiti women feel that the internet provides them with opportunities to experience things they would not have been able to do in their ordinary lives and to explore various topics that may have been considered taboo for them to pursue.[31] The anonymity of women's online presence may be one of the most significant reasons for the increased internet use by women in Kuwait. Anonymity is defined as the state when a person is unidentifiable.[32] Some studies have associated online anonymity with anti-social behaviour.[33] Conversely, other studies have found that anonymity fosters social inclusion by allowing people to selectively self-present in order to better manage the impression they make.[34] This is especially important in Kuwait's virtual spheres, as several scholars have found that political participation is not acceptable for woman due to gender issues.[35] Anonymity online allows women to overcome traditional social differences and to participate in what has traditionally been considered a masculine domain. Taking the previous observations into account, this study hypothesises the following:

H1: Women who are more anonymous online will have higher levels of online participation than women who are less anonymous online.

Methodology

The current study surveyed 800 Kuwaiti women aged 18 years and over and randomly selected.[36] The sample was generated by telephone interviews and conducted between 15 June and 8 July, 2013.[37] Although many factors influence survey data collection in Kuwait, the survey method suited the present project because it allowed the collection of a national sample and investigated women's political behaviour, media use and demographics.[38]

The survey's questionnaire comprised 39 questions that focused on five main sections: Social media use, media use,[39] political attitudes,[40] political participation, and demographics. Social media variables used in the study helped to profile Kuwaiti women's social media use habits and characteristics. Respondents were asked about their social media use,[41] time spent on the internet[42] and their internet accessibility.[43] Social media were examined for exposure to mainstream media in order to determine their relationship with political participation.

Anonymity was also measured here.[44] There has been much research on the role of anonymity in communication.[45] This study found that anonymity fosters online social inclusion because it allows people to self-select their identities for better impression management. This study also investigated respondents' exposure to news and political information in order to examine the effect of such exposure on participation.[46] They were asked about the average amount of time they 'spent on digital media to get news and political information yesterday'.[47] They were also asked about the average amount of time they 'spent on social media to get political news and information yesterday'. Further questions asked respondents about their political interest,[48] political discussion[49] and socio-political factors.[50]

This study distinguishes between online participation and offline participation activities in order to investigate the different effects of participation.[51] Respondents were asked 'how often during the past six months' they had participated in each of 11 online political activities.[52]

In the current sample of Kuwaiti woman, two thirds (67.1 per cent) were married and most (70%) had children aged under 18; their average age was 33 years. Over one third (37.4%) had a Bachelor's degree, and over six in ten (62.8%) worked full-time. In addition, 37.4 per cent of the women were college graduates, while 29.3 per cent held a two-year Diploma (Community College). In all, 12.2 per cent of women were high school graduates, while only 6.6 per cent had some high school education. Nearly one third (31.8%) earned between $3,575 and $5,357 (31.8 per cent) per month, followed by those earning between $2,681 and $3,571 (22.8 per cent), and those earning between $875 and $1,250 (15.9 per cent). However, a significant number of these Kuwaiti women (28.8 per cent) reportedly earned $5,360 or more monthly. Due to government allowances and support for the unemployed, housewives, students and the elderly, only 4.5 per cent of women earned less than $1,785 monthly.

Women's Media Consumption Habits

The results showed that Kuwaiti women do not use mass media very much. Our results indicated that 41 per cent of women do not listen to the radio, 44.9 per cent do not read print newspapers and 47.6 per cent do not read e-newspapers. Although the difference appears to be small, women spend slightly more time per day reading e-newspapers than they spend reading print newspapers. This reflects the popularity of technology in Kuwait and the extensive prevalence of digital media.

The findings also indicated that the majority of respondents have internet access (86 per cent), and 87 per cent of them use social media. Slightly less than a quarter (23.9 per cent) spent one to two hours online daily, while 30.9 per cent spent the same amount of time on social media. 65.6 per cent of respondents use their smartphones to access social media. The findings are consistent with other recent studies that have found social media and the internet to be the main public spaces for discussing sensitive political topics in the Arab region.[53] In fact, Alqabra argues that social media have led to many changes and increased political discussion in Kuwait.[54]

In terms of internet accessibility, when internet access was analysed by education and income, the results clearly indicate that women with higher levels of education are more likely to have access to the internet.[55] The majority of respondents (65.6 per cent) used their smartphones to access social media, followed by those who use laptops (14.9 per cent), tablets (11.2 per cent) and desktop computers (10.6 per cent). Twitter was the most dominant social media site for Kuwaiti women, with 59.8 per cent of respondents using Twitter, followed by Instagram (49.9 per cent). Facebook was used by only 18.5 per cent of them, followed by YouTube (16.3 per cent) and Google+ (13.6 per cent). These findings are consistent with other reports that have found the female penetration rate of Facebook in Arab countries to be low compared to the global trend.[56]

The majority of respondents also have social media access (87 per cent); many of them do not reveal their real identities when they access these sites, and 76.6 per cent of respondents do not share their full names on social media. Conversely, 20 per cent of respondents use no personal information, 18.3 per cent of them use their full names, 16.8 per cent use nicknames that indicate gender, and 10 per cent used nicknames that do not indicate gender; only 6 per cent use nicknames that might be someone's name, 5.1 per cent use their full real names together with additional information and 4 per cent use partial real names plus additional personal information.

In addition, respondents were asked whether they posted a personal photograph 'identifying' them when they used their preferred social media sites. 61.3 per cent of respondents do not use a personal photo that identifies them on social media.

Political Characteristics of Kuwaiti Women

Previous studies have shown that political characteristics are related to political participation and that the media reinforce interest in politics and voting intentions.[57] The majority of Kuwaiti women in this study were registered voters (75.2 per cent), compared with 22.6 per cent who were not. Only 1 per cent of women had not been able to register or could not remember whether they were registered to vote or not (1.2 per cent). When respondents were asked about their political ideology, less than four in ten (39 per cent) declined to indicate their political ideology, while 36 per cent said they were independent. Around one in seven (14 per cent) of respondents said they were conservative or very conservative (7 per cent).

The analysis shows that the majority of respondents (64.2 per cent) perceived religion to have 'a lot' of influence on their daily lives, while around one in three (29 per cent) of the respondents perceived religion to have 'little influence' or 'some influence' (6 per cent). Only 1.7 per cent of them perceived religion to have 'no influence at all' on their daily lives. In terms of political interest, over four in ten respondents (43.9 per cent) were moderately interested in politics, followed by those who were slightly interested (16.7 per cent) and those who are not interested in 'at all' (15.2 per cent).

The survey included a question about political talk[58] and the results showed that around one in three (31 per cent) of the respondents did not talk about politics 'at all', while 27.7 per cent of them did so a 'few times a week', followed by those who did so 'once a week' (25 per cent), 'once a day' (9 per cent) and 'more than once a day' (7 per cent).

When asked about the socio-political factors that have the most influence on women's ability to participate in politics, respondents considered religious norms to have the highest influence on their ability to participate in politics (62.5 per cent). They also indicated that the current political situation had the second highest influence on their ability to participate (57.5 per cent), followed by the factor of husband, father or brother, and cultural and social norms (both 55 per cent). Other factors were children, friends and 'the fact that I'm a woman' (45 per cent). The findings, consistent with previous research on women's political participation in Kuwait, suggested that family, husbands and social norms have impacts on women's decisions and their ability to participate in politics.[59]

Political Participation

This section examines data on the sampled Kuwaiti women's political participation. Among all online political activities, respondents watched political videos 'the most'. Among all online political activities, 21 per cent of internet users at least 'occasionally' watched political videos online, followed by '*like* political content' (17 per cent), 'share political content online' (16.3 per cent), 'went online to *fact check* claims made by online' (15 per cent), 'contacted a politician online privately' (11 per cent), 'took part in an online political discussion' (9.4 per cent), 'used internet to invite people to political discussion' (8.6 per cent), 'created a political content online' and 'participated in an online campaign' (both 8.2 per cent). Joining political forums was the least common activity, with only 5.9 per cent of online users reporting that they had at least 'occasionally' joined a forum.

The differences among online political participation activities were relatively small and the overall results indicated that women have a very low rate of online political participation.[60] This low level of participation in online activities reflects the relatively low level of female political involvement in the country. It is important to note that women lack civic skills and political interests due to their relatively recent experience with political matters.

Key Prediction Factors for Political Participation

A further stage in this analysis was performed to establish whether the specific factors predicted reported the influence of online political participation. A five-step hierarchical regression model was computed to achieve this.[61] The findings indicated that respondents' political characteristic variables explained 11.6 per cent of the total variance in the online political participation model.

The analysis showed that political interest ($\beta= .26$, $p < .001$) and political talk ($\beta= .11$, $p < .01$) were significantly associated with higher online participation. Exposure to political content online was also significantly associated with higher online participation ($\beta= .14$, $p < .001$). Thus, respondents who looked for political content online were more likely to have higher online political participation levels than respondents who looked for other content. Socio-political factors explained 5.5 per cent of the variance in online political participation. Respondents who reported that their families influence their ability to participate in politics were more likely to participate in online political activities ($\beta= .11$, $p < .01$).

The findings also showed that demographic variables explained 3.8 per cent of the total variance in online participation. Registered voters were

Table 7:1 Hierarchical Linear Regression Predicting Online and Offline Participation

Predictors	Online Participation
Demographics	
– Registered voters	.18***
Incremental R2 (%)	3.80***
Political Characteristics	
– Political talk	.10**
– Political interest	.28***
Incremental R2 (%)	11.6***
Mainstream Media	
– Digital newspapers	.14***
Incremental R2 (%)	3.20***
Socio-Participation Factors	
– Family influence	.11**
– Online privacy	.22***
– Anonymity	.08*
Incremental R2 (%)	5.50***
Digital Media Use	
– Digital skills	.17***
– Seeking online content (political)	.14***
Incremental R2 (%)	4.30***
Total R2 (%)	28.4***

Note: Online participation is measured on an 11-point scale ranging from 11 (low online participation) to 55 (high online participation). Offline participation in measured on an 11-point scale ranging from 11 (low offline participation) to 55 (high offline participation). Cell entries represent before-entry standardised ordinary least square regression coefficients. *p < .05. **p < .01. ***p < .001, two-tailed. N = 576.

positively associated with higher levels of online participation (β= .18, p < .001). However, the other demographic characteristics such as age, education, income and marital status were not associated with online participation. Therefore, political interest (β= .28, p < .001), political talk (β= .10, p < .001), family influence (β= .11, p < .001), exposure to political information, and voting registration are all factors related to higher online political participation. In terms of mainstream media, exposure to e-newspapers was associated with higher levels of online political participation (β=. 14, $p < .001$), whereas exposure to print newspapers, radio and TV was not. Respondents who read more e-newspapers were more likely to have higher levels of online participation. Finally, regarding the relation between social media use and higher levels of online participation (RQ2), the findings indicated that there was no association between internet use and online participation (β= -.03, ns).

Hypothesis 1, which predicted that women who are more anonymous online would have higher levels of online participation, was supported (β= .08, $p < .05$). Thus, women who are more likely to be anonymous online were more likely to have higher levels of online political participation.

Discussion

In recent years, research has increasingly focused on the relationship between social media and political participation in open democracies.[62] The present research explored the potential relationship between social media use and political participation among women in a conservative society, Kuwait. Kuwait offers an excellent opportunity to test how technology can influence the power of traditional values and cultural norms by providing disengaged segments of the population such as women with the resources needed to engage in politics at a lower cost of participation.

Several studies have linked internet penetration rates and technological advancement with democracy and greater liberalisation, and have neglected to focus on the behaviour of internet users. The internet and social media revolution in the Arab word has brought a lot of attention to the power of technology to change societies and has raised questions about the influence of the technological revolution on the region in terms of politics, social change and culture. Overall, the present research found that Kuwaiti women consume a low amount of mainstream media. However, television rated highest in their media consumption, which supports previous research findings in Kuwait.[63] Women's average daily consumption of e-newspapers was higher than that of print newspapers. This supports evidence that e-newspapers are taking over the readership of traditional print newspapers.

In terms of the relationship between media use and political participation, this study found that e-newspapers are positively associated with higher online political participation, suggesting that the consumption of digital sources of information (especially by Kuwaiti women) is related to higher levels of online participation. Although previous research has consistently found that the total time spent online was associated with higher levels of online participation, this study did not find such an association.

The study found that respondents who have higher levels of political interest and those who talk more about politics are more likely to participate in online political activities. This is consistent with the argument put forward by some scholars that online participation is a reflection of offline politics and reinforces people's pre-existing offline attitudes.[64] Those who are interested in politics offline have been found to be more likely to participate in online politics. Politically active women in Kuwait are usually liberated, elite women. However, it is important to explain that 'elite' in Kuwait does not necessary mean those with high incomes and the socially advantaged. Political elites in Kuwait can be described as being more socially engaged, politically interested and publicly known. Those women are more likely to participate in non-profit organisations, volunteer for social work and participate in events sponsored by women's organisations.

Finally, this study indicated that the influence of the family on women's ability to participate in politics is positively associated with higher rates of online political participation. This suggests that family is perceived as an important factor in determining levels of political participation. Kuwaiti women usually have male guardians who may influence their voting decisions and degree of political participation.

The study's main finding is that anonymity was moderately – albeit significantly –related to higher online participation. Although anonymity has been tested before with regard to its relationship with blogging and online behaviour, it has not been applied to political participation. Anonymity provides women with an opportunity to overcome social and cultural barriers online. Women who hide behind nicknames online can express their opinions and participate in political activities without fear of social judgement.

Conclusion

There is an increasingly optimistic view that the internet is radically changing the nature of political participation. This view holds that the internet mobilises traditionally disengaged sectors of society (such as women) and provides them with new platforms for participation.[65] Conversely, there is an opposing view that considers the effect of the internet on democracy to be minimal. This study found that the internet's influence on women's political participation was actually very small. This is in contrast to previous research conducted in Western countries.[66]

The findings in this study suggest that the so-called 'online democracy' advocated by the cyber optimists needs to be re-evaluated for regions such as the Middle East. The internet offers a vast amount of information, a sense of empowerment and plenty of space for the expression of opinions and opportunities for mobilisation. Nevertheless, the internet is limited in its ability to transform the way politics actually works. Kuwait has made great efforts to provide internet accessibility and support technological advancement, which has resulted in a highly wired society. This research has shown that women have high levels of internet accessibility, high levels of social media accessibility and high rates of smartphone penetration. However, internet use and accessibility were not associated with higher levels of online political participation.

Hence, this lack of association between use/accessibility and participation can be interpreted in many ways, including the need to reassess the type of political activities in which people engage online. The net utopians who believe that the internet will change the world and spread democracy need to re-evaluate the type of activities people pursue online; i.e. special attention should be paid to analysing the difference between those who use the net for political activities and those who simply use it for e-shopping. Although oil-rich states such as Kuwait do not suffer from issues such as the affordability or accessibility of the internet or low literacy rates, there are other barriers to full online inclusion in the country.

However, our study found that anonymity had a significant impact on the level of online political participation. Anonymity promotes women's involvement in Kuwait because it allows women to evade social pressures and cultural restrictions. Anonymity offers women the chance to express their opinions and form their own political identities. As a result, women who participate in politics online – even if they do so anonymously – might be empowered to do so openly and publicly.

There are several reasons for the low level of women's involvement in politics. First, political activities had long remained the exclusive preserve of elite women in Kuwait, which in turn led to the marginalisation and exclusion of other women. Second, the ongoing conflict among religious leaders in the Muslim world concerning the eligibility of women to participate in politics has led to women's disengagement. Cultural and traditional heritages play an important role in women's socialisation. Lisa Alturki explains that ritual practices and social relations have played an important role in the socialisation of Gulf women throughout history.[67] Women developed many communities of social relationships outside their families, which provided them with support and communication. Therefore, these social communities and relationships were, to a large extent, substitutes for women's public involvement and participation. Fourth, men dominated politics for a long time, and women have only recently gained their political rights to vote and be nominated for the National Assembly, in 2005. Therefore, there is still some cultural resistance to women's active involvement in politics.

Notes

1 Y. Alkout, 'Women Political Movements' Speech: Alfezeai "Women Are Still Men's Subordinates"', *Alwatan Online Newspaper* (Kuwait, 4 April 2013).

2 Abdulredha Asiri, *The Political System in Kuwait: Principles and Practices* (Kuwait: Alwatan, 2007).

3 Mohammed Alajimi, *Political Participation in Kuwait: A Study of Reality and the Future* (Cairo, Egypt: Aldar Alalamiya, 2009).

4 Ibid.

5 Alajimi; Paul Salem, 'Kuwait: Politics in a Participatory Emirate', *Carnegie Endowment for International Peace*, 2007, 3 <http://carnegieendowment.org/files/cmec3_salem_kuwait_final1.pdf>.

6 Abdulla Alshayji, 'Kuwait: A Democratic Model in Trouble. Carnegie Endowment for International Peace. Analysis on Arab Reform', *Carnegie Endowment for International Peace*, 2009 <http://carnegieendowment.org/2009/02/03/kuwait-democratic-model-in-trouble/f9l5>.

7 World Population Review, 'Kuwait Population Review', *World Population Review*, 2013 <http://worldpopulationreview.com/kuwait-population-2013/>.

8 Salem.

9 Abeer Aldweelah, 'The Degree of Political Awareness among Kuwaiti Working Women in Higher Education and its Effect on Students', *Kuwait Center for Research and Studies*, 2009.

10 Aldweelah.

11 Ashraf Saad and Noshin Kilany, 'Kuwaiti Women and Their Green Chair Struggle', *Arabic Sky News*, 2012 <http://www.skynewsarabia.com/web/article/56899/>.

12 Shadad Alfadhly, 'Social Networks Effects on National Security', *Alaan Online Newspaper*, 18 February 2011 <http://www.alaan.cc/>; *Asharq Alawsat Newspaper*, 'Women's Rights in Kuwait: A Long History of Controversy', 25 February 2005 <http://www.aawsat.com/details.asp?article=284791&issueno=9586#.UcuE9WC6Rl0>.

13 Saad and Kilany.

14 S. Alqabra, 'Social Cohesion in Kuwait: From Establishment to the Current Movements in 2011', *Almesbar Studies and Research Center*, 2012, pp. 14–49.

15 Annual Statistical Abstract, 'Population: Kuwait Annual Statistical Report', *Press and Publication Department at Kuwait Statistical Bureau*, 2011 <http://www.csb.gov.kw/Socan_Statistic_EN.aspx?ID=19>.

16 *Alwatan Online Newspaper*, 'The 2013 Parliament in All Kuwaiti Dialects', 27 July 2013 <http://alwatan.kuwait.tt/articledetails.aspx?Id=294154>.

17 Mohammed Alajimi, *Kuwaiti Women and Political Participation: A Scientific Analysis* (Beirut, Lebanon: Dar AlJadeed, 2000).

18 Peter Dahlgren, 'The Internet, Public Sphere, and Political Communication: Dispersion and Deliberation', *Political Communication*, 22 (2005), 147–162.

19 Pippa Norris, *A Virtuous Circle: Political Communications in Post-Industrial Societies* (New York, NY: Cambridge University Press, 2000).

20 Caroline Tolbert and Raamona McNeal, 'Unraveling the Effects of the Internet on Political Participation', *Political Research Quarterly*, 56 (2003), 175–185 <10.1177/106591290305600206>.

21 Tolbert and McNeal.

22 See e.g., Tolbert and McNeal; Michael Xenos and Patricia Moy, 'Direct and Differential Effects of the Internet on Political and Civic Engagement', *Journal of Communication*, 57 (2007), 704–718.

23 Xenos and Moy.

24 Eva Anduiza and others, 'Online Resources, Political Participation and Equality', in *Paper presented at the American Political Science Association annual conference* (Boston, MA, 2008), pp. 28–31.

25 Kate Kenski and Natalie Stroud, 'Connections between Internet Use and Political Efficacy, Knowledge, and Participation', *Journal of Broadcasting & Electronic Media*, 50 (2006), 173–192 <doi:10.1207/s15506878jobem5002_1>.

26 Bruce Bimber, 'The Internet and Political Transformation: Populism, Community, and Accelerated Pluralism', *Polity*, 31 (1998), 133–160; Michael Jensen, James Danziger and Alladi Venkatesh, 'Electronic Democracy in America: Civil Society, Cyber Society and Participation in Local Politics' (Irvine: Center for Research on Information Technology and Organization, University of California, 2005).

27 Bimber, 'The Internet and Political Transformation: Populism, Community, and Accelerated Pluralism.'

28 *Asharq Alawsat.*

29 Richard LeBaron, 'Another Election "crisis" Kuwait', *Atlantic Council*, 2012 <http://www.acus.org/viewpoint/another-election-'crisis'-kuwait>.

30 Bruce Bimber and Lauren Copeland, 'Digital Media and Traditional Political Participation over Time in the U.S.', *Journal of Information Technology & Politics*, 10 (2013), 125–137 <doi:10.1080/19331681.2013.769925>.

31 Deborah Wheeler, 'The Internet and Youth Subculture in Kuwait', *Journal of Computer-Mediated Communication*, 8 (2003) <doi:10.1111/j.1083–6101.2003.tb00207.x>.

32 Hua Qian and Craig Scott, 'Anonymity and Self-Disclosure on Weblogs', *Journal of Computer-Mediated Communication*, 12 (2007), 1428–1451 <doi:10.1111/j.1083-6101.2007.00380.x>.

33 Ibid.

34 Ibid.

35 Alajimi, *Kuwaiti Women and Political Participation.*

36 Before the survey was administered, respondents were invited to take part in the study and two screening questions were asked: whether the respondent was a Kuwaiti and whether she was 18 years of age or older. Those who did not meet these basic selection criteria were excluded from the study.

37 Overall, of the 22,752 women who were contacted (some up to three times) to take part in the study, 800 women completed the questionnaire, which results in 4 percent response rate.

38 The demographic characteristics of Kuwaiti women were measured using ten variables: education; marital status; children; age; voting registration status; employment; political ideology; residence; income; and religious influence.

39 Traditional media exposure was measured by asking respondents about how much time they spent with media 'yesterday'. Respondents were asked this question for each of the following types of media: TV, radio, print newspapers, digital newspapers, and social media. They rated their exposure to each type of media on a 9-point scale, ranging from 'no exposure at all' (1) to 'more than 6 hours' (9).

40 Scholars have suggested that political interest is an important predictor of political participation. Therefore, this study examined respondents' political interest and its relationship to political participation. Respondents were asked to rate their interest in what is going on in government and politics.

41 To measure social media use, respondents were asked to rate, on a 9-point scale, ranging from 'none' (1) to 'more than 6 hours'(9), how much time they spend on social media in an average day and which social networking sites they use 'at least sometimes' (Facebook, Twitter, Google+, LinkedIn, YouTube, Pinterest, Tumblr, Instagram, Keek, KIK and blogs).

42 Scholars have argued that is it important to study access and the extent of internet use. The time women spend online is important because more people have access than actually use the internet.

43 To measure social media access, respondents were asked if they 'ever use social media sites'. Answers were coded ('yes =1 and 'no' = 0).

44 To measure anonymity in this study, respondents were asked two questions. First, they were asked to rate on a 8-level scale the amount of personal information they usually provide on social networking sites. The eight levels of anonymity, which were identified in a previous study was done by Qian and Scott: 'full real name plus additional personal information'; 'full real name'; 'partial real name plus additional personal information'; 'partial real name'; 'nickname that could be someone's name'; 'nickname that indicates gender'; 'nickname that doesn't indicate gender' and 'no personal information'. Second, respondents also were asked whether they had a personal picture identifying them on social networking sites.

45 Qian and Scott.

46 Studies have found that there is a positive association between exposure to news and information and political participation. Scholars have argued that the internet provides cheaper access to political information and news, which in turn influences individuals' level of information acquisition and political participation.

47 Political information and news questions were measured on a 5-point scale ('none' = 1 to 'six hours' = 5).

48 This interest was assessed on a 5-point scale ('not interested at all' =1 to 'extremely interested' = 5) (recoded).

49 Respondents rated their political discussion on a 5-point scale ('not at all' = 1 to 'more than once a day' = 5).

50 This study adapted a set of possible factors that may have an influence on women's ability to participate in politics. The socio-political factors were measured by asking respondents 'how much influence has each of the following factors had on your ability to participate in politics in Kuwait. Participants were provided with eleven factors: 'Family members'; 'husband, father or brother'; 'children'; 'friends'; 'social norms'; 'cultural norms'; 'the current political situation'; 'religious norms'; 'lack of time'; 'the fact that I am a woman'; and 'others'. Each factor was measured on a 4-point scale ('no influence at all' = 1 to 'a lot of influence' = 4) (recoded).

51 See e.g., Corinna Di Gennaro and William Dutton, 'The Internet and the Public: Online and Offline Political Participation in the United Kingdom', *Parliamentary Affairs*, 59 (2006), 299–313; Lars Willnat and others, 'Online Media and Political Participation: The Case of Malaysia', *Mass Communication and Society*, 16 (2013), 557–585 <doi:10.1080/15205436.2012.734891>.

52 These were have been identified in previous studies: 'joined a political forum online'; 'visited a political website'; 'created political content online'; 'participated in an online campaign'; 'used the internet to organise or invite people to political events'; 'contacted a politician privately online'; 'went online to fact check claims made by politicians'; 'watched a political video online'; 'shared political content/videos/photos online'; '*liked* a political article, picture or any political content online' and 'took part in an online political discussion'. Each activity was measured on a 5-point scale ('never' = 1 to 'very frequently' = 5). The answers to all 11 questions were then combined into an online political participation index, ranging from low (11) to high degrees of participation (55) (Cronbach's alpha = .91).

53 Zeynep Tufekci and Christopher Wilson, 'Social Media and the Decision to Participate in Political Protest: Observations from Tahrir Square', *Journal of Communication*, 62 (2012), 363–379 <doi:10.1111/j.1460-2466.2012.01629.x>.

54 Alqabra.

55 On a scale from 1 (low education level) to 6 (high education level), the average education level for those who have access to social media was higher (M = 3.8) than women without social media access (M = 2.9).

56 Racha Mourtada and Paul Salem, 'Social Media in the Arab World: The Impact on Growth, Women and Social Change', *Arab Social Media Report*, 2012, pp. 269–274 <http://www.iemed.org/observatori-en/arees-danalsi/arxuis-adjuncts/anuari/med.2012/mourtada salem-en>; Fadi Salem and others, 'The Role of Social Media in Arab Women's Empowerment', *Arab Social Media Report*, 2011.

57 David Weaver, 'What Voters Learn from Media', *Annals of the American Academy of Political and Social Science*, 546 (1996), 34–47; Tolbert and McNeal.

58 Scholars have argued that political discussion and arguments have increased women's political interest and participation. The level of political discussions was assessed by asking respondents how often they spoke to their friends and family about politics during the past week.

59 See for example, Alajimi, *Kuwaiti Women and Political Participation*; Aldweelah.

60 On a scale that ranges from 11 (low) to 55 (high online participation), the average rate of women's participation in online politics was very low (M = 15).

61 The first set of predictors represents respondents' demographic characteristics (age, education, marital status and income) and their voting registration status. The second level of predictors relate to the respondents' political

characteristics such interest and level of political talk. The third level of predictors concerns the respondents' level of daily exposure to mainstream media such as TV, radio, print newspapers and digital newspapers (ranging from none to more than 6 hours per day). The fourth block relates to the social-political factors that influence participation, such as family influence on the ability to participate and anonymity. The fifth block signifies respondents' internet use.

62 See e.g., Willnat and others; Di Gennaro and Dutton; Eva Anduiza, Marta Cantijoch and Aina Gallego, 'Political Participation and the Internet', *Information, Communication and Society*, 12 (2009), 860–876.

63 Alajimi, *Political Participation in Kuwait.*

64 Such as Anduiza, Cantijoch and Gallego; Jensen, Danziger and Venkatesh; Weaver; Bruce Bimber, 'Information and Political Engagement in America: The Search for Effects of Information Technology at the Individual Level', *Political Research Quarterly*, 54 (2001), 53–67.

65 Anduiza, Cantijoch and Gallego.

66 Such as the study done by Tolbert and McNeal.

67 Lisa Alturki, 'Arab Women in the Nineteen-Twenties Presence and Identity', *Beirut: AlWihda AlArabiya Study Center*, 2010.

8

The New Media as Alternative Medium in the GCC Region

Mokhtar Elareshi and Khalid Al-Jaber

Since the Arab uprisings began in late December 2010, Arab news media platforms have undergone great change. The internet, through the social media (e.g., Facebook and Twitter) and other platforms, was adopted to mobilise and organise mass protests during the uprisings.[1] This may have been the first instance of such a medium being used on a huge scale by ordinary people, in a phenomenon that has become known as 'citizen' journalism.[2] Furthermore, the emergence of satellite TV services and the internet have brought new realities to the region's changing media landscape.[3] The internet is noticeably becoming increasingly dominant in many Arab countries,[4] where it is widely used, especially by young Arabs, for news and entertainment and to communicate with others.[5]

Moreover, the change in political circumstances in several Arab regimes impelled the leaders of other Arab nations to follow suit, listening to their people and modifying their media controls.[6] Evidence has emerged that the introduction of the internet in Arab society has had important consequences in terms of changing people's attitudes and behaviours.[7] The use of social media, mainly Facebook and Twitter, by local citizens has affected the relationships between individuals and between them and their governments.[8] These new news services constitute new platforms that can be used as tools to express people's concerns about everyday life and their political future.

This study was designed to understand the extent to which Arab audiences have taken up an expanded and more diverse supply of news though specific channels such as satellite TV and the internet. What is the significance of online social network sites as news sources and communications channels for ordinary people? What role can and do they play as part of a set of news-gathering channels for news consumers? How have these platforms been used to produce and present their own news? How important are they as news sources for mainstream news media and as platforms for mainstream news media to disseminate their news? The study reported here has sought to provide a more recent comparative analysis of internet use and different news consumption habits in three GCC countries in an attempt to provide more details on the Gulf countries, their audiences and their media.[9]

Literature Review

Although there has been a good deal of literature on media development in the Arab world,[10] little has been written specifically about the social media habits of GCC people and the growing media sector in the region, especially after three years of the so-called 'Arab Spring', when freedom of expression and independent media were the theme of several of the uprisings.[11]

Following the spread of satellite TV news services in several Arab countries in the mid-1990s, there were predictions that these platforms would change the media landscapes in the Arab world.[12] In this context, the GCC countries have led the way in that they have provided their consumers with the news and information they are looking for by adopting the new technology in their developing systems.[13] In addition, the establishment of the internet in these countries, especially with free access, has provided a new platform for personal communications and the search for information and news. Recently, GCC countries, like some other Arab nations, have witnessed the phenomenon of the establishment of many different websites, the purposes of which differ for the public and the authorities.[14] Governmental bodies and institutions, for example, have been prompted to create their own sites, alongside those of private companies and profit and non-profit institutions. These websites have attracted various users, especially e-commerce sites.

It is worth saying that the internet (via social media web pages) may pose a further threat to Arab governments in different respects, such as how they deal with women and alternative political views. The social media (e.g., Facebook and Twitter) have opened up a new platform for interpersonal communication, exposing people to information and entertainment content that may not be available via offline media; for example, young Arab women have discovered a new social empowerment through the internet.[15]

It is essential to enquire whether Arab governments have adopted the internet through social networking sites to compete with existing online news services; alternatively, does this initiative represent a move towards electronic government and public service distribution? There are no clear-cut answers to these questions, but one might say that the internet has been adopted by Arab governments to follow the move towards the massive use of new technology that is capable of reaching all kinds of people inside and outside the region.[16] It is also a response to the huge volume of information coming from outside the region, especially those websites that are run by opposition groups.[17] Some Arab governments such as the UAE have realised the importance of the internet for accessing and communicating with the public via their social websites.[18]

Moreover, Facebook and Twitter are used by private citizens mainly for personal information and entertainment needs and as an interpersonal communications system. Facebook, for example, has been among the most popular social networking sites in the Arab world, followed by Twitter, especially over the last five years.[19] Saudi internet users are among the most active Twitter users in the world, second only to those in Indonesia. The use of Facebook and Twitter to facilitate communication has been the topic of recent scholarly attention, especially the relationship between the use of social networking and political change.[20] Some argue that Twitter was an important platform during the protests in Egypt.[21] Numerous individuals, especially intellectuals, politicians, artists and writers, have created their own websites to highlight their community roles and publish their creations and opinions to a wide audience. Therefore, the internet is a platform for e-governments, commercials and businesses.[22]

New Media Sources in GCC Countries

The GCC countries have recently experienced significant change and growth in the availability of media sources, especially in terms of news and entertainment.[23] The emergence of satellite technology and the internet has transformed media landscapes in these countries.[24] This has produced a variety of responses to the overwhelming impact of new technologies.[25] The rapidly growing popularity of Facebook and Twitter, for example, can be seen as a significant outcome for users in this region, where the internet can now be used in everyday life. There has been a significant expansion of the choice of content to which users can gain access. For example, Facebook and Twitter have provided their users with opportunities to engage in more conversations, discussions and debates about their future issues.[26] This gives the consumer greater control over access and exposure to content, paralleled by the diminishing direct control of state governments.[27]

Furthermore, the adoption of Information Communication Technology (ICT) and the internet in the GCC nations today is considerably different from that which prevailed in these states in the early 2000s.[28] For instance, news and information are no longer dominated by state media that adhere to the state's views.[29] Such changes have forced Arab governments, policy-makers, including those in GCC countries, and media operators themselves to reconsider their policies and practices.[30] For example, Saudi internet users have been given more freedom to express their opinions, while other GCC countries such as UAE and Kuwait have restricted their internet users. In 2012, the UAE government amended the law on internet crime, which carries a three-year prison sentence for anyone using or designing websites with a view to ridiculing or harming the reputation of the state or the head of state or his deputy, any of the governors of the seven Emirates, anything related to the country's flag or the national anthem, or any symbols of the state.[31]

When the first generation of ARABSAT was launched in the mid-1980s, almost all Arab TV governments had gone international, with around 60 satellite TV Arabic services on air by the end of 1997.[32] Further development occurred with the emergence of Pan-Arab satellite TV news services in the mid-1990s – Abu Dhabi TV in 1995, Al-Jazeera in 1996 and, later on, Al-Arabiya TV in 2003 – and the internet service, especially in the mid-2000s;

governments have lost some of their control over these media outlets and are unable to exercise the same degree of censorship as before.[33] As a result, GCC audiences customarily enjoy visiting different news suppliers for news and entertainment in their leisure time. Thus, they spend a great deal of time surfing the internet compared to other platforms.[34] In GCC countries, TV consumption averages between 206 and 237 minutes per day.[35]

There are several reasons for surfing the internet and using social media (e.g., Facebook and Twitter). For example, entertainment, socialising, personal communications and looking for information have been the most popular reasons for doing so in the Arab world.[36] The internet is extremely popular because it provides news and information for a majority of people.[37] However, the internet contexts in the GCC States have been somewhat under government control.[38] They have highlighted concerns about the image of the State, most often equated with that of its ruler, an unelected monarch.[39]

Competition from the internet, loss of control over information flow, criticism of inefficient national TV systems, erosion of audience loyalty, and the clamour by entrepreneurs for a role in emerging pan-national commercial media operations have led to the establishment of a new media environment in all GCC countries.[40]

All this represents a significant shift from how the media used to look in the GCC countries.[41] Although the rise of satellite TV services has transformed the news landscape in the GCC countries, another news source has become known and named as the most important source for news and entertainment – the internet.[42] For example, the year following the start of the 2011 Arab uprisings witnessed a huge increase in the number of Arab users who access and engage with the internet and use social media platforms (e.g., Facebook and Twitter) for news and entertainment.[43] For instance, in 2009 alone, the number of Arabs using the internet stood at approximately 6 million. Wael Ghonim predicts that there will be 100 million Arab internet users by 2015.[44] Moreover, the report provided by the International Telecommunication Union (ITU) estimates that around a third of all Arab people are internet users. Facebook is used by 70 per cent of young adults aged between 15 and 29.[45] In 2011, the number of internet users increased by 68 per cent. Moreover, in regard to the usage of social media, the Centre for International Media Assistance (CIMA) indicated that the most popular trending hashtags in September 2011 were Bahraini users, with just over half a million mentions in tweets, and Kuwaiti users, with 140,000 mentions.[46]

Furthermore, formerly offline media such as newspapers and satellite TV services are now largely online and are attempting to operate as multiplatform channels to promote stories and engage with their widespread audiences and citizens, who use various means to obtain and share information and knowledge.[47] This new era of news broadcasting was set in motion with the launch of Al-Jazeera.net in early 2000. The success of this channel encouraged other, similar news operations to attempt to gain a foothold in the Arab and Western worlds, and in a more competitive news market in general Al-Jazeera TV has been joined by services such as BBC News 24 Channel, CNN, Al-Arabiya TV, Al-Hurra TV, France24 News TV and others.[48] Based on the previous discussion, this study compares the results of two different studies conducted in 2009 and in 2013 to explore the habits of different news media sources among residents in three GCC countries. The study was underpinned by a number of specific research questions:

RQ1: Have the habits of news consumption of GCC audiences changed recently?
RQ2: How much time is spent on different news media?
RQ3: How are news sources in the GCC countries perceived?
RQ4: Which sources are considered the most reliable among GCC countries?

Methodology

Two major surveys on the use of news sources in the Middle East countries were conducted. The first survey, a self-completion online questionnaire, was carried out with Arabic-speaking respondents in Bahrain, Qatar and Saudi Arabia, utilising the websites of three major media organisations to direct respondents to the site housing the questionnaire. From an initial contact sample of 2,146 respondents, filters were deployed to block out responses from respondents living outside these three countries, yielding a final sample of 1,752 participants. These comprised 568 respondents from Bahrain, 553 from Qatar and 631 from Saudi Arabia. Data were collected between 10 December 2009 and 12 March 2010.

The second survey comprised a questionnaire survey conducted face to face and by telephone (in Qatar) with 3,755 Gulf respondents, aged between 18 and 81. Originally, the survey was carried out in eight Arab countries: Bahrain, Egypt, Jordan, Lebanon, Qatar, Saudi Arabia, Tunisia and UAE. This chapter will only compare and present findings for reported news consumption habits linked to three Gulf countries: Bahrain (1,250 respondents), Qatar (1,253 respondents) and Saudi Arabia (1,252 respondents).

Questionnaire

The first survey was a pre-structured questionnaire that included several types of questions (28). For example, respondents were asked to state their main news media consumption, their general news interests, their gratifications and expectations from consuming different platforms, their opinions about televised news services, their motivations for watching televised news services, their perceptions of the quality of news on these televised news services and their demographic status. The questions were measured on common four-, five-, or seven-point scales.[49] This chapter reports findings from the news consumption questions and personal details only.

In the second survey, the participants were asked to identify their main sources of news and information, their general patterns of media use, their news habits, and their use of the internet and social media. The survey sample was selected to represent the population demographically, in terms of gender, age and region. Within that population, a random sampling approach was adopted. The survey was conducted during December 2012 and February 2013 in Saudi Arabia and Bahrain, and from March 2013 to April 2013 in Qatar. Weighting was applied in Qatar and Saudi Arabia to ensure that the sample was representative in terms of ethnic group, gender, age and region.[50]

Respondents were asked to indicate which news sources they used the most and how much time they spent on different news media. They were asked to state the number of hours they spent on each medium.

Respondents were also asked to state how often they used different sources for news and information and how much they consumed different news media from a list of news sources.[51]

With regard to perceptions of news media, three statements describing the news media in the Arab world were given to all respondents in order to examine their perceptions. The statements were: 'the quality of news reporting in the Arab world has improved over the past two years'; 'news media in your country are credible'; and 'the media in your country can report the news independently without interference from officials'.[52] Finally, respondents were required to state which news sources they considered generally reliable.[53]

Before proceeding, a couple of matters should be taken into consideration about the two surveys in terms of data collection and the similarities and differences between them. First, the 2009 survey predated the 2011 uprisings in the Arab world. Therefore, all the findings of the 2009 survey pertained to opinions expressed prior to the uprisings, in Bahrain for instance. In 2013, however, the respondents' views may have been affected by the uprisings, which may give a misleading account of what news sources they used. In addition, the 2009 survey was more precise than the 2013 survey in inquiring about which TV news services were used. For example, local and pan-Arab TV services were addressed separately in the 2009 survey. Great attention was paid to the use of the internet in the 2013 survey, while much of the focus of the 2009 survey was on offline news media. Therefore, comparisons may be problematic, as it was important to examine the respondents' views before, during and after the uprisings. This is a great opportunity to measure the news consumption over different periods.

Results

Media usage

Although television still plays a dominant role in modern life in the Arab world because of the high literacy rates, the internet via social media networks (e.g., Facebook and Twitter) has become a major source of information for GCC audiences. In the second study, when asked whether the news habits of GCC audiences have changed recently, the respondents indicated that, overall, consumption habits have clearly changed (RQ1). In this period, respondents broadly watched more TV services than they did in 2009 in all three countries. This may have been due to the 2011 uprisings when people tried to find more news and information about their businesses and political future.

It is interesting to note that the internet was ranked first on both measures and ahead of other media platforms such as TV, radio, newspapers and magazines (Table 8:1). This is an indication that the internet was used and surfed every day in the region more widely than most offline media during this period. These findings (study 2013) have confirmed those of earlier research suggesting that TV in the Arab world including GCC countries remains the most popular medium for news and entertainment.[54] Respondents in GCC countries indicated that they have spent a lot of time watching TV services over the last four years.

It is also apparent that local media, including radio, newspapers and local TV, were used more often during this period (2013) in all three countries, while mobile devices were noticeably used to obtain more news and information. However, this has not changed in the three countries over the last few years. Mobile devices can be deployed to receive news from all the major news services.

There were several significant gender differences regarding the reported use of different media in 2013. By country, Qatari males (91 per cent) were more likely than females (80 per cent) to utilise the internet via social media networks for news and information. Similar results were found in the 2009 study.

In Bahrain, males (85 per cent) were more likely than females (78 per cent) to use the internet and social media networks, and to listen to radio (87 per cent vs. 79 per cent respectively); they were slightly more likely to read newspapers (88 per cent vs. 86 per cent respectively). These figures have not changed significantly from those reported in the 2009 study, as the Chi-square tests revealed. For instance, it is still the case that more Bahraini males than females consume news via the internet, radio and newspapers.

In Saudi Arabia, interestingly, males (100 per cent) were slightly more likely than females (99 per cent) to watch TV programmes, utilise the

Table 8:1 Reported Consumption of Different News Platforms

News Sources	All %		Saudi %		Bahrain %		Qatar %	
	2009	2013	2009	2013	2009	2013	2009	2013
Internet & social media networks	72	83	72	82	69	82	74	86
Pan-Arab TV news services*	70	96	76	99	64	99	69	90
Newspapers	27	69	23	59	27	87	30	62
Local & national TV services	17	–	18	–	16	–	18	–
Mobile	16	17	15	15	20	20	14	14
Radio	14	70	12	61	16	84	13	64
Non-Arabic TV services	7	–	5	–	8	–	8	–
Magazines	3	46	2	36	4	68	4	34

* In 2009, respondents were asked to be more precise about their TV viewing, while in 2013 they were asked more generally. Pan-Arab TV here also included local and national TV services. In 2009, the question was, 'Thinking about the sources to which you turn to get your news, how frequently do you use each of the news sources listed below for news nowadays?' (1 = daily and 7 = don't use). In 2013, the question was, 'During a typical week, how much time do you spend on the following activities?' (Number of hours per day or week was calculated).

– (Study 2009; N = 1,752) (study 2013; N = 3,755)

internet (e.g., Facebook and Twitter) (86 per cent vs. 79 per cent respectively), listen to radio (72 per cent vs. 49 per cent respectively), read newspapers (74 per cent vs. 41 per cent respectively), and read books (40 per cent vs. 30 per cent respectively). Similar findings were cited in the 2009 study. The Chi-squire tests were run on these figures, and no significant differences were found, which means that the differences in results are due to chance.

Overall, in both surveys it seems that males in this region were more likely than females to use the internet and social media networks (e.g., Facebook and Twitter), watch TV programmes, listen to radio, and read newspapers and books, while females were more interested in reading magazines. In a similar vein, other studies have found that Arab males and females consume different news platforms.[55]

There were also significant age group differences in media use in 2013. In Qatar, those aged 18–24 (91 per cent) were more likely than those aged 35–44 (88 per cent) to use the internet and social media networks, listen to radio (65 per cent vs. 61 per cent respectively) and read magazines (34 per cent vs. 33 per cent respectively). In Bahrain, 98 per cent of those aged 18–24 were more likely than those aged 35–44 (84 per cent) to surf the internet (e.g., Facebook and Twitter) for news or information, read books (90 per cent vs. 71 per cent respectively) and read magazines (84 per cent vs. 74 per cent respectively). These figures indicate that the news consumption habits of young adults in these countries have not changed significantly as the results were found to be very close to those of the 2009 survey. The Chi-square tests were run on the two surveys and no significant differences were found.

In Saudi Arabia, those aged 18–24 (100 per cent) were more likely than those aged 35–44 (99 per cent) to watch TV programmes, use the internet (e.g., Facebook and Twitter) (96 per cent vs. 80 per cent respectively), read magazines (44 per cent vs. 34 per cent respectively) and read books (39 per cent vs. 33 per cent respectively). Similar results were also found in the 2009 study, thus indicating that respondents' habits have not changed significantly. These findings are consistent with several other studies, which also showed that the majority of news viewers were in the younger and mature age groups compared to the older consumer age group.[56]

Respondents also indicated how much time they spend on offline platforms (RQ2). Television, as mentioned earlier, is by far the most consumed offline medium in the three GCC countries. Not only are TV services virtually ubiquitous in these states, but respondents also spent far more time watching TV than any other medium. They spent roughly over three hours a day consuming different TV programmes.

On average, Bahraini respondents spent roughly 27 hours per week on TV programmes, followed by Saudi respondents at 25 hours and Qatari respondents at 17 hours. However, weekly consumption of radio was higher among Qatari respondents (12 hours), than among Bahrainis (11 hours) and Saudis (6 hours). Bahraini respondents (15 hours) spent more time reading books than Qataris (9 hours) and Saudis (5 hours). Overall, respondents in the three countries spent much less time (less than 1 in 10 per week each) on reading newspapers and magazines than on other platforms.

Perceptions of news media

There has been a noticeable improvement in standards of news media reporting in the Arab world in the last five years.[57] Audiences seem to be very optimistic, in the era of the internet and Information Communication Technology (ICT), about the news consumption in their countries. When asked about their perceptions of news consumption, respondents in the three GCC countries indicated different views and perceptions (RQ3). Overall, the quality of news reporting has improved in the past two years, a view shared by the majority of respondents (67 per cent). Sixty per cent of all respondents agreed that news media in their countries are more credible, and more than half (53 per cent) of them agreed that their media are now able more or less to report the news independently without strong interference from officials.

In Saudi Arabia, for example, 84 per cent of respondents indicated that the quality of news reporting in the Arab world has improved over the past two years; 62 per cent of Qatari respondents and 56 per cent of Bahraini respondents concurred with this view. Several studies have found that credibility is highly associated with the emergence of new satellite technologies and Pan-Arab TV services. Pan-Arab TV services were highly rated as credible sources of information.[58] However, the clear finding in the 2009 survey was that local media were being abandoned in favour of pan-Arab TV services as they lacked credibility, attractiveness and professionalism.

Seven in ten (71 per cent) Saudi respondents agreed that news can be independently reported without strong interference from officials, compared to 50 per cent of Qatari respondents. Meanwhile, only 38 per cent of Bahraini respondents agreed with this statement. These findings are a notable indication that news media in the GCC countries have changed positively. This may be due to the pressure put on governments and authorities to give people more freedom to express their views.[59] However, the picture seems to be different in Bahrain, where people still believe that their news media are tightly controlled by the local government.[60]

Perceptions of the quality of news media are mostly consistent among gender and age groups within each country. For example, Saudi males (80 per cent) were more likely than females (66 per cent) to believe that their news media were more credible and able to report the news more independently (79 per cent vs. 60 per cent). Both males and females strongly agreed (over 80 per cent) that the quality of their news reporting has improved in the last few years.

In 2013, 60 per cent of both Qatari males and females indicated that the quality of news reporting has improved in the last few years, while just over half of them believed that the news media in their regime are more credible and can provide reports independently of their governments' influence and control. These perceptions were less prevalent in Bahrain where only a third of both females and males (32 per cent and 30 per cent respectively) indicated that the quality of news reporting has improved. Fifty-five per cent of females and 50 per cent of males agreed that their news media are more credible, while 39 per cent of males compared to 36 per cent of females agreed that their news media are able to report news stories independently of officials.

With regard to age groups, those Saudi respondents aged 35–44 and 18–24 (both over 80 per cent respectively) strongly agreed that the quality of news reporting has improved in the last few years. More than two thirds (75 per cent) of both groups agreed that their news media are more credible, while those aged 35–44 (75 per cent) were more optimistic about their news media's independence than those aged 18–24 (68 per cent). In Bahrain, more of those aged 18–24 (66 per cent) agreed that the quality of news reporting has improved than those aged 35–44 (57 per cent) and that their news media are more credible (60 per cent vs. 53 per cent respectively), while 40 per cent of both age groups agreed that their news media are able to report independently. In Qatar, 63 per cent of those aged 35–44 compared to 57 per cent of those aged 18–24 agreed that the quality of news reporting has improved and their news media are credible (52 per cent vs. 50 per cent), while more of those aged 18–24 (49 per cent) than those aged 35–44 (41 per cent) agreed that their news media can report the news independently.

Perceptions of reliability of news sources

Levels of reliability attributed to news information sources broadly correspond with their perceived importance, although the general evaluation is far from a ringing endorsement (RQ4). The internet and social media networks (e.g., Facebook and Twitter) are seen as sources of information that are almost as reliable as television (66 per cent vs. 70 per cent respectively) for providing various news and information. Newspapers and radio were ranked in almost equal third place on this measure (slightly over 50 per cent), while books (44 per cent) and magazines (29 per cent) were seen as less reliable sources.

By country, male Saudi respondents (81 per cent) were more likely than females (73 per cent) to report the internet as a reliable source of information, followed by newspapers (72 per cent vs. 48 per cent), radio (68 per cent vs. 57 per cent respectively), and books (50 per cent vs. 41 per cent respectively). Magazines were considered reliable sources of information by the same percentages of both (41 per cent). Saudi respondents seem to have held similar perceptions about offline and online media since 2009. For statistical confirmation, a Chi-square test was run on these figures and showed no significant differences. This means that the differences in results are due to chance.

In Bahrain, the internet emerged as the news source reportedly most likely to be reliable (70 per cent), with females (71 per cent) being more likely than males (69 per cent) to say as much. Television was seen as the second most reliable source of news and information by both genders (two thirds). Female respondents (57 per cent) were slightly more likely than males (55 per cent) to report newspapers as a reliable source, and were more likely to say so about radio (54 per cent vs. 53 per cent respectively), books (44 per cent vs. 42 per cent respectively) and magazines (31 per cent vs. 27 per cent respectively). These findings differed from those of the 2009 study, where Bahraini respondents assigned high credibility to TV as the most consumed and reliable medium. The differences in views may have been due to the recent uprising that took place in Bahrain 2011, where many people expressed their views via the internet, especially Twitter.[61]

Among Qatari respondents, the internet and newspapers were ranked in almost equal second place after television (55 per cent), but they were not equally well perceived. The internet was seen as a reliable source for news and information more by males (55 per cent) than by females (46 per cent). Similarly, in the 2009 survey male respondents were more likely than females to rely on TV news (e.g., pan-Arab TV services) for their news and information.

With regard to age groups by country, in Saudi Arabia the internet was more likely to be seen as a reliable source of news and information by those aged 18–24 (85 per cent) than by those aged 35–44 (77 per cent); this was followed by books (51 per cent vs. 43 per cent), and magazines (43 per cent vs. 35 per cent), while radio was equally well perceived (63 per cent).

In Qatar, those aged 18–24 (63 per cent) were more likely than those aged 35–44 (53 per cent) to indicate TV as a reliable source, followed by the internet (e.g., Facebook and Twitter) (53 per cent vs. 49 per cent respectively), newspapers (52 per cent vs. 48 per cent respectively) and radio (47 per cent vs. 44 per cent respectively), while those aged 35–44 (46 per cent) were more likely than those aged 18–24 (41 per cent) to say the same about books and magazines (19 per cent vs. 17 per cent respectively).

In Bahrain, the internet (e.g., Facebook and Twitter) was more likely to be seen as a reliable source for news and information by those aged 18–24 than by those aged 35–44 (67 per cent), followed by books (47 per cent vs. 43 per cent respectively), while those aged 35–44 (69 per cent) were more likely than those aged 18–24 (60 per cent) to say the same about TV, followed by radio (69 per cent vs. 47 per cent respectively), newspapers (58 per cent vs. 49 per cent respectively) and magazines (26 per cent vs.

25 per cent respectively). For many years, online news lagged behind television as a primary source of information, even among young people.[62] In the last few years, however, online news outlets in the Arab world have experienced a sharp growth in traffic.[63] Today, the internet is named the primary news source for local, national and international news by those with high levels of education in the Arab GCC countries, especially in Bahrain.[64]

Discussion

This study has explored the changing nature of news consumption patterns suggested by two different surveys in three countries: Saudi Arabia, Bahrain and Qatar. The findings indicated that most respondents follow news information on multi-platforms on a regular basis. Therefore, the news consumption habits of GCC countries have changed recently due to the increased influence of the internet and social media (e.g., Facebook and Twitter). This study confirmed that the internet (e.g., Facebook and Twitter) has overtaken other offline media, including broadcast and print media.[65] Given that, it is perhaps not surprising that the internet is considered important for news and entertainment. Gulf internet users often spend time online for news and entertainment.[66] With regard to watching television and using the internet (e.g., Facebook and Twitter), the findings of both studies were similar to those in other studies.[67]

When asked how much time respondents spent on different news media, further analysis confirmed that the majority of respondents spent a great deal of time consuming different news media. Among offline media, they spent more than three hours a day using the internet (e.g., Facebook and Twitter), watching various TV programmes, listening to radio, and reading books, newspapers and magazines. Past studies found that many young adults spend several hours a day utilising the internet for social media purposes and to watch different satellite broadcasters.[68]

One significant result emerging from this study is that the respondents surveyed in both studies indicated that they were satisfied with their news media. For example, most of them agreed that the quality of news reporting in their countries has improved in the last few years. Again, this may be linked to the uprisings that occurred in several Arab regimes, which allowed people to use different media platforms to express their views.

Respondents also clearly indicated that their news media are seen as more credible sources that are independent of state officials. This finding is consistent with earlier research that found that some Pan-Arab TV services and the internet and social media (e.g., Facebook and Twitter) were seen as the most credible sources of news in the Arab world.[69] These findings support the notion of Tsfati and Cappella, who stated that when audiences believe the mainstream media, they consume mainstream news, but when they disbelieve the media, they seek alternatives.[70]

This study also sought to discover which news sources are seen as more reliable than others. The internet (e.g., Facebook and Twitter) and television have emerged as the most important channels for news and entertainment. The reliability of the internet is professed by young adults who spend many hours surfing the internet for more information and news about local, national, international events. Such people, who live in the well-wired Gulf, consider the internet to be even more reliable than TV for news and information, particularly in the case of Bahrain.

The findings of this study clearly indicate that television faces great competition from the internet, especially among young people in Saudi Arabia, Bahrain and Qatar where the internet attracts the highest audience in the Arab world and internationally.[71] However, the idea that one generation tends to rely on newspapers, another on TV and another on the internet was confounded, as the majority of respondents in both surveys access a mixture of sources and devices to obtain their news. It is fair to say that people's choice of news medium depends significantly on the topic and the nature of the story.[72]

Conclusion

This study has given an account of the reported use of news media by GCC residents in three different countries – Saudi Arabia, Bahrain and Qatar – paying special attention to their use of the internet and offline media (television, radio and newspapers). It has shown that the spread of news sources in the GCC countries has established a new sort of customer in a manner that goes beyond national boundaries. It seems that respondents who consume news and information through one platform are more likely to consume information through other available media platforms.

This is an indication that the GCC respondents are looking for news via multi-platforms, and that they are likely to try different media to triangulate perspectives on a particular topic in order to assess what these sources are really offering.

Overall, the internet and television are seen as the most important platforms for news and entertainment. They are also considered to be the most reliable. In general, Saudi respondents were more satisfied than Qataris and Bahrainis with their news media. Saudis also considered their media to be more credible and independent than they had done previously. This does not mean that these regimes are now favouring free expression. Following the Arab uprisings, freedom of expression has not yet become accepted and tolerated by those in power, as reported by the Freedom House.[73] A great deal of expression is clearly occurring, but it is increasingly lacking in freedom. Freedom of expression may have been the prevailing sentiment immediately following the uprisings but it is certainly not the prevailing sentiment in places such as the GCC countries. For example, protocol journalism is still very much alive in most Arab countries governed by Kings and Emirs. This is because the media outlets are still dominated by state ownership or by individuals loyal to the state and their leaders.

Notes

1 Barrie Gunter and Roger Dickinson, 'The Changing Nature of News and the Arab World', in *News Media in the Arab World: A Study of 10 Arab and Muslim Countries*, ed. by Barrie Gunter and Roger Dickinson (New York: Bloomsbury, 2013), pp. 1–20; Shopie Mohsen, 'The Role of New Information and Communication Technologies and Social Media during the Arab Spring' (Unpublished master's dissertation, University of Ottawa, Canada, 2013); Fouad Ajami, 'The Arab Spring at One: A Year of Living Dangerously', *Foreign Affairs*, 91 (2012), 56–65; Sean Aday and others, *New Media and Conflict after the Arab Spring* (United States Institute of Peace. Washington, DC, 2012).

2 Aday and others.

3 Mohsen.

4 Mohammed T. Simsim, 'Internet Usage and User Preferences in Saudi Arabia', *Journal of King Saud University: Engineering Sciences*, 2011, 101–107; Aday and others; Mokhtar Elareshi, Abdul-Karim Ziani and Barrie Gunter, 'The Use of Mobile Phone and Internet in Getting Local News in GCC Regions: A University Student Study', *Journal of Media and Communication Studies*, 3 (2015), 001–010.

5 Khalid Al-Jaber and Khalid Al-Sayed, *Arab Media in a Turbulent World* (Doha, Qatar: Al-Sharaq Publishing Ltd, 2013); Yasmine Ryan, 'How Tunisia's Revolution Began', *Al-Jazeera English*, 2011 <http://english.aljazeera.net/>; Ajami.

6 Silvia Colombo, 'The GCC Countries and the Arab Spring: Between Outreach, Patronage and Repression', in *Paper prepared for the Istituto Affari Internazionali* (Rome, Italy, 2012).

7 Simsim; Colombo.

8 Wael Ghonim, *Revolution 2.0: The Power of the People Is Greater than the People in Power: A Memoir* (New York: Houghton Mifflin Harcount, 2012).

9 The data analysed here were taken from two surveys: 1) data were conducted in 2009 by Khalid Al-Jaber; and 2) data from a survey conducted by Northwestern University, Qatar, in 2013.

10 William Rugh, *Arab Mass Media: Newspapers, Radio, and Television in Arab Politics* (London: Praeger, 2004); Douglas Boyd, *Broadcasting in the Arab World: A Survey of the Electronic Media in the Middle East* (Iowa: Iowa State University Press, 1999).

11 Mohsen; Colombo; Eva Bellin, 'Reconsidering the Robustness of Authoritarianism in the Middle East: Lessons from the Arab Spring', *Comparative Politics*, 44 (2012), 127–149 <doi:http://dx.doi.org/10.5129/001041512798838021>.

12 Moḥamed Zayani, *The Al-Jazeera Phenomenon: Critical Perspectives on New Arab Media* (London: Pluto Press, 2005).

13 Khalid Al-Jaber and Mokhtar Elareshi, *The Future of News Media in the Arab World* (Germany: LAMBERT Academic Publishing, 2014); Colombo; Mohsen.

14 Khalid Al-Jaber, 'Satellite TV and New Media in Supporting of the Arab Spring', in *Paper presented at the Media and Democratic Transition in the Arab Spring Countries Conference* (Media Department, University of Qatar, Doha, Qatar, 2013); Nader Ibrahim, 'Does Social Media Carry out Change in the Gulf?', 2013 <http://www.bbc.co.uk/arabic/middleeast/2013/12/131230_gulf_social_media.shtml>.

15 Khulood Miliany, 'The Impact of the Internet on Saudi Students' Use of Mass Communications', in *Paper presented at the Tenth Annual International Conference on Communication and Mass Media 14–17 May* (Athens, Greece, 2012).

16 Al-Jaber; Miliany; Mohsen.

17 Ibrahim.

18 Colombo.

19 Miliany; Ibrahim.

20 Colombo.

21 Zeynep Tufekci and Christopher Wilson, 'Social Media and the Decision to Participate in Political Protest: Observations from Tahrir Square', *Journal of Communication*, 62 (2012), 363–379 <doi:10.1111/j.1460-2466.2012.01629.x>.

22 Ibrahim.
23 Al-Jaber.
24 Jeffrey Ghannam, *Digital Media in the Arab World One Year after the Revolutions* (Washington, DC: Center for International Media Assistance, 2012).
25 Gunter and Dickinson.
26 Khalil Rinnawi, 'Arab Internet: Schizophrenic Trilogy', in *Arab Media*, ed. by Noha Mellor and others (Cambridge: Polity Presss, 2011), pp. 123–148; Ghonim.
27 Ghannam; Miliany; Ibrahim.
28 Aday and others.
29 Gunter and Dickinson.
30 Joe Khalil, 'News Television in the Arabian Gulf Period of Transitions', *Global Media Journal*, 8 (2006); Ghonim.
31 Ibrahim; Matt Duffy, 'Media Laws and Regulations of the GCC Countries: Summary, Analysis and Recommendations', *Doha Centre for Media Freedom*, 2013 <http://www.dc4mf.org/sites/default/files/gcc_media_law_en_0.pdf>.
32 Muhammad Ayish, 'Communication Research in the Arab World a New Perspective', *The Public Journal*, 5 (1998), 33–57.
33 Larry Diamond, 'Introduction', in *Liberation Technology: Social Media and the Struggle for Democracy*, ed. by Larry Diamond and Marc F. Plattner (Baltimore: Johns Hopkins University Press, 2012), pp. ix–xxvi; Ghonim; Ibrahim.
34 Khayrat Ayyad, 'Internet Usage vs. Traditional Media among University's Students in the United Arab Emirates', *Journal of Arab and Muslim Media Research*, 4 (2011), 41–61; Thomas Johnson and Shahira Fahmy, 'The CNN of the Arab World or a Shill for Terrorists?', *The International Communication Gazette*, 70 (2008), 338–360.
35 Everette Dennis, Justin Martin and Robb Wood, 'Media Use in the Middle East: An Eight-Nation Survey', 2013 <http://menamediasurvey.northwestern.edu/>; Miliany.
36 Al-Jaber; Ayyad; Ghonim.
37 Ayyad.
38 Khalil; Ibrahim.
39 Ibrahim.
40 Mounir Adhoum, 'Deregulatory Trends of Television Broadcasting in North Africa: The Case of Tunisia's Response to Direct Broadcasting Satellite Television' (USA: Ohio University, 1996); Gunter and Dickinson; Ghonim.
41 Kai Hafez, 'Arab Satellite Broadcasting: Democracy without Political Parties', *Transnational Broadcasting Studies*, 15 (2006); Fadi Salem, Racha Mourtade and Sara Alshaer, 'Transforming Educationin the Arab World: Breaking Barriers in the Age of Social Learning', *Arab Social Media Report*, 2013 <http://www.arabsocialmediareport.com/UserManagement/PDF/ASMR_5_Report_Final.pdf>.

42 Omar Alghazzi, 'De-Westernizing New Media Discourse: The Case of Citizen Journalism in the Arab World', in *Paper presented at the annual meeting of the International Communication Association* (Hilton Metropole Hotel, London, 2013); Miliany; Mubarak El-Hazmi, *Media in Saudi Arabia: A Longitudinal Study of the Origins and Development* (Jeddah, Saudi Arabia: King Abdul Aziz University, 2002); Tourya Guaaybess, 'A New Order of Information in the Arab Broadcasting System', 2002 <http://hdl.handle.net/1814/1822>; Osman Hafez, *Development of the Press in the Kingdom of Saudi Arabia* (Jeddah, Saudi Arabia: Al-Madina Printing and Publishing, 1989).

43 Ghannam; Gunter and Dickinson; Elareshi, Ziani and Gunter.

44 Ghonim.

45 Fadi Salem and others, 'The Role of Social Media in Arab Women's Empowerment', *Arab Social Media Report*, 2011; Miliany.

46 Ghannam; Ibrahim.

47 Ghannam; Ghonim.

48 Muhammad Ayish, 'American-Style Journalism and Arab World Television: An Exploratory Study of News Selection at Six Arab World Satellite Television Channels', *Transnational Broadcasting Studies*, 2001; Mokhtar Elareshi and Julian Matthews, 'The Changing News Landscape of Libya', in *News Media in the Arab World: A Study of 10 Arab and Muslim Countries*, ed. by Barrie Gunter and Roger Dickinson (London: Continuum, 2013), pp. 109–134.

49 For more information on the full questionnaire, please see *The Future of News Media in the Arab World* by Al-Jaber and Elareshi, 2014.

50 For more information, see http://menamediasurvey.northwestern.edu/.

51 The list contained watching TV services, listening to radio stations, reading news via newspapers, magazines and books, and surfing the internet.

52 Respondents were asked to rate each of these statements on a five-point scale (1 = strongly disagree to 5 = strongly agree).

53 The reliability here was measured on a scale of 1 to 5 where 1 = none of it is reliable and 5 = all of it is reliable.

54 Al-Jaber; Mokhtar Elareshi, *News Consumption in Libya: A Study of University Students* (Newcastle: Cambridge Scholars Publishing, 2013); Imad Karam, 'Arab Satellite Broadcasting, Identity and Arab Youth' (City University London. UK, 2007); Hussein Amin, 'Mass Media in the Arab States between Diversification and Stagnation', in *Mass Media, Politics and Society in the Middle East*, ed. by Kai Hafez (New Jersey: Hampton Press, 2001), pp. 23–44; Louay Bahry, 'The New Arab Media Phenomenon: Qatar's Al-Jazeera', *Middle East Policy*, 8 (2001), 88–99; Guaaybess.

55 Ali M. Najai, 'Television and Youth in the Kingdom of Saudi Arabia: An Analysis of the Uses of Television among Young Saudi Arabian Viewers', *1982* (Madison: University of Wisconsin, 1982); Miliany.

56 Hala Abdel Rahman, 'Uses and Gratifications of Satellite TV in Egypt', *Transnational Broadcasting Studies*, 1998; Arab Advisors Group, 'Reports on

the Arab World's Communications and Media Markets', 2007 <http://www.arabadvisors.com>; Ali Jamal and Srinivas Melkote, 'Viewing and Avoidance of the Al-Jazeera Satellite Television Channel in Kuwait: A Uses and Gratifications Perspective', *Asian Journal of Communication*, 18 (2008), 1–15; Miliany.

57 Miliany; Elareshi and Matthews; Ayyad.

58 Noureddine Miladi, 'Satellite TV News and the Arab Diaspora in Britain: Comparing Al-Jazeera, the BBC and CNN', *Journal of Ethnic and Migration Studies*, 32 (2006), 947–960.

59 Ghannam; Ibrahim.

60 Gunter and Dickinson; Ibrahim.

61 Ibrahim.

62 Miliany.

63 Ayyad; Rasha A Abdulla, *The Internet in the Arab World: Egypt and Beyond* (New York: Peter Lang, 2007); Racha Mourtada and Fadi Salem, 'Social Media, Employment and Entrepreneurship: New Frontiers for the Economic Empowerment of Arab Youth?', *Arab Social Media Report*, 2012 <http://www.dsg.ae/en/publication/Description.aspx?PubID=307&PrimenuID=11&mnu=Pri>.

64 Ayyad; Ibrahim.

65 Ghonim.

66 Dennis, Martin and Wood.

67 Karam; Jamal and Melkote; Miliany; Elareshi and Matthews; Al-Jaber.

68 Karam; Elareshi and Matthews; Al-Jaber.

69 Muhammad Ayish, 'News Credibility during the Iraq War: A Survey of UAE Students', *Transnational Broadcasting Studies*, 12 (2004); Shahira Fahmy and Thomas Johnson, 'Show the Truth and Let the Audience Decide: A Web-Based Survey Showing Support among Viewers of Al-Jazeera for Use of Graphic Imagery', *Journal of Broadcasting & Electronic Media*, 51 (2007), 245–264; Amal Jamal, 'Media Culture as Counter-Hegemonic Strategy: The Communicative Action of the Arab Minority in Israel', *Media, Culture & Society*, 31 (2009), 559–577.

70 Yariv Tsfati and Joseph Cappella, 'Do People Watch What They Do Not Trust? Exploring the Association between News Media Skepticism and Exposure.', *Communication Research*, 30 (2003), 504–529.

71 Ibrahim.

72 Ghonim.

73 Freedom House, 'Freedom in the World 2013', 2013 <http://freedomhouse.org/report/freedom-world/freedom-world-2013#.U0uSdfm-1cY>.

9

Social Media, Surveillance, and Spying in the Bahrain Uprising

Marc Owen Jones

> Sami Abd al-Aziz Hassan was the leader of the 'Yokogawa Labor Union of Bahrain', a trade union at the Middle East division of Japanese engineering firm Yokogawa. He was sacked from his job in early 2013 after he was identified as the author of anonymous Tweets exposing alleged labour law violations by his employer. His Twitter account was targeted with IP spy links sent publicly via Twitter mentions.[1]

Irrespective of political stance, both government supporters and activists turned to social media and the internet to follow the Bahrain uprising that began in mid-February 2011. The number of Twitter users in Bahrain shot up,[2] and dozens of Facebook groups materialised, the majority of which were posting updates, information, photos and updates related to unfolding events. Bahrain's youth networks were rapidly becoming increasingly networked youths. Indeed, media coverage of the 'Arab Spring' tended to popularise the social media aspect of the struggle, with many news outlets focusing on the role of Twitter and Facebook in the revolutions. Much of their discourse subscribed to the technological utopian position, which views social media and the internet as a positive force that democratises information, reinvigorates citizens' political engagement, encourages freedom of expression and brings people together.[3]

Others were somewhat cynical, arguing that social media were merely a tool, and not necessarily integral to the efficacy of the revolutions as whole. Few, however, fully assumed the technological dystopian or neo-Luddite position, which posits that technological developments such as the internet simply serve to 'confound the problems of space, access and interaction by alienating people from each other and even themselves'.[4] In addition to fears that technology may actually work against integration, the dystopian position describes the fear that Web 2.0 technologies may be used as part of the 'informational-control continuum' and thus shape media content through 'propaganda, psychological operations, information intervention, and strategic public diplomacy'.[5]

The dystopian potential of technology has recently been examined by Evgeny Morozov, who highlights the failure of cyber-utopians to predict how authoritarian regimes might use the internet as a tool for propaganda, surveillance and censorship.[6] Indeed, the post-Snowden era has highlighted the extent of web surveillance by governments. Having said that, the internet cannot be reduced to a simple dystopian-versus-utopian binary, however. Instead, one must acknowledge that it can work simultaneously as a tool of both empowerment and control – depending on who is using it and what objectives they are seeking to achieve. As Rebecca MacKinnon states:

> People, governments, companies, and all kinds of groups are using the Internet to achieve all kinds of ends, including political ones.... Pitched battles are currently under way over not only who controls its [the internet's] future, but also over its very nature, which in turn will determine whom it most empowers in the long run – and who will be shut out.[7]

Examining the nature of these 'pitched battles' on a case-by-case basis is a useful endeavour, as temporal and contextual factors influence the manner in which the internet and social media are used. Given that the 2011 uprising in Bahrain has not succeeded in achieving regime change, it makes sense to focus on how hegemonic forces have utilised social media to subjugate both dissent and dissenters in the months following 14 February. This chapter therefore focuses more on the dystopian potential of technology, and looks at how social media, in particular Twitter and Facebook, have assisted the Bahraini government, hegemonic institutions and those representing the hegemonic order in maintaining their position of dominance. In particular, it examines how the Al Khalifa regime has used social media for the purposes of surveillance, censorship and propaganda.

The Growth of Web Activism and Control in Bahrain

Ever since the internet arrived in Bahrain, it has been used by political activists as a space for resistance. Forums such as bahrainonline.org were used to post photos of rallies and acts of government oppression carried out by the state security apparatus.[8] Since the start of the protests, all of these forums have assumed either a pro- or anti-government identity. In a very real sense, Bahraini cyberspace has become segregated. This segregation is not formalised, yet the nature of interactions in Bahrain's forums is firmly based on political and social loyalties, and as such there are often implicit expectations of what one should and should not say. Twitter, for example, is a different format, and its functionality made it an extremely useful tool in the 'Arab Spring'.

The surge of users generated by protests on the street resulted in a proliferation of interactions online, the basis of which was often the political context that inspired the user to join. Unlike forums, however, Twitter is not a closed community. As a result, interactions between those holding opposing opinions and political allegiances are not restricted. On the contrary, they are common. In Bahrain, the resulting interactions were often characterised by volatility, hostility and aggression. Despite these aspects, Twitter is perhaps the most effective place for activists and Bahrainis to communicate in real time with both local and global actors who may be outside their immediate networks.

This is especially important in light of the state's tight control of the national media, which increased during the 2011 crackdown. Indeed, the regime temporarily closed down *Al-Wasat*, the only Bahraini newspaper remotely critical of the regime. Its editor, Mansoor al-Jamri, was charged by the general prosecutor for publishing false information that 'harmed public safety and national interests'.[9] Opposition figures have also been excluded from the state media, which creates 'frustration… and results in these groups resorting to other media outlets such as social media'.[10] This inability to seek representation through official media outlets inevitably increases the importance of digital spaces and social media. This was especially apparent following the declaration of the National Safety Law in Bahrain on 15 March 2011.[11] The law, which was the precursor to a broader crackdown, saw the destruction of important political and religious structures, as well as a clampdown on public gatherings of any sort. However, given Bahrain's history, the law was by no means exceptional as the internet in Bahrain has always been the target of government legislation and regulation. Cybercafés in Bahrain are strictly regulated and subversive websites and live streaming/chat services blocked. In short, anything that may be deemed to violate Articles 19 and 20 of the country's press rules, which include 'instigating hatred of the political regime, encroaching on the state's official religion, breaching ethics, encroaching on religions and jeopardising public peace or raising issues whose publication is prohibited by the provisions of this law'[12] may be subjected to government censure and censorship.

Hence, just as physical places posed a threat to the regime and were destroyed by the regime, so too, do digital spaces, which are new frontiers for activism, and are the location from which people might challenge the homogenising power of authoritarianism. In order to counter the threat embodied by these digital spaces, the Bahraini government and those representing the hegemonic order are employing tactics to control them. These tactics are numerous but can generally be identified under the umbrella of 'surveillance', for they are all attempts to instil normative and acceptable repertoires of behaviour both through observation and through the creation of a fear of observation.

Surveillance and Sousveillance

Surveillance is the process by which organisations and governments observe individuals or groups of individuals. It is an asymmetric process that affords power to the observer but not the observed and is therefore a process by which the observer asserts his/her domination over the observed. The means by which an organisation conducts surveillance is multifaceted, but technological developments have facilitated the speed and efficacy of the process, allowing more efficient and pervasive observation. Indeed, the rise of what Jan van Dijk first termed the 'Network Society' has given both organisations and the state unprecedented opportunities to carry out surveillance.[13] As David Lyon argues, the information society is also the surveillance society.[14]

The historical role of technology in surveillance is perhaps most famously illustrated by Bentham's Panopticon, a building whose geometry allowed a prison guard to watch the inmates without them knowing. Timothy Mitchell describes the Panopticon as the 'institution in which the use of coercion and commands to control a population was replaced by the partitioning of space, the isolation of individuals, and their systematic yet unseen surveillance'.[15] Mitchell's work on Egypt draws heavily on the work of Michel Foucault, who outlined the importance of the power differential within the context of the 'unseen'. Ben Barton and Marthalee Barton summarise Foucault's argument, stating that the 'asymmetry of seeing-without-being-seen is, in fact, the very essence of power,' and the 'power to dominate rests on the differential possession of knowledge'.[16] As well as stressing the importance of asymmetry, Foucault states that '[the] major effect of the Panopticon is to induce in the inmate a state of conscious and permanent visibility that assures the automatic functioning of power'.[17]

In other words, it is not just being watched that is enough to induce obedience to authority but, rather, the *possibility* of being watched. An example of such an apparatus could be seen in Saddam Hussein's Iraq, where a mosque with an unusually high minaret was built in order to keep track of the Shi'a in Karbala.[18] The Hasan mosque, itself a modern-day Panopticon, functioned alongside a highly repressive state intelligence apparatus (*mukhabarat*), which is a common presence in the majority of Middle Eastern countries. Bahrain is no exception, and its *mukhabarat* have been integral to the functioning of Bahrain's intelligence system. Ian Henderson, the British head of security in Bahrain, instituted 'pseudo-gangs', and although Bahrain is a liberal state by regional standards, with fewer restrictions on internet access,[19] it still suffers from many of the same repressive measures that serve to limit both dissent and political mobilisation. Even before mid-February, Bahrain had blocked websites deemed to be politically controversial and arrested on a number of occasions the well-known blogger Ali Abdulemam.[20]

This censorship indicates the threat that new technologies pose to regimes around the world. They must therefore adopt new methods of observation, ones that preferably permit coercion with minimal resort to violence. While such observation was traditionally carried out via the naked eye, 'surveillance techniques have increasingly become embedded in technology'.[21] Oscar Gandy[22] and Mark Poster[23] argue that the growth of information technology and databases has led to an asymmetrical monitoring of behaviour. This surveillance allows particular organisations, be they corporate or bureaucratic, to 'not only commodi[tise] the personal information of those observed, but also [to] use such information to inform practices of social control and discrimination'.[24] Facebook and Twitter therefore offer a potential opportunity for organisations to extract information which can be used to further the agenda of the particular institutional body collecting the data.

So, just as the Panopticon allowed the asymmetric observation of a prison's inmates, the modern-day neo-Panopticon can be seen as the use of observational technologies to discourage certain forms of behaviour in a wide range of places, from malls to high streets, forums and social media.[25] While the essence of this surveillance is based on the fact that it is asymmetrical, the use of new technologies by individuals to observe those in authority represents a sort of inverse Panopticon, one where citizens can challenge the government痴 monopoly on information.[26] This idea is described as 'sousveillance', "from the French words for 'sous' (below) and 'veiller' (to watch)".[27] 'Sousveillance', itself a form of 'reflectionism', is a term invented by Steve Mann to describe the process of using technologies to confront organisations by documenting their actions or the consequences of their actions.[28] In other words, it gives those who are observed the power to become the observer and to resist the authority of the state. However, Mann also discusses the idea of 'personal sousveillance', which is the use of technology such as social media to document one's own day-to-day experience. An example of this is the Bahraini activists who photographed themselves at the Pearl Roundabout.

Yet, as William Marczak and his colleagues note, 'targeted surveillance of individuals conducted by nation-states poses an exceptionally challenging security problem, given the great imbalance of resources and expertise between the victims and the attackers'.[29] Indeed, such seemingly banal 'personal sousveillance' can be re-appropriated by the regime and its supporters and used as part of its own surveillance apparatus. This is nowhere more evident than in Bahrain, where the increasing polarisation of society has resulted in citizens using social media as a tool of peer-to-peer (P2P) and vigilante sous/surveillance.

Social Media, Surveillance and Counter-Revolutionary Vigilante Sousveillance

Government spying

The rise of new technologies posed new challenges for the government, which turned to novel tactics to uncover activists using social media. An investigation by the advocacy and transparency group Bahrain Watch revealed that at least 11 activists have been jailed since October 2012 for writing anonymous Tweets referring to King Hamad as 'dictator' (*Taghiyya*) or 'fallen one' (*saaqiT*) in Arabic. The tactics, most likely orchestrated by the Ministry of Interior's Cyber Crime Unit, were crude: Malicious links generated from freely available online services were sent out by government-operated accounts to those engaging in 'subversive' activity. If the target clicked on the malicious links, the victim's IP address would then be revealed to the attacker. According to Bahrain Watch:

> When an individual connects to the internet on his computer or phone, they are temporarily assigned an IP address by the phone company or internet provider whose service they are using (e.g., Batelco, Zain, Menatelecom, etc). Bahraini law requires that every time an IP address is assigned, the internet service provider must record the name of the subscriber of the internet connection, as well as the date and time. This information must be preserved for at least one year, and the security forces must be able to directly access this information at any time.[30]

In addition to this 'IP spying' technique being used on Twitter, malicious links were also sent out from accounts and numbers 'through Facebook, e-mail, and likely via other services including YouTube, InstaMessage, and mobile messaging services including BlackBerry Messenger and WhatsApp'.[31] Some activists, who were recently arrested, were sent malicious links from trusted accounts that appear to have been hacked by government agents.[32] The breadth of those accounts targeted with malicious links is staggering. So far, the government has used this tactic to target 'journalists, labour unions, human rights groups, activists, licensed opposition groups… whistleblowers, Sunni groups, vigilantes and even residents opposed to the seizure of their homes to build a government housing project'.[33] Even parody accounts, such as that of @SheikhKhalifaPM, an account that pokes fun at the Prime Minister, were targeted. Ever irreverent, @SheikhKhalifaPM responded by saying 'Bloody typical… hot young women only get in touch with me when they want something from me… like maybe my IP address'.[34]

Similarly, the Ministry of the Interior was found to be using FinSpy, malware developed by UK-Based Gamma International. FinSpy can secretly take remote control of a computer, copy its files, activate the microphone, take screenshots, intercept Skype calls, and log every keystroke.[35] FinSpy was often sent to activists via malicious files disguised as email attachments of potential interest to the target. In one example, FinSpy was attached to an email that appeared to come from the bona fide Al-Jazeera journalist Melissa Chan before being sent to activists.[36]

Bahrain Watch's investigation also revealed that the Bahrain government used FinSpy to infect the country's most prominent lawyers, activists, and politicians. These included Ibrahim Sharif, the head of the country's liberal Wa'ad party, Muhammad al-Tajir, a leading human rights lawyer, Hadi al-Musawi, head of the human rights department of Al-Wifaq, Bahrain's largest opposition society, and Hasan Mushaima, an incarcerated opposition leader deemed by Amnesty International to be a prisoner of conscience.[37] Sai'd Shehabi was also among three Bahraini exiles granted asylum in the UK, all of whom had their computers targeted, illustrating how Bahrain's repressive reach extends well beyond its borders. Other people were also targeted in Belgium and Germany.[38]

The authorities have also taken advantage of vulnerabilities in the social media app Zello, which allows people to use their phones like walkie talkies.

Bahrain Watch expressed concern that 15 activists had been arrested after they were lured to a false meeting set up by the police who posted the message through the account of a compromised member. Following this, police even posted messages via the app claiming that they were coming to get the activists 'one by one'.[39]

Trolling

Broadly speaking, trolling can be defined as a form of aggressive internet communication where people using anonymous accounts engage in abusive behaviour towards other users. It is a form of what Rebecca MacKinnon calls 'cyber-harassment' and can vary in severity, ranging from provocative comments to outright bullying'.[40] Trolling in Bahrain 'usually comes from anonymous accounts, and its severity can range from death threats and threats of rape, to spiteful comments and personal abuse'.[41] For example, one Twitter user feared for the safety of her child when an anonymous troll started tweeting about how he (the troll) knew where the child went to school. He even named the school and gave details of its layout and location. Another activist reported how trolls created five parody accounts, all of which were dedicated to ridiculing her. In an attempt to rectify this, the victim had to send to Twitter on each occasion proof of identity to get rid of the anonymous accounts. Tiring of this, Twitter eventually suggested she just tweet under a separate or anonymous identity, essentially admitting defeat at the hands of the troll(s).

Bahrain's Twitter trolls have acquired such a reputation that they have prompted many international journalists or activists reporting on Bahrain to write/blog about them, including Jillian York, David Goodman and Brian Dooley.[42] Following the release of the Bahrain Independent Commission of Inquiry (BICI) report on 23 November 2011, Al-Jazeera reporter Gregg Carlstrom tweeted: 'Bahrain has by far the hardest-working Twitter trolls of any country I've reported on'. Global Voices editor for the Middle East and North Africa, Amira Al Hussaini, tweeted: 'Yawn: cyberbullying = censorship! Welcome to the new era of freedom in #Bahrain'. A number of people told me how trolling stopped them from tweeting politics, with one user stating: 'Don't know how long Marc, my heart is heavy. Even my moderate views get attacked by trolls'.

Few people who engage in trolling have accounts that reveal their true identity, and it is precisely this anonymity that makes many people suspicious. There are perhaps thousands of anonymous accounts, all of which have very few followers, and they usually have avatars that symbolise their support for the regime (such as a picture of one of the royal family). Despite the fact that the regime enjoys some degree of legitimacy in Bahrain, there is a belief that many of these accounts are created by the security forces or PR companies to bully activists and give the illusion of widespread support for the government.[43] Given that the US military is developing software that will allow it to 'secretly manipulate social media sites by using fake online personas to influence internet conversations and spread pro-American propaganda',[44] it comes as no surprise that the private sector may seek to profit from it. Indeed, it was revealed that BGR Gabara, a British PR firm reportedly working for the Bahraini government, planned to organise a 'Twitter campaign' on behalf of Kazakh children.[45]

What these findings illustrate is that trolling can result in people changing their tweeting habits. A number of people interviewed described how they were less likely to tweet anything against the regime after being trolled. Others changed their Twitter privacy settings so that their tweets would not be seen by the global public. This demonstrates how hegemonic forces can use social media to influence the flow of anti-government rhetoric, thus contributing to the state's censorship apparatus dissuading people from tweeting; this also creates an informational vacuum, one that can then be filled with pro-regime propaganda/PR. Even expatriates living in Bahrain stopped blogging anything critical following discussions with their family about the possible implications.

Name and shame

Perhaps one of the most pernicious things to have come out of the uprising is the Hariqhum Twitter account. Hariqhum, which literally means 'the one that burns them', is a self-proclaimed defender of Bahrain who spends his days disclosing information about traitors in Bahrain. This includes posting photos of people seen at anti-government rallies, circling their faces and disclosing their addresses, their places of work and their phone numbers. However, the account has achieved such notoriety that it has become well known in Bahrain. An example of his impact was revealed to me by one informant who said, 'My friend she left the country after her husband who works in a bank became a target of this 7araghum [*sic*]. I don't think she'll ever come back'. The climate of fear that existed when this message was sent should not be underestimated, for it was a time when thousands of Bahrainis were being fired from work for taking in part in strikes, even though the strikes were 'within the permissible bounds of the law'.[46]

While many have tried to unveil Haraqhum's identity, no one has been successful. It is believed to be a number of people taking it in turns to manage the account. Hariqhum has become an institution in itself in Bahrain, with people using it to report suspected 'traitors', and also to obtain information about these 'traitors'. One such example was provided by someone whose father used to occupy a high position in a Bahraini company. He was contacted by someone who had information about a potential 'traitor' working in the company,

> this guy sends a message to my Dad pasted from Haraqhum about an [insert company name] employee... He was sending it to my dad because my dad is still well connected, so can make things happen... So he was telling my dad 'Do the needful' (i.e. get him fired)

Prior to Hariqhum, there were other examples of people with anonymous Twitter accounts receiving messages disclosing their name and identity (e.g., imagine you had gone to great lengths to protect your identity on Twitter and then someone you don't know contacts you and tells you your name, phone number and address). On describing Haraqhum, the Report of the Bahrain Independent Commission of Inquiry stated:[47]

> In some cases, a photograph of a protester was posted with a comment asking for the name of the person, and other Twitter users then posted the requested information. Witnesses reported to the Commission that persons who had been named or identified by Harghum [*sic*] would then avoid sleeping at their home address for fear of an attack. Harghum [*sic*] also allegedly advertised a MoI hotline, which people could call in order to report on persons engaged in anti-government activity.

The Harghum [*sic*] Twitter account targeted anti-government protesters and even disclosed their whereabouts and personal details. Harghum [*sic*] openly harassed, threatened and defamed certain individuals, and in some cases placed them in immediate danger. The Commission considers such harassment to be a violation of a person's right to privacy while also amounting to hate speech and incitement to violence.[48]

As of December 2014, the government has done nothing about the account, even though the commission stated that Haraqhum 'produced material that international law requires to be prohibited and which is in fact prohibited under Bahrain law.' It is interesting to note that similar 'name and shame' groups existed on Facebook,[49] yet it is easier to have Facebook remove these groups. Twitter, on the other hand, makes it hard to remove such groups unless they are reported for spam. This has led to many pro-government supporters leading campaigns encouraging people to report human rights activists such as Nabil Rajab and Maryam al-Khawaja for spam. Despite Facebook's more sympathetic policy on getting rid of such groups, it was reportedly used to identify the workplace and home of 20-year-old poet Ayat al-Qurmezi, who had angered the authorities by reading out a poem criticising King Hamad. Visitors to this Facebook page were told to write the 'traitor's name and work place.' Soon afterwards, masked men arrested her.[50]

'Passive' observation and offline factors

In anticipation of the protests, the Bahraini government created a number of Twitter accounts, most notably one for the Ministry of the Interior (MoI) – the body responsible for Bahrain's security forces. While the MoI's account tended to publish news without interacting with other people, this did not stop people from interacting with the MoI. Between the months of February and April, it was common for pro-regime supporters to use Twitter to 'report' people they thought were traitors to the MoI. The following Tweet is an example of this:

> @hussainm89 Dear @moi_bahrain can you please arrest this MOFO Hussain Mirza born 1989, he is a traitor

Although it is doubtful that the Ministry takes such complaints seriously, the impact of the threat of surveillance is very real, as someone once made clear: 'Be careful Marc. Don't argue a lot. A lot of people from MoI on Twitter. And if you mention the king, justice etc, you might be unable to enter the country. Just be careful plz'.

Offline factors refer to a number of pressures that do not necessarily occur online but still work to encourage censorship by discouraging people from using social media (the phrase self-censorship is problematic as it implies that there is no stimulus that causes the censorship, thus shifting the responsibility from the hegemonic order to the individual). In March, a photo of 'web terrorists' was circulated on Twitter. These included Manaf al-Muhandis, Mahmud Yusif and Muhammad Masqati – all prominent Twitter users or bloggers who were subsequently arrested.[51] They were all detained for varying lengths of time, and none of them tweeted anything controversial or very political for a considerable time following their release. Prominent blogger ʿAli ʿAbd Al-Imam, who is currently believed to be in hiding, was sentenced in absentia to 15 years in prison for 'spreading false information and trying to subvert the regime'. However, he re-emerged in 2013 after escaping to Britain from Bahrain.[52] In addition, blogger Zakariya Rashid Hasan Al-Asheri was tortured to death in prison on 9 April 2011.[53] As a result of the above arrests, important representatives of the activist community disappeared, further diminishing the visibility of credible online activism and prompting much fear among other online activists, who became far more reluctant to tweet anything critical of the regime. The death of Zakariya also resulted in Reporters without Borders putting Bahrain on a list of 'enemies of the internet'.[54] Other offline factors include family pressure not to use social media (particularly Twitter), and widespread fear that the government is able to hack accounts and access personal information. One informant stated: 'I used to Tweet but then when some of my friends got arrested my father sat me down and gave me a looong [*sic*] talk, guilting me into deleting all my tweets'.

The 'unknown'

Other, perhaps more sinister, elements faced by activists are the clandestine operations undertaken by companies such as Olton, a UK-based intelligence-gathering/PR firm that has a contract with the Bahrain Economic Development Board. One activist told me:

> There's this British company called Olton. I don't know exactly what they do except that they employ Bahrainis loyal to the regime to do something with social media. The person recruiting them is ex-UK military.

Despite the government of Bahrain's Tender Board's description of Olton's work being 'to develop an electronic system to track international media', one of their employees is known to have worked for the Ministry of the Interior, the body responsible for Bahrain's security forces.[55] Furthermore, Olton was at the IDEX Arms Fair in Abu Dhabi where the company was reported to be marketing its 'web-trawling' software as something that could head off unrest in the Middle East. It would do this by monitoring social media in order to identify ringleaders.[56] Fears that Twitter and Facebook were being monitored were further exacerbated after at least 47 students were expelled from Bahrain Polytechnic for 'participating in unlicensed gatherings and marches'. This was 'based on evidence mostly obtained from social media pages like Facebook'.[57] Some were dismissed for simply 'liking' an anti-government post on Facebook.[58] Many reported that they were expelled after the authorities had shown them printouts of their Facebook pages.

Propaganda and Disinformation

Blurring this line between propaganda, PR, 'data-mining' and intelligence-gathering was 'Liliane Khalil', a hoax journalist who used blogs, Twitter and email to build up a convincing online persona. Although she had claimed to be the US editor of a pro-government blog called the Bahrain Independent, an investigation revealed that she was a hoax.[59] Although Liliane Khalil's exact identity remains unknown, there is evidence linking her to Task Consultancy, a Bahraini company that was paid by the Bahraini government to formulate a PR plan.[60] Liliane Khalil also interviewed a number of activists on the understanding that she wanted to hear 'their side of the story'. However, several of those interviewed reported that she passed on their personal information to a pro-regime Twitter user – who then broadcast it on Twitter, stating that the interviewees were traitors.

Similarly, the government has hacked or taken over accounts used by activists and then utilised them to disseminate pro-government propaganda. YouTube videos were edited and taken out of context in order to demonise protesters. Conspiratorial recordings became popular and were often propagated by government officials. In one case, a video showing protestors allegedly waving Bahrain flags with 12-point flags instead of five was widely circulated,[61] its significance being that the 12 points signify the 12 Shi'a imamas, and thus the flag-waving suggested a seditious Shi'i conspiracy.[62] Even though the flags in the video did not even contain 12-point flags, Samira Rajab, at the time an upper house legislator, went on Al-Jazeera to claim that this was evidence of a conspiracy. However, it was pointed out the flag she held only had ten points.[63] In another example, a video was circulated on YouTube allegedly showing people applying make up to children in an attempt to suggest that activists were faking their injuries and that the government was attacking children. It transpired that the video was an edited video from Nazareth, Israel, showing children being made up for an event. Despite this, the video soon received over 17,000 hits, not including mirrored copies.[64] As I said in 2011:

> the presence of such disinformation is very harmful in times of conflict, for it is also a time when people are feeling vulnerable, defensive and afraid. I have even seen Trolls termed 'e-thugs' in recent days, perhaps not surprising since the term 'thug' has now become an important part of the Middle Eastern protest lexicon. The trolls are exploiting both our need for information, which surely increases in times of crisis, and also the dearth of credible information on the issues. This lack of credible official information compounds the issue, and as the government continues to remain absent, the scramble for answers is both desperate and blind.[65]

The Surveillance and Sousveillance State

For activists, the use of social media as a tool for activism or representation is fraught with danger. The tactics adopted by hegemonic forces in Bahrain contributed to a climate of fear and distrust, one that disrupted social media space by assimilating it as part of the regime's surveillance apparatus. Trolling, for example, is not only a form of social control that exercises its power through intimidation, but also serves as a reminder that one's behaviour is always being watched, and that any potential dissent will never be expressed without fear of observation. Even the mere presence of an MoI Twitter account was enough to regulate some people's behaviour by reminding them that they were being monitored. The incarceration of key online activists also reminded Bahrainis of the potential costs of utilising social media for dissent, thus asserting that the transgression of a certain set of normative behaviours (in this case acquiescence) would not be tolerated.

The impact in Bahrain of trolling and naming and shaming illustrates the dangers of these forms of 'cyber-vigilantism', which will only become more detrimental as social cohesion in Bahrain is further eroded. Hariqhum is a particular worry, for it has become a quasi-official institution, one whose continued existence and endorsement by some supporters of the regime represents tacit support of its utility as a method of social control. Just as plain-clothes thugs operate alongside the police in suppressing protests, accounts such as Hariqhum's worked alongside the regime's intelligence-gathering apparatus, appropriating citizens' 'personal sousveillance' and using it to persecute, vilify and threaten. Although Hariqhum's identity still remains unknown, the opaque way in which the regime has so far conducted the crackdown and the blurring of lines between law enforcement and state-endorsed vigilantism have heightened the suspicions of activists, many of whom believe that Hareghum actually operates with MoI approval. Whether this is the case is in many ways irrelevant. This is because perception plays a fundamental role in surveillance, for what we perceive and what is actual form the underlying mechanism of the Panopticon, which seeks not only to watch but also to make people *believe* they are being watched.

Another alarming trend is the clandestine role played by predominantly Western PR and security firms, many of which are 'exploiting the burgeoning but unregulated surveillance market'.[66] Bahrain also enlists the services of companies such as Nokia Siemens, whose SMS monitoring technology was used by the state's security apparatus to intercept the communications of suspected dissidents.[67] Olton, the British company offering expertise in social media, and recently acquired by Protection Group International, sold a 'reputation management' service. This aimed to promote 'positive' online commentary while 'mitigating the negative'.[68] The fact that it is also an 'intelligence-gathering' company has serious implications for freedom of speech. As I have stated elsewhere:

> The threat posed by unscrupulous PR companies to freedom of speech should not be underestimated. It is bad enough that they distort the public sphere in exchange for money, yet it is the rise of companies like Olton that is the most alarming, for when does intelligence gathering become evidence gathering? Furthermore, when does 'reputation management' involve facilitating the silencing of those narratives that oppose the desired rhetoric of the paying client?[69]

The recent revelation that that British PR firm Bell Pottinger was offering to help companies hijack citizen petitions in order to influence European Union law raises questions about a similar incident that occurred in Bahrain last year.[70] This involved the circulation of a petition on Twitter that claimed to be a proposal listing the demands of Bahrain's youth for an forthcoming reconciliation initiative called the National Dialogue. Over a thousand people signed it, though many of the signatories were anonymous, sock-puppet accounts. The following day, the National Unity Gathering (Bahrain's new pro-government political party) used the petition as a basis for determining what Bahraini youth wanted (unsurprisingly, they did not want political change – just security).[71] The notion that anonymous online accounts may be rubber-stamping policies in order to give them a veneer of democratic legitimacy illustrates the ease with which social media can be used to manufacture consent. Although this may seem like the stuff of Orwellian fantasy, one must not underestimate the dangers of a growing, global surveillance industry, one that capitalises on the desire of authoritarian regimes around the world to monitor, control and suppress dissent.

Fighting the spread of such technology is costly and time-consuming. The Rights Group Privacy International (PI) launched a legal case against HM Revenues and Customs (HMRC) in the UK over its refusal to provide 'details about potentially unlawful exports of spyware tools made by Gamma International'.[72] In May 2014, the British High Court ruled in favour of PI, stating that HMRC's refusal to release information was 'unlawful'.[73] Now Privacy International has filed a criminal complaint with the UK National Cyber Crime Unit, asking it to investigate the targeting of three UK-based Bahrainis with Gamma International's FinFisher computer 'spyware'.[74]

Conclusion

Through the aforementioned methods, government agents and government supporters alike are able to preserve the status quo by extending the means by which they conduct surveillance. Such methods are attempts to impose normative forms of behaviour in spaces that allow the performance of identities that challenge the hegemonic order. These spaces, which include Shi'i religious structures, the Pearl Roundabout and social media, all represent what Foucault described as heterotopias, i.e., places that challenge 'safe space' and allow the flourishing of resistance identities that challenge the hegemonic order.

This capacity of social media to function as a space of resistance did not go uncontested in Bahrain, and hegemonic forces also used them to enhance and 'mobilise identities to facilitate the extraction of resources from the society to confront the external (and in Bahrain's case, internal) threat'.[75] So while social media allow activists to 'overcome the powerlessness of their solitary despair… and fight the powers that be by identifying the networks that are', it also allows hegemonic forces to resist change.[76] Furthermore, Bahrain illustrates how it is not simply faceless authoritarian regimes that resist political change, but citizens too, especially those who benefit both economically and socially from maintaining the status quo. Indeed, just as those advocating political change might use social media to create networks of resistance, those representing the hegemonic order are able to mobilise their own networks of domination.

Perhaps one of the saddest aspects of all this was the way in which information shared amidst a climate of optimism, such as photos of peaceful protesters at the Pearl Roundabout, was re-appropriated by the likes of Hareghum and reframed within a context of treachery, terrorism and betrayal. Such abuses of social media not only remind Bahrainis of the potential costs of sharing information publicly but also demonstrate how trust is an increasingly scarce commodity. The nature of this breakdown of trust was nowhere more evident than on Facebook, and numerous interviewees shared stories of how they purged their 'friend lists', both through anger at their newly developed political outlook and through fear that certain persons might gain access to potentially 'incriminating' photos or information. The erosion of trust is itself a crucial part of the effects of surveillance, for the inability to trust others promotes increased isolation of the individual, which can unravel social cohesion and discourage the formation of strong activist networks that advocate social justice.

Although it must be emphasised that these negative effects are very real, they by no means undermine the importance of social media as a tool for sousveillance. It is an instrument of both empowerment and control, yet the extent to which it functions as either depends greatly on the cultural, geopolitical, technological and temporal context in which it is being used. The role of social media is ambivalent, and although they have been an incredibly positive force in Bahrain, documenting their successes would necessitate a separate article. Unfortunately, the government's claims of reform since 2011 have been rendered hollow by lacklustre implementation of the BICI report. New media laws appear to legitimise even tighter state control over the media. The creation of an 'independent regulator',[77] the 'Supreme Council for Media and Communication',[78] following recommendations in the BICI report, is questionable considering that all members are essentially appointed by the King.[79]

As things stand, pro-democracy activists still face a great many obstacles in their search for spaces from where to represent themselves. The brutal daily crackdowns in the villages, the destruction of the Pearl Roundabout and the demolition of mosques all represent attempts to control space and render it ahistorical, conformist and safe. For the regime, these are all spaces of crisis, transformation and change, or heterotopias. Social media are no different, and they too can be regulated and controlled. As the struggle for democracy continues in urban space, so it also continues in cyberspace. In many ways, the battle is *for* cyberspace, for it is a battle between the principles of empowerment and control, the continuation of which underlines the argument that social media are a tool of both emancipation and repression.

Notes

1 Bahrain Watch, 'The IP Spy Files: How Bahrain's Government Silences Anonymous Online Dissent', *Bahrain Watch*, 2013 <https://bahrainwatch.org/ipspy/viewreport.php>.

2 *Al-Wasat News*, 'The Number of Bahrainis Using Twitter Has Increased by 80% during Recent Events', 6 June 2011.

3 Manuel Castells, *The Rise of the Network Society* (Oxford: Blackwell, 1996); Lawrence Grossman, *The Electronic Republic: Reshaping Democracy in the Information Age* (New York: Penguin Books, 1995); Howard Rheingold, *The Virtual Community: Homesteading on the Electronic Frontier* (New York: Harper

Collins, 1993); Diana Saco, *Cybering Democracy: Public Space and the Internet* (Minneapolis: University of Minnesota Press, 2002).

4 Saco, p. xv.

5 Vian Bakir, *Sousveillance, Media and Strategic Political Communication: Iraq, USA, UK* (London: Continuum, 2010), p. 8.

6 Evgeny Morozov, *The Net Delusion: The Dark Side of Internet Freedom* (Jackson, TN: Public Affairs, 2011).

7 Rebecca MacKinnon, *Consent of the Networked: The Worldwide Struggle for Internet* (New York, NY: Basic Books, 2012), p. 27.

8 Fahad Desmukh, 'The Internet in Bahrain: Breaking the Monopoly of Information', *Foreign Policy*, 2010.

9 Trade Arabia, 'Al-Wasat Journalists to Stand Trial in Bahrain', *Trade Arabia*, 2011 <http://www.tradearabia.com/news/MEDIA_196756.html>.

10 Information Affairs Authority, *Bahrain Independent Commission of Inquiry – BICI* (Manama, 2012), p. 422.

11 Bahrain News Agency, 'HM King Hamad Declares State of National Safety', 2011.

12 Information Affairs Authority, 'Press Rules and Regulations', 2002 <http://www.iaa.bh/policiesPressrules.aspx>.

13 Dijk van J A G M, *De Netwerkmaatschappij, Sociale Aspecten van Nieuwe Media [Dutsh]*, 3rd edn (Houten NL, Zaventem BEL: Bohn Stafleu van Loghum, 1997).

14 David Lyon, *Surveillance Society: Monitoring in Everyday Life* (Buckingham: Open University Press, 2001).

15 Timothy Mitchell, *Colonising Egypt* (Berkeley: University of California Press, 1991), p. x.

16 Ben Barton and Marthalee Barton, 'Modes of Power in Technical and Professional Visuals', *Journal of Business and Technical Communication*, 7 (1993), 138–162 <doi:10.1177/1050651993007001007>.

17 Michel Foucault, *Discipline and Punish: The Birth of the Prison* (New York: Vintage Books, 1977), p. 201.

18 Bakir, p. 17.

19 Albrecht Hofheinz, 'Arab Internet Usage: Popular Trends and Public Impact', in *Arab Media and Political Renewal: Community, Legitimacy and Public Life*, ed. by Naomi Sakr (London: I.B.Tauris, 2007), pp. 56–79, p. 60.

20 Desmukh, 'The Internet in Bahrain: Breaking the Monopoly of Information'.

21 Steve Mann, Jason Nolan and Barry Wellman, 'Sousveillance: Inventing and Using Wearable Computing Devices for Data Collection in Surveillance Environments', *Surveillance & Society*, 1 (2003), 331–355.

22 Oscar H. Jr Gandy, *The Panoptic Sort: A Political Economy of Personal Information* (Boulder, CO: Westview Press, 1993).

23 Mark Poster, *The Mode of Information: Poststructuralism and Social Construct* (Chicago, IL: University of Chicago Press, 1990).

24 Lee Humphreys, 'Who's Watching Whom? A Study of Interactive Technology and Surveillance', *Journal of Communication*, 61 (2011), 575–595 <doi:10.1111/j.1460-2466.2011.01570.x>, p. 576.

25 Mann, Nolan and Wellman, p. 332.

26 Ibid., p. 333.

27 Ibid., p. 332.

28 Steve Mann, '"Reflectionism" and "diffusionism": New Tactics for Deconstructing the Video Surveillance Superhighway', *Leonardo*, 31 (1998), 93–102.

29 William Marczak and others, 'When Governments Hack Opponents: A Look at Actors and Technology', in *Paper presented at the 23rd USENIX Security Symposium 20–22 August* (San Diego, CA, 2014) <http://www.icir.org/vern/papers/govhack.usesec14.pdf>.

30 Bahrain Watch, 'The IP Spy Files: How Bahrain's Government Silences Anonymous Online Dissent.'

31 Ibid.

32 Ibid.

33 Ibid.

34 As Sheikh Khalifa tweeted: 'Bloody typical…hot young women only get in touch with me when they want something from me… like maybe my IP address', [Tweet by @SheikhKhalifaPM], 18 September 2014.

35 Vernon Silver, 'Gamma Says No Spyware Sold to Bahrain; May Be Stolen Copy', *BloombergBusiness*, 2012 <http://www.bloomberg.com/news/2012-07-27/gamma-says-no-spyware-sold-to-bahrain-may-be-stolen-copy.html>.

36 William Marczak and Morgan Marquis-Boire, 'From Bahrain with Love: FinFisher's Spy Kit Exposed?', *Citizenlab*, 2012 <https://citizenlab.org/2012/07/from-bahrain-with-love-finfishers-spy-kit-exposed/>.

37 Fahad Desmukh, 'Bahrain Government Hacked Lawyers and Activists with UK Spyware', *Bahrain Watch*, 2014 <https://bahrainwatch.org/blog/2014/08/07/uk-spyware-used-to-hack-bahrain-lawyers-activists/>.

38 European Center for Constitutional and Human Rights, 'Gamma/FinFisher: No Investigation into German-British Software Company', *European Center for Constitutional and Human Rights*, 2014 <http://www.ecchr.de/surveillance-technology/articles/human-rights-organisations-file-oecd-complaints-against-surveillance-firms-gamma-international-and-trovicor.html>.

39 William Marczak, 'Bahrain Watch Issues Urgent Advice for Activists to Stop Using @zello due to Security Flaw', *Bahrain Watch*, 2014 <https://bahrainwatch.org/blog/2014/09/07/bahrain-watch-issues-urgent-advice-for-activists-to-stop-using-zello-due-to-security-flaw/>.

40 MacKinnon.

41 Marc Jones, 'Bahrain Activists' Trouble with Trolls', *Index on Censorship Uncut*, 2012 <http://uncut.indexoncensorship.org/2012/05/bahrain-marc-owen-jones-twitter-trolls/>.

42 Jillian York, 'Twitter Trolling as Propaganda Tactic: Bahrain and Syria', 2011 <http://jilliancyork.com/2011/10/12/twitter-trolling-as-propaganda-tactic-bahrain-and-syria/>; David Goodman, '"Twitter Trolls" Haunt Discussions of Bahrain Online', *The New York Times Blog*, 2011 <http://thelede.blogs.nytimes.com/2011/10/11/twitter-trolls-haunt-discussions-of-bahrain-online/>; Brian Dooley, "Troll' Attacks on #Bahrain Tweets Show Depth of Government Attempts to Silence Dissent', *The World Post*, 2011 <http://www.huffingtonpost.com/brian-dooley/troll-attacks-on-bahrain_b_1099642.html>.

43 Thor Halvorssen, 'PR Mercenaries, Their Dictator Masters, and the Human Rights Stain', *The World Post*, 2011 <http://www.huffingtonpost.com/thor-halvorssen/pr-mercenaries-their-dict_b_863716.html>.

44 Nick Fielding and Ian Cobain, 'Revealed: US Spy Operation That Manipulates Social Media', *Guardian*, 17 March 2011 <http://www.guardian.co.uk/technology/2011/mar/17/us-spy-operation-social-networks>.

45 Melanie Newman and Oliver Wright, 'PR Firm's Plan to Target Sting after Gig Boycott', *The Independent*, 8 December 2011 <http://www.independent.co.uk/news/uk/politics/kazakhstan-pr-firms-plan-to-target-sting-after-gig-boycott-video-6273824.html>.

46 Information Affairs Authority, *Bahrain Independent Commission of Inquiry – BICI*, p. 240.

47 Ibid., p. 381.

48 Ibid., p. 391.

49 Suzi Dixon, 'Facebook "Used to Hunt down Bahrain Dissidents"', *The Telegraph*, 4 August 2011 <http://www.telegraph.co.uk/expat/expatnews/8681230/Facebook-used-to-hunt-down-Bahrain-dissidents.html>; Andrew Hammond, 'Bahrain Media Play Role in Tension after Protests', *Reuters*, 2011 <http://in.reuters.com/article/2011/05/05/idINIndia-56790720110505>.

50 Al-Jazeera English, 'Shouting in the Dark. Television Programme', *YouTube*, 2011 <http://www.youtube.com/watch?v=xaTKDMYOBOU>.

51 Reporters without Borders (2011a), 'Bahraini and Syrian Authorities Try to Impose News Blackout', 4 April. <http://en.rsf.org/bahraini-and-syrian-authorities-04-04-2011,39946.html>.

52 Information Affairs Authority, *Bahrain Independent Commission of Inquiry – BICI*, p. 238.

53 BBC, 'Bahrain and Belarus Named Enemies of the Internet', BBC News Channel, 2012 <http://www.bbc.com/news/technology-17350225>.

54 Dixon.

55 Freedom House, 'Freedom on the Net 2013: Bahrain', *Freedom House*, 2013 <https://www.freedomhouse.org/sites/default/files/resources/FOTN 2013_Bahrain.pdf>.

56 Fahad Desmukh, 'Myths and Lies in the Bahrain Infowars', *blogspot*, 2011 <http://revolutionbahrain2.blogspot.se/2011/04/myths-and-lies-in-bahrain-infowars.html>.

57 Desmukh, 'Myths and Lies in the Bahrain Infowars'.

58 Yousef Al-Saraf, 'Bahrain Watch Welcomes Partner Privacy International's Legal Action on Government Surveillance', *Bahrain Watch*, 2014 <https://bahrainwatch.org/blog/2014/10/14/bahrain-watch-welcomes-partner-privacy-internationals-legal-action-on-government-surveillance/>.

59 Al-Saraf.

60 Jones, 'Bahrain Activists' Trouble with Trolls'.

61 Desmukh, 'Myths and Lies in the Bahrain Infowars'.

62 Ibid.

63 Hussein Ibish, 'The Bahrain Uprising: Towards Confrontation vs Accommodation', *A Henry Jackson Society Strategic Briefing*, 2011 <http://www.henryjacksonsociety.org/cms/harriercollectionitems/Bahrain1c.pdf>.

64 Bahrain Watch, 'Fabrigate', *Bahrain Watch*, 2014 <https://bahrainwatch.org/media/#!sameerarajab>.

65 Desmukh, 'Myths and Lies in the Bahrain Infowars'.

66 Goodman.

67 Jamie Doward and Rebecca Lewis, 'UK Exporting Surveillance Technology to Repressive Nations', *Guardian*, 7 April 2012 <http://www.guardian.co.uk/world/2012/apr/07/surveillance-technology-repressive-regimes>.

68 Vernon Silver and Benjamin Elgin, 'Torture in Bahrain Becomes Routine with Help from Nokia Siemens', *BloombergBusiness*, 2011 <http://www.bloomberg.com/news/2011-08-22/torture-in-bahrain-becomes-routine-with-help-from-nokia-siemens-networking.html>.

69 Kevin Rawlinson, 'Revealed: Lobbyists' Plans to Hijack "people"s Petitions', *The Independent*, 10 April 2012 <http://www.independent.co.uk/news/uk/home-news/revealed-lobbyists-plans-to-hijack-peoples-petitions-7628058.html>.

70 Gulf Daily News, 'Security Is Top Wish of Young', *Gulf Daily News*, 15 June 2011 <http://www.gulf-daily-news.com/NewsDetails.aspx?storyid=307981>.

71 From Protection Group International (PGI), 'Olton', *From Protection Group International (PGI)*, 2012 <http://www.olton.co.uk/services/reputation-management>.

72 Marc Owen Jones, 'Bahrain's PR Machine Threatens Free Speech', *Index on Censorship Uncut*, 2012.

73 Gareth Morgan, 'HMRC Faces High Court Challenge over Spy Software Sales', *V3.co.uk2*, 2013 <http://www.v3.co.uk/v3-uk/news/2261787/hmrc-faces-high-court-challenge-over-spy-software-sales>.

74 Stephen Saideman, 'Conclusion: Thinking Theoretically about Identity and Foreign Policy', in *Identity and Foreign Policy in the Middle East*, ed. by Shibley Telhami and Michael Barnett (Ithaca, NY: Cornell University Press, 2002), pp. 196–200, p. 170.

75 Dave Neal, 'Court Rules HMRC Must End FinFisher Spy Software Stonewalling', *V3.co.uk2*, 2014 <http://www.v3.co.uk/v3-uk/news/2344407/court-rules-hmrc-must-end-finfisher-spy-software-stonewalling>.

76 Al-Saraf.

77 Foucault.

78 Manuel Castells, *Communication Power* (New York, NY: Oxford University Press, 2009), p. 341

79 POMED in their report, *One Year Later: Assessing Bahrain's Implementation of the BICI Report (November, 2012)*, speak of a seven-member Higher Media Board, containing four people appointed by the King, with the other three being appointed by the Prime Minister, the President of the Shura Council and the President of the Council of Ministers. However, the Bahrain governments report, *BICI Follow-Up Report (November, 2012)*, speaks of a nine-member 'Supreme Council for Media and Communication' consisting of nine members appointed by royal order.

10

Social Media and Political Change in the Gulf

Samah Ahmed

The role of social media in political discourse in the Gulf region has been widely reported on across the media and by academics in a vast array of studies highlighting the evolution of internet consumption in the Gulf Cooperation Council (GCC) and the wider Middle East.[1] It is clear that the GCC online community is becoming increasingly politicised. It can be argued that many people, frustrated at the lack of political debate in traditional media, are going online to voice their issues and concerns. People's transition to social media as a news source is driven by their preference for eyewitness accounts of news and 'citizen journalism' – reports from people via Twitter, Facebook updates, Flickr photographs and other real-time updates to their own networks. The rising use of social media by news-producers themselves suggests that those who make the news as well as those who consume it want less intermediary and more direct access. While social media have no doubt played a key role in anti-government movements and politics in parts of the GCC such as Bahrain, where online forums and blogs have been utilised extensively for nearly a decade,[2] it will require more than social media alone to put the concept of democracy into practice. This chapter therefore examines how social media in the GCC region have changed the political reforms and whether they have fostered political change.

The proliferation of social media began in the 1990s, mostly in the form of simple log-and-chat applications, used and developed by communities of computer programmers and technology enthusiasts. By the early years of the twenty-first century, the mainstream public began to rapidly adopt and adapt to the world of social networking, with the launch of sites such as Friendster, LinkedIn and MySpace. By 2003, 10 per cent of the world were internet users.[3]

The term 'social media' refers to internet sites where people interact freely, sharing and discussing information about news, each other and their lives, using a multimedia mix of personal words, pictures, videos and audio.[4] The term 'social media' has created a significant buzz in the GCC region, from corporate marketers to government departments to law enforcement; all have been keen to join the newest offering from the internet. Both young and old have embraced the social media phenomena, and user-generated content has become the social commentary of the era, with social media as its home.

While the 'Arab Spring' in 2011 swept through country after country in the wider Middle East and North Africa, the GCC countries remained relatively passive, with the exception of Bahrain, the Eastern Province of Saudi Arabia and Oman. While the unrest in Bahrain has been the most intense, it was triggered in large part by economic and sectarian factors; sectarian marginalisation was also a catalyst of protests in Saudi Arabia's Eastern Province, and the demonstrations in Oman were triggered initially by economic grievances. While the Egyptian protests ran under the slogan 'Bread, Freedom and Human Dignity'[5] and the Tunisian protest adopted the slogan 'The people want to overthrow the regime', in contrast no definitive slogans were associated with the protests that occurred in the GCC countries.[6] Furthermore, the speed at which the protests in the GCC countries were quelled, with the exception of Bahrain, indicates that the people did not lend mass support to the protest leaders. Alternatively, it might be argued that the quick concessions made by the state, specifically responding by offering financial packages to key sectors of society and engaging in limited political, economic and welfare reforms, ensured that the revolts were quickly extinguished.[7]

The importance of social media in this latest wave of political upheaval has seen political theorists and social scientists lining up in opposing camps. Malcolm Gladwell is a prominent sceptic of the importance of social media in progressive social and political change. In an October 2010 article in the *New Yorker*, he pointed out that 'the platforms of social media are built around weak ties. Social networks are effective at increasing participation by lessening the level of motivation that participation requires'.[8]

One of the leading social-media movement proponents is New York University Professor Clay Shirky, author of *Here Comes Everybody*. Shirky asserts that 'the more promising way to think about social media is as long-term tools that can strengthen civil society and the public sphere' and 'social media can compensate for the disadvantages of undisciplined groups by re-ducing the costs of coordination.[9] For political movements, one of the main forms of coordination is what is called 'shared awareness', the ability of each member of a group to not only understand the situation at hand, but also understand that everyone else does too.[10] Social media increases shared awareness by propagating messages through social networks.

The Communication Landscape and Policy in the GCC Region

The GCC is made up of the six nations, which were formed in 1981 to foster a cooperative framework to facilitate co-ordination, integration and inter-connection between the member states.[11] The population of the GCC has grown rapidly since 1990, more than doubling from 21 million to 46 million by 2011.[12] Social media platforms have seen a dramatic rise in the number of users from the GCC region, believed to be attributed to several factors, including increase in internet penetration rates, bandwidth, literacy rates, online media sophistication, and socio-economic status.

A study by Dennis and his colleagues at the Northwestern University in Qatar has found internet use in the GCC region to be almost universal, especially in the United Arab Emirates (UAE) where 91 per cent of those surveyed stated that they use the internet, and its use is nearly as widespread in Qatar (86 per cent), Bahrain (82 per cent) and Saudi Arabia (82 per cent).[13] Internet penetration in the GCC countries is also considerably high; a 2013 report from Ipsos MENA found that overall internet penetration rate was 61 per cent, a figure significantly higher than the 39 per cent reported for the Middle East and North Africa (MENA) region as a whole.[14] For example, Facebook was a platform most used by UAE users (41 per cent), followed by Kuwaiti users (34 per cent), Qatari users (29 per cent), Bahraini users (26 per cent), Saudi Arabia users (19 per cent) and, lastly, Omani users (17 per cent).[15]

Additional factors that account for the high rates of internet use include the demographics of the GCC region, with 54 per cent of the population being under the age of 25[16]; moreover, substantial expatriate communities, who constitute 59 per cent of the total population of the GCC, may also contribute significantly to the numbers of online users from within the region.[17]

Bahrain

Online media in Bahrain is governed by the Press and Publications Law of 2002, which stipulates prison sentences of up to five years for anyone publishing material that is offensive to Islam or the King, or that is perceived as undermining state security or the monarchy. By 2008, the Bahraini Telecommunications Regulatory Authority (BTRA) had licensed 22 internet service providers in Bahrain (ISP).[18]

Bahrainis use the internet to debate sensitive issues and to exchange content that is not available in the traditional media. The most popular platform is the banned *bahrainonline.org* – the largest independent news forum, with over 50,000 members – where coverage of regular street protests is posted along with oppositionist articles.[19] Multiple independent online news sites have emerged in the last few years, but many have had to close due to harassment by the authorities. For example, the sites *Alsaheefa.net* and *Awaal.net* were closed after three journalists were charged with inciting hatred of the government, insulting the regime, and fostering sectarianism in 2008. Websites such as Twitter, Facebook and YouTube have been well utilised by Bahraini individuals and human rights organisations such as the Bahrain Center for Human Rights (BCHR) to organise protests and promote civil rights. These tools have started to play an even more significant role following the pre-election crackdown in 2010; after many forums and critical websites were blocked, many Bahrainis turned to Twitter and Facebook to voice their opinions and campaign against the government actions.

Internet services were first introduced to Bahrain in 1995 by the Bahrain Telecommunications Company (BTC), known as *Batelco*. Bahrain has a fixed broadband penetration rate of approximately 88.9 per cent[20] and an impressively high literacy rate of 94.6 per cent.[21] Furthermore, while the online community of Bahrain is relatively small compared to larger countries, it is extremely dynamic and has only further proliferated with the protest movement of 2011, with the number of users on Facebook reaching 377,620 as of March 2013, representing a penetration rate of 51.2 per cent, and around 72,468 active users on Twitter as of June 2012.[22]

In 1997, only two years after the internet had been introduced in the country, a Bahraini internet user became the first to be arrested after sending information to a political opposition group outside of the country.[23] The Ministry of Information made its first official attempt to block websites containing content critical of the government in 2002, and today over 1,000 websites are blocked, including individual pages on certain social-networking sites.[24]

The country's polarisation following the events of February and March 2011 is evident online, with the two sides vying to ensure that their voices are heard. Restrictions on Bahraini internet users escalated in 2011, following widespread protests against the ruling family of King Hamad bin Isa Al Khalifa. The authorities engaged in mass arrests, military trials, and widespread intimidation tactics in an attempt to silence popular demands for greater political rights and democratic freedoms, including a new Constitution and an elected government.

United Arab Emirates (UAE)

Emiratis are fiercely nationalistic and proud of their country's achievements over the past 42 years. Unlike Saudi Arabia, Kuwait or Bahrain, there is often little debate on the country and its long-term direction but more insight into social issues particularly those which affect the country's citizens. The UAE continues to have the highest number of free trade zones related to media in the region, highlighting the strong presence of the media sector in the country.

Over 90 per cent of internet users in the UAE use social networking sites on a regular basis. Since 2009, the frequency of visiting social networking sites has increased substantially. 21 per cent of users now visit a site four to five times a day, compared to just 3 per cent in 2009. Expat Arabs are amongst the highest users in terms of frequency of use, as well as those under the age of 35. Overall, there has been a significant increase in the mean time spent using social networking sites from 5.4 times per week to 11.9 times per week.[25]

The telecommunication services in the UAE are regulated by the Telecommunication Regulatory Authority (TRA), which was established in 2003 by Federal law and is tasked with ensuring the adequacy of telecommunications services throughout the country and establishing and implementing a regulatory and policy framework. The United Arab Emirates' long-term strategy to diversify its economy has seen the government investing heavily in the development of the Information and Communications Technology (ICT) industry. As more and more of the population has taken up social media as a tool for self-expression, the rulers and legal authorities have put in place policies and laws to address and control the online environment, namely the Federal Decree No. 5 of 2012 on combating cybercrimes.[26]

Kuwait

Kuwait boasts one of the highest literacy rates in the region, at close to 95 per cent, as a result of the extensive government support for the education system. Despite its relatively high broadband penetration at 81 per cent of households, Kuwait is the lowest ranked (62) of all the GCC countries in terms of the networked readiness for ICT, largely due to the limited development of ICT infrastructure and the absence of competition in the fixed-line sector.[27] Recent signals from the government such as the setting-up of an independent regulator for the telecoms sector and the introduction of competition in the fixed-line sector are seen as positive in terms of introducing innovative products, pushing services and increasing competition in the telecoms sector.

By many measures, Kuwait has had a more developed civil society than those found elsewhere among the GCC countries. It has a critical press enjoying relative freedom, a tradition of public debate in the diwaniyas (a room or hall area for receiving guests, neighbours and friends to discuss current events and exchange views), established political groupings, and an active parliament, which exercises significant influence and control over governance by the ruling family.[28] Of the GCC nations, Kuwait is the only country to achieve a 'Partly Free' press status ranking from the international advocacy group Freedom House.[29]

Qatar

The Supreme Council for Information and Communications Technology was established in 2005 to draft laws and regulations establishing new ISPs, handle e-crimes, and ensure protection from the internet. Residents of Qatar spend a considerable amount of time online – about 19 hours a week at home (the same as television), 17 hours per week at work for those who are employed, and for students seven hours per week at school. Westerners spend twice as much time as do Qatari nationals online at school (11 hours compared to five hours per week typically), and they also spend slightly more time than other groups on the internet at home (22 hours per week).

As stated by Dennis and his colleagues in 2013, the use of social networking is common among residents of Qatar. Seventy-six per cent of all internet users in Qatar use social networking sites.[30] The frequency of social networking online is higher among Westerners (85 per cent of internet users) and lower among Qatari nationals (67 per cent). Facebook dominates social networking, as 86 per cent of adults who network use this platform. However, while nine in ten non-nationals are on Facebook, only two thirds of Qatari nationals (65 per cent) use this site. Qatari nationals are far more likely than non-nationals to be using Twitter (65 per cent).[31]

Those in Qatar seem to be cautiously optimistic about the benefits the internet brings to the flow of information, ideas and influence with respect to 'powerful institutions' and 'public issues'. Six in ten internet users in Qatar (60 per cent) agree that 'people like you can better understand the nature of powerful institutions' and a similar number feel that people 'can have more influence on society' (58 per cent) and 'have more say about public issues' (57 per cent) by accessing the internet. Half believe the internet can influence the extent to which 'institutional leaders will care what they think'.[32]

Despite providing the headquarters for international news broadcaster Al-Jazeera, Qatar's domestic press environment remains notably restricted. Reporters without Borders ranked Qatar at 110 out of 179 countries in terms of press freedom and the country sits firmly in the 'Not Free' category according to the Freedom House index.[33]

Oman

According to the initiative for an Open Arab Internet, Oman has a population of 2.4 million, 600,000 of whom are non-Omanis. Oman depends heavily on oil, yet its per-capita income is the second lowest compared to the rest of its GCC neighbours. For over three decades, the state-owned Oman Telecommunications Company (OTC), the official internet service provider (ISP), has been in charge of developing the telecom sector in Oman. Omantel, previously the General Telecommunications Organisation (GTO), started offering telecommunications services in 1970 and internet services in 1997. Mobile and fixed-line services cover 95 per cent of the country; however, relative to the rest of the GCC, internet penetration rates are still low. According to Internet World Stats, Oman had just over two million internet users as of June 2012, with a penetration rate of 68 per cent, and 584,900 Facebook subscribers, equating to 18.9 per cent penetration.[34]

The Ubar Portal, developed in 2007 by the government, provides some electronic government services such as e-tendering, e-taxation and municipal services. In 2003, the Omani government launched the Digital Oman Strategy (DOS) project that was to lead to the education of Oman's digital society about the web and achieve the goal of launching 750 government websites. To supplement the government's initiative, a group of students, academics, IT professionals, businesses and some government institutions joined together in April 2008 to launch Oman's first IT knowledge internet platform. The project's aim was to bridge the information technology knowledge gap between students, professionals, and the industry sector.

The initiative was relaunched in 2010 to accelerate the country's level of digital penetration and readiness. This initiative along with the 2010 National Broadband strategy has seen a rapid rise in broadband penetration in Oman over the last few years.[35]

Saudi Arabia

The media environment within Saudi Arabia continues to be one of the most tightly controlled in the region. Due to the limitations on free interaction between men and women in Saudi Arabia, the internet plays a significant role in social interaction. Saudi Arabia has enjoyed a rapid growth of internet and communications technologies in recent years. Broadband penetration access had increased to 51 per cent of the population by 2012,[36] up from 24 per cent in 2009.[37]

Overall, infrastructure is not considered a major barrier to access except in remote and sparsely populated areas. Internet penetration is highest in major cities such as Riyadh and Jeddah, as well as in the oil-rich Eastern Province. In the wake of popular uprisings throughout the Arab world, the government of Saudi Arabia enforced strict limits on free speech and organised protest. While the recent wave of demonstrations has not changed the political landscape of Saudi Arabia as it has in other countries of the region, there was a notable rise in online engagement between 2010 and 2012; for example, the number of registered Facebook users had increased from around 2.25 million in June 2010 to 5.5 million by June 2012.[38]

Government Agencies and Social Media Adapted

Many of the GCC governments are undergoing a process of trial and error as they cope with an increased flow of information online that is not always comfortable for their leaders. And while information is being shared faster than it can be contained, the GCC governments are in a state of equilibrium, attempting to balance freedom of information, flow of information and control of information. The various governments in the region have grappled with the loss of authority online, in some cases suggesting that the only way to address false and fraudulent information about their nations on social media is to set up authorities specifically to regulate information on social media channels.

While there is a strong drive by GCC governments to adapt and develop effective e-government programmes, some have been more successful than others. The strong vision of Sheikh Mohammed bin Rashid Al Maktoum, Ruler of Dubai, Vice President and Prime Minister of the UAE, has seen the Dubai Government strongly engaging the public, with 51 per cent of respondents surveyed by Dubai School of Government stating that they use online e-services to access information on offline services, and 29 per cent saying that the internet has facilitated effective interaction with government services.[39] The UAE was noted as an e-government leader in a world e-government rankings survey, advancing 21 positions to the ranking of 28th globally and 5th in Asia. The rapid progress of the United Arab Emirates highlights how effective e-government can help support development. With double the population and three quarters of the GDP per capita, the United Arab Emirates has achieved around the same level of online services as those offered in Norway, a global leader in 8th position.[40]

Saudi ministers and officials are also gradually embracing new media platforms. Saudi Minister of Culture and Information, Abdulaziz Khoja, has more than 65,000 Twitter followers, and he keeps them continuously updated with general and sometimes personal observations about his daily activities. But although social media use is starting to grow among regional leaders, its adoption remains the exception to the rule and use of the technology has been largely haphazard.

Saudi Arabia and Qatar have both undertaken to expand citizen-centric services, as reflected in their notable performance in the 2012 United Nations e-Government Survey, which raising their global rankings to 41st and 48th respectively.[41] The principle goals of the Saudi Arabian e-government offerings are to increase the productivity and efficiency of the public sector, boost the return on investment in ICT and provide easy-to-use, timely and accurate services.

Qatar has also taken steps to ensure its presence online by creating an independent telecommunications regulator, ictQATAR, in 2004. ictQATAR's entry into the world of social media began in 2008, when it set up a Facebook page and began to use YouTube. It also became one of the first government entities in Qatar to have a presence on major international sites such as Flickr – as well as the Arabic forums. By mid-2010, ictQATAR had a presence on 19 regional or international social media sites. The organisation effectively serves as the custodian for technology in Qatar, its mandate being to increase awareness of the organisation in Qatar, reach citizens, and establish a platform for feedback and to engage in a dialogue.[42]

A noteworthy development in the Saudi e-services is the e-Dashboard portal, which verifies the identity of the citizen and serves as a single sign-on portal where citizens can access all services provided. The Saudi government also offers an Open Data Initiative (ODI), which provides citizens with documents and reports from ministries and government agencies, all publicly available. It encourages e-participation to gather public opinion through surveys, public consultations and blogs.

The United Arab Emirates and Bahrain rank 28th and 36th respectively in the 2012 global e-government development index.[43] The UAE has taken significant steps at the federal level to ensure that it is at the forefront of engaging with the citizens, communicating with clients and the public, and engaging them in delivering government programmes and services. In 2011, the Emirates e-Government, in collaboration with Dubai School of Government, produced a policy document entitled *Guidelines for Social Media Usage in United Arab Emirates Government Entities*[44] for government entities to leverage the benefits of social media and avoid their potential risks and threats. However, a report by Tahseen Consulting showed that the social media presence of major UAE government entities was still poor in terms of volume of active output.[45]

Virtual State/Social Media, Surveillance and Social Control

The recent turmoil in many parts of the Arab world has illustrated the power of a free flow of information. Residents throughout the region circumvented state control of media via new social technologies such as Facebook, Twitter and YouTube. The effects have been well documented and continue to progress. The lack of free media in the Middle East helped exacerbate the region's problems. While not without its drawbacks, a society with a free and active press might benefit from the news media's scrutiny. A free press can ask questions about problems in a society such as corruption, discrimination and a lack of jobs. With free and open debate, these issues can be addressed and alleviated. In many countries – including most Arab nations – the heavy hand of state media control blocks this important duty of the news media.

Had information flowed more freely prior to the 'Arab Spring', some of the unrest might have been avoided. More than any other part of the Arab world, the GCC countries illustrate the approach of advocating state control of media. To varying degrees in these countries, the state exercises tight control over the media. These governments generally value the cohesiveness and accord of society more than any potential benefits of a free press. Their governmental systems – hereditary monarchies rather than elected leaders – also lend themselves to this type of media control in which certain *redlines* are not to be crossed.

However, with the unrelenting advance of technology and communication, the days of simply 'controlling the message' appear to be disappearing. Governments will not be able to stop the trend toward increased flow of information, but they may be able to choose how best to respond to the new environment. In the 'Arab Spring' era, Qatar is the only GCC nation that has issued a proposal to change its media laws to create more freedom for journalists. Saudi Arabia and Oman have made changes to control their press and digital platforms more tightly. Bahrain has announced plans to change its laws to improve freedom for journalists but has also indicated signs of tighter control. The UAE and Kuwait have taken actions to restrict freedom of expression but have made no firm legal moves in one direction or the other.[46]

In Kuwait, where criticism of the Emir is illegal, the authorities have cracked down on opposition activities on Twitter and other social media platforms, resulting in multiple arrests and prison sentences over recent years. In March 2013, Kuwaiti opposition activist and former parliament member Hamad al-Khalidi was sentenced to two years in prison for insulting the Emir on Twitter.[47] In a similar vein, in November 2012, revisions to the UAE cybercrime law left activists and general internet users liable to imprisonment for posting content that is deemed to have endangered state security, criticised the nation and its leaders, or insulted Islam or other religions.[48] In 2013, activist Abdullah al-Hadidi was sentenced to 10 months in prison for spreading information on Twitter 'in bad faith'. Al-Hadidi was the first activist to be convicted under the new cybercrime law. When he was detained, he was covering the trial of 94 people – including his own father – who were accused of plotting to overthrow the regime.[49]

Over 20 online activists and bloggers were detained in Bahrain, following the March 2011 crackdown on protests, after calling for political reform on Twitter. And after the government introduced stricter penalties for insulting the King or national symbols, six activists were sentenced to a year in prison in May 2013 for insulting the monarch on Twitter. The six were charged by Bahrain's lower criminal court with 'misusing the right of free expression'.[50]

As the number of Saudi Twitter users grows, the government is reportedly exploring ways to end anonymous use of the service. In March 2013, a spokesperson for the Interior Ministry described the platform as a tool for stirring social unrest, and in May 2013 the leader of Saudi Arabia's religious police condemned users of social media, especially Twitter, on religious grounds. The regime regularly targets Twitter users who challenge state authority or social and religious norms. In September 2012, Bader Thawab was arrested and put on trial for using social media to disturb national unity after tweeting 'down with the House of Saud'.[51] Many Gulf governments view social media as a threat, approaching them as a danger to be restrained and using them as a pretext for taking action against dissenters.[52]

Digital Dystopia

The overriding fear amongst governments in the region is that the internet will be the new primary source of information. Where government agencies once dictated which information was available in the public domain, the internet and, specifically, social media have become the primary source of information. A survey of 22 Arab nations, by the Mohammed bin Rashid School of Government, found that 36 per cent of respondents used the internet as their primary source of news.[53] Dealing with rumours or facts, with stories ranging from the dates of public holidays to the spread of public health information (as in the case of Middle East Respiratory Syndrome),[54] the internet has become the most utilised and fastest way of obtaining and spreading information. In a region where tight control of the population is seen as paramount for ensuring national security, the perceived threat is obvious.

Internet Censorship: The Line that Cannot be Defined

The media laws vary from country to country, but one aspect that is undeniably common to all six GCC nations is the speed with which media laws are being developed and tightened. In fact, the laws are evolving at such a fast pace that the general population is often oblivious to where the law stands. Cases where individuals have filmed and uploaded videos to social media sites such as YouTube and Facebook, only to then be arrested for breaking cybercrime laws, have brought to the forefront the total lack of awareness and understanding of media laws. Internet censorship is a prevalent practice that is duly implemented by telecommunication operators across all GCC countries. It is noteworthy that all major telecommunication providers are either majority- or fully-owned government entities.

Public life in the GCC states is regulated by restrictive laws on media, public assembly, the formation of civil groups, and political participation. Social media provide the opportunity for virtual social interaction and expression by Gulf residents that is limited outside the home. However, like others around the globe, Gulf nationals primarily use social media for a mixture of entertainment and information-seeking and sharing. The most popular political content reveals interests in reforming policies rather than in radical change. One of the most tweeted hashtags in Saudi Arabia recently (The salary is not enough), triggering 17 million tweets in a matter of weeks and becoming the 16th most popular Twitter trend in any language, called attention to the Kingdom's poor and demanded that the government raise Saudi purchasing power via higher public sector salaries.[55]

Not surprisingly, social media platforms are viewed with mistrust by governments because they are extremely difficult to control. As a consequence, governments in the Gulf have acted aggressively to arrest and jail those seen as threats on multiple occasions. While most of these arrests have had a political nature, other bloggers and tweeters have been arrested on charges of insulting Islam. But this may have a political angle to it as well: A Shi'i Muslim was arrested in Bahrain having been accused of slandering the Prophet Muhammad's wives in a forum in retaliation for Sunni attacks on Shi'i,[56] while a Saudi tweeted what were regarded as blasphemous remarks against the Prophet Muhammad – the Saudi fled the country but was extradited from Malaysia and detained amid calls for his execution.[57] A Kuwaiti received a 10-year jail sentence for insulting the Prophet Muhammad and criticising the rulers of Saudi Arabia and Bahrain. Kuwait has also applied legal charges for challenges expressed on social media: A Kuwait University professor was detained on charges of using a Twitter account to slander the Emir, while a distant member of the ruling family was arrested for tweeting offensive political views. In Oman, six people were convicted in September 2012 of slander and of violation of the 'information technology' law, and were sentenced to jail terms of one and a half years as well as being fined 1,000 Omani riyals.[58]

In the UAE, people spreading what is regarded as false information on the internet are often warned by public officials that such an act is considered a criminal offence under the UAE laws, especially if it causes public panic; Article 29 of the Federal Legal Decree No. 5 for 2012 states that those proven guilty face imprisonment and a civil fine of up to Dh1 million.[59] The laws are used to deter people from spreading reports or untruthful information on social media and the internet.[60]

Conclusion

While technology has undoubtedly given more and more individuals a voice, it is still the people who drive actual change. Approximately one third of the citizenry in Bahrain, Oman, and Qatar, and one quarter in Kuwait and the UAE, are between the ages of 15 and 29.[61] Young Gulf activists tend to pursue political agendas that are more far-reaching than those of traditional opposition elements and older generations. Yet they generally call for legislative, judicial and other structural reforms rather than all-out revolution. Technology is not an autonomous power that can inherently be used to accomplish a democratic state, or even drive legislation. In fact, historically, there is evidence that technologies have usually been shaped and used by those in power to maintain their positions of power. A question that therefore arises is whether new information communication technology platforms, such as social media, are actually any different from this; have they indeed created a new information age where existing structures and political processes can be fundamentally changed?

While some governments may believe that the monitoring of social media will enable them to control the citizens' cultural and social orientations, in turn controlling their political positioning, they are likely to find that the counter-effect of the explosion in the dissemination of information will be the outcome. Hence, it can be said that achieving effective online regulation depends on the flexibility of these governments and the margin of freedom they are willing to allow.

In short, social media have to a certain extent changed social and political interaction in the Gulf, just as it has changed around the world. The region's citizens and residents have much more freedom to talk about issues online. The Gulf's governments and their business interests have also become adept at using social media to promote their own messaging and market themselves, to somewhat limited effect in the case of governmental agencies. The region's citizens are aware that even online they are being monitored and most of them will tread carefully about what they say and how they say it. Others will go online anonymously.[62]

For governments, social media have become a statement source on societal pressures, and the message to nationals is clear – talk about whatever you want but do not criticise. Examples have been made of those who do. However, while the governments have the ability to cut off social media and even close access to some parts of the internet, it is unlikely that any government in the GCC will go as far as to ban social media channels. Creating viable civil societies in the GCC cannot be accomplished by social media alone. The ability to successfully navigate social transitions will rely on other players from the citizenry and governments, and the region's populations will need to become more open and vocal about their online rights.

Resistance to change and lack of digital knowledge, along with the cultural norms, all add to the different barriers the GCC countries will continue to face. However, as education starts to play a vital role in many of these countries, there will be more and more people who are educated about the digital media channels available to them.

Notes

1 Jane Kinninmont, 'To What Extent Is Twitter Changing Gulf Societies', *Chatham House*, 2013 <http://www.chathamhouse.org/publications/papers/view/189413>; Nadine Abdalla, 'Social Protests in Egypt before and after the

25 January Revolution: Perspectives on the Evolution of Their Forms and Features', *Dossier*, 2012 <http://www.iemed.org/observatori-en/arees-danalisi/arxius-adjunts/anuari/med.2012/abdalla_en.pdf>; James Canton, *Managing the Game-Changing Trends That Will Transform Your World* (Boston, MA: Da Capo Press, 2015); Fadi Salem, Racha Mourtade and Sara Alshaer, 'The Arab World Online (2014): Trends in Internet and Mobile Usage in the Arab Region', *Arab Social Media Report* (Dubai, 2014) <http://www.mbrsg.ae/getattachment/ff70c2c5-0fce-405d-b23f-93c198d4ca44/The-Arab-World-Online- 2014-Trends-in-Internet-and.aspx>.

2 Sean Aday and others, *New Media and Conflict after the Arab Spring* (Washington, DC: United States Institute of Peace, 2012).

3 Brahima Sanou, 'ITU World Telecommunication /ICT Indicators Database. ICT Facts and Figures', *ITU*, 2013 <https://www.itu.int/en/ITU-D/Statistics/Documents/facts/ICTFactsFigures2014-e.pdf>.

4 See, <http://www2.uncp.edu/home/acurtis/NewMedia/SocialMedia/SocialMedia History.html>.

5 Abdalla.

6 Marc Owen Jones, 'Putting a Price Tag on Repression', *Your Middle East*, 2012 <http://www.yourmiddleeast.com/opinion/marc-owen-jones-putting-a-price-tag-on-repression_14547>.

7 Silvia Colombo, 'The GCC Countries and the Arab Spring: Between Outreach, Patronage and Repression', in *Paper prepared for the Istituto Affari Internazionali* (Rome, Italy, 2012).

8 Sarah Joseph, 'Social Media, Political Change, and Human Rights', *Boston College International & Comparative Law Review*, 35 (2012), 145–188 <http://lawdigitalcommons.bc.edu/cgi/viewcontent.cgi?article=1667&context=iclr>.

9 Clay Shirky, 'The Political Power of Social Media', *Foreign Affairs*, 2011 <http://www.foreignaffairs.com/articles/67038/clay-shirky/the-political-power-of-social-media>.

10 Priyanka Singh and Yagya Dwivedi, 'Social Media and Awareness in Global Society', *International Journal of Humanities & Social Sciences*, 1 (2013), 48–56<http://www.academia.edu/4243682/social_media_and_awareness_in_global_society>.

11 Cited from: The Cooperation Council for the Arab State of the Gulf: Secretariat General, <http://www.gcc-sg.org/eng/index895b.html?action=Sec-Show&ID=3>.

12 Cited from: The Cooperation Council for the Arab State of the Gulf: Secretariat General, <http://sites.gcc-sg.org/Statistics/>.

13 Everette Dennis, Justin Martin and Robb Wood, 'Media Use in the Middle East: An Eight-Nation Survey', 2013 <http://menamediasurvey.northwestern.edu/>.

14 Ipsos, 'Online Audience Measurement in the Arab World', *Ipsos MediaCT*, 2013 <http://fac.ksu.edu.sa/sites/default/files/online-audience-measurement.pdf>.

15 Fadi Salem and Racha Mourtada, ‘Social Media in the Arab World: Influencing Societal and Cultural Change’, *Arab Social Media Report*, 2012 <www.arabsocialmediareport.com/userManagement/PDFD/ASMR 4 updated 29 08 12>.

16 Markaz Research, ‘Kuwait Financial Centre Markaz Research’, *Markaz* <http://www.bloomberg.com/research/stocks/private/snapshot.asp?privcapId=40384263>.

17 Ali Al-Khouri, ‘Population Growth and Government Modernisation Efforts. The Case of GCC Countries’, *IRACST- International Journal of Research in Management & Technology*, 2 (2012) <file:///C:/Users/AVSGuest/Downloads/Population Growth and Government Modernisation Efforts.pdf>.

18 Open Net Initative, ‘Internet Filtering in Bahrain’, *OpenNet Initative*, 2009 <https://opennet.net/countries/bahrain>.

19 Freedom House, ‘Freedom on the Net: Bahrain’, 2011.

20 Natalija Gelvanovska, Michel Rogy and Carlo Rossotto, ‘Broadband Networks in the Middle East and North Africa, Accelerating High-Speed Internet Access’, *The World Bank*, 2014 <http://www.worldbank.org/en/region/mena/publication/broadband-networks-in-mna>.

21 UNESCO, ‘Adult and Youth Literacy: National, Regional and Global Trends, 1985–2015’, *UNESCO*, 2013 <http://www.uis.unesco.org/Education/Documents/literacy-statistics-trends-1985–2015.pdf>.

22 Fadi Salem and Racha Mourtade, ‘Citizen Engagement and Public Services in the Arab World; The Potential of Social Media’, *Arab Social Media Report*, 2014 <http://www.mbrsg.ae/getattachment/e9ea2ac8-13dd-4cd7-9104-b8f1f405cab3/Citizen-Engagement-and-Public-Services-in-the-Arab.aspx>.

23 Freedom House, ‘Freedom on the Net: Bahrain.’

24 Index on Censorship, ‘Bahrain: Government Orders over 1,000 Websites Blocked’, 2009 <http://www.indexoncensorship.org/2009/09/bahrain-government-orders-over-1000-websites-blocked/>.

25 Maryam Fahad, *Arab Media Outlook*, 2011.

26 Federal Decree – Law No. 5 of 2012 on Combating Cybercrimes.

27 Benat Osorio, Soumitra Dutta and Brunov Lanvin, ‘The Networked Readiness Index 2013, Benchmarking ICT Uptake and Support for Growth and Jobs in a Hyperconnected World’, *World Economic Forum*, 2013 <http://www.searo.who.int/entity/health_situation_trends/country_profiles/e_health/wef_gitr_2013_nri_structure.pdf>.

28 Kuwait Government Online, ‘Customs and Traditions in Kuwait’, 2015 <doi:2015-03-26>.

29 Freedom House, ‘Freedom in the World: Kuwait’, 2013 <https://freedomhouse.org/report/freedom-world/2013/kuwait#.VRk4hvnF-Sp>.

30 Dennis, Martin and Wood.

31 Ibid.

32 Ibid.

33 Reporters without Borders, '#Free Austin Tice', 2013 <http://en.rsf.org/press-freedom-index-2013,1054.html>.

34 Internet World State, 'Oman', 2012 <http://go.hrw.com/atlas/norm_htm/oman.htm>.

35 Oxford Business Group, 'The Report: Oman', 2014 <http://www.oxfordbusinessgroup.com/oman-2014>.

36 Gelvanovska, Rogy and Rossotto.

37 Sanou.

38 Salem and Mourtada.

39 Salem, Mourtade and Alshaer.

40 United Nations, 'United Nations E-Government Survey 2012: E-Government for the People', *United Nations Department of Economic and Social Affairs*, 2012 <http://www.un.org/en/development/desa/publications/connecting-governments-to-citizens.html>.

41 United Nations.

42 ictQATAR, 'Creating a Strategic Presence on Social Media. Supreme Council of Communication Technology', *ictQATAR*, 2011 <http://www.ictqatar.qa/en>.

43 United Nations.

44 Ibrahim Elbadawi, 'Guidelines for Social Media Usage in United Arab Emirates Government Entities', *Emirates e-Government*, 2012 <http://www.fahr.gov.ae/Portal/Userfiles/Assets/Documents/884dd373.pdf>.

45 Wesley Schwalje and Walid Aradi, 'An Arab Open Government Maturity Model for Social Media Engagement', *Tahseen Consulting*, 2013 <http://www.tahseen.ae/an arab open government maturity model for social media engagement.pdf>.

46 Matt Duffy, 'Media Laws and Regulations of the GCC Countries: Summary, Analysis and Recommendations', *Doha Centre for Media Freedom*, 2013 <http://www.dc4mf.org/sites/default/files/gcc_media_law_en_0.pdf>.

47 Gulf News, 'Kuwait: Kuwait Tweeter Jailed for Emir Insult: Opposition's Hamad Al Khalidi Sentenced to 2 Years', *Gulf News*, 30 March 2015 <http://gulfnews.com/news/gulf/kuwait/kuwait-tweeter-jailed-for-emir-insult-opposition-s-hamad-al-khalidi-sentenced-to-2-years-1.1164979>.

48 <http://incelaw.com/ourknowledge/publications/new-cyber-crimes-legislation>.

49 Gulf Center for Human Rights, 'UAE- Human Rights Defender Abdullah Al-Hadidi Released after 10 Months in Jail', *Gulf Center for Human Rights*, 2013 <http://gc4hr.org/news/view/516>.

50 Al-Jazeera.net, 'Bahrain Sentences Twitter Users to Prison', 2013 <http://www.aljazeera.com/news/middleeast/2013/05/201351512272986561l.html>.

51 Global Vocies Online, 'Saudi Charged for "down with the House of Saud" Tweet', 2013 <http://globalvoicesonline.org/2013/02/16/saudi-twitter-user-arrested-accused-of-following-tempters/?utm_source=twitterfeed&utm_medium=twitter>.

52 Lori Boghardt, 'Saudi Arabia's War on Twitter', *The Washington Institute*, 2013 <https://www.washingtoninstitute.org/policy-analysis/view/saudi-arabias-war-on-twitter>.

53 Salem, Mourtade and Alshaer.

54 Saad Al-Dosary, 'MERS: Social Media Responsible for False Info', *Arab News*, 2014 <http://www.arabnews.com/news/559246>.

55 Boghardt.

56 Rebecca Di Leonardo, 'Bahrain Court Jails Man for Insulting Wife of Prophet Muhammad', *JURIST*, 2012 <http://jurist.org/paperchase/2012/08/bahrain-court-jails-man-for-insulting-wife-of-prophet-muhammad.php>.

57 Kate Hodal, 'Malaysia Deports Saudi Journalist Accused of Insulting Prophet', *Guardian*, 13 February 2012 <http://www.theguardian.com/world/2012/feb/12/malaysia-deports-saudi-journalist-prophet>.

58 Reuters, 'Oman Jails Six Men for Internet Slander: Activist', 2012 <http://www.reuters.com/article/2012/09/10/us-oman-court-idUSBRE8890KT20120910>.

59 1 United Arab Emirates Dirham equals 0.27 US Dollar.

60 *Gulf News*, 'Rumour-Mongers Causing Public Panic Will Be Prosecuted, Authorities Warn. Gulf News', 2014 <http://gulfnews.com/news/gulf/uae/crime/rumour-mongers-causing-public-panic-will-be-prosecuted-authorities-warn-1.1332562>.

61 Boghardt.

62 Nick Higham, 'BBC Poll: Web Brings More Freedom and More Surveillance', *Magazine*, 2014 <http://www.bbc.com/news/magazine-26824802>.

11

The Future of Social Media in the GCC Region

Mokhtar Elareshi and Barrie Gunter

This book has presented a series of original studies that examined the use of internet and social media sites in the Gulf region since the 2011 'Arab Spring'. These studies have adopted a range of approaches to investigate how platforms such as Facebook and Twitter have been adopted and utilised by special interest groups, the general public, governments and their agencies, and the established mass media. Social media sites have emerged in the Gulf States as well as elsewhere in the Arab world as channels for personal communications, tools for political activists, and alternative news platforms. While social media have in many ways empowered ordinary citizens, they have also become tools of the authorities. Governments can and do use them as surveillance mechanisms to monitor the current status of political opinion about their policies and actions. The established news media use them as new communications channels to reach their audiences. It is reasonable to conclude that social media have begun to transform communications networks in this region, albeit not yet to the level that they have done in other parts of the world.

Much has been made of the role played by social media in relation to recent political uprisings that have occurred across the Arab world. Claims have been made by some observers that blogging, microblogging, and online social networking played critical roles in facilitating political activism. There is ample evidence that these online tools played a part in enabling activists to communicate with each other and with the outside world about the events in which they were engaged. The extent to which the outcomes of these political changes – which varied from one Arab nation to the next – would have occurred without these digital instruments is less clear. Claims that social media were critical components of these political processes have had a mixed response. Yet, as the studies reported in this book have indicated, social media platforms have enabled some disenfranchised sectors of Arab societies to gain a voice they had previously lacked.

This book has highlighted the fact that social media sites were used during the events of the 'Arab Spring' to spread news and information among people. Such applications have prevailed ever since. As internet penetration has spread across Arab societies, more and more of their citizens have turned to online sources for news and information. As the most enthusiastic adopters of new digital technologies, young people have become especially enamoured of these new information sources. In some Arab countries, most notably Kuwait, social media have been adopted by women as channels through which their interests can be promoted. Social media have also been used in attempts to bring together disconnected Arab communities in a spirit of unity.

Evidence emerged in this book that social media such Facebook and Twitter are more likely to have been a factor in the first day of mass protests in Egypt in early 2011. Philip Howard and his colleagues examined the subversive use to which social media were put and pointed out how authoritarian regimes, such as that in Bahrain, harnessed social media for the purpose of surveillance while their opponents practised sousveillance, such as uploading videos of police brutality, as discussed in Chapter 9.[1] In this regard, social media have been favoured by participants in and supporters of different political, social and activist movements – in the case of Bahrain again. For example, Melisssa Wall and Sahar El Zahed[2] pointed to the use of YouTube as a new platform for politics and citizens because of its 'visual and intensely intimate' nature. This revolution in the use of new technology purportedly unfolds in the realm of the imagination because it gives people free minds to contemplate these matters.

This book also clearly indicates that, following the 2011 uprisings, the GCC region has witnessed transformational changes ranging from political *openness* to economic booms, which seem to conflict with the opposition to current government strategies and decisions, as discussed in Chapter 10.[3] Some Arab citizens have used social media as one of a range of communication tools to challenge established authorities in relation to the free flow of information, their own political and social rights, economic inequalities, and the prevailing forms of government.

Concerns about the free flow of information have undoubtedly underpinned the growing popularity of pan-Arab news services. A general feeling that government-controlled news services provide a narrow and selective news agenda as compared with non-Arab international news agencies that have become increasingly visible in this region has led to pressures on national Arab governments to relax controls over news provisions. Research reported in Chapters 5 and 8 illustrated how new sources of news have been adopted and represent both challenges to and opportunities for the established news providers in Arab countries. Young people welcome news through online sources. Equally, they have a strong appetite for news from more traditional media, especially television. However, their news appetites are satisfied better by new news suppliers than by old ones. There is another empowerment aspect to online information flows; i.e. citizens can become both news *consumers* and news *producers*.

In the last few years, news information has been produced not only by the news media industry but also by ordinary people who have taken the lead and become known as citizen journalists. This application of online media was promoted by their utility to political activists during the periods of political unrest from 2011. The focus of news produced by ordinary people here centred on political, socio-cultural and everyday life. These developments have affected the established news industry in the Arab world and have motivated the main providers to modify their news practices and the news agenda they produce.

The growth of social media use, not simply within the frame of orchestrated political activism, but more widely among ordinary people, presents a source of tension and concern for governments in the Gulf region. The reason for this is simple. If people begin sharing political, economic and social ideas among themselves interpersonally on a large scale, this form of communication may prove to be a powerful source of reflection on existing social and political values and beliefs. This phenomenon, in turn, could result in wide-ranging societal pressures for change in the way these countries are governed. For this reason, the region's governments have increased their own involvement in online media both as sources of information and as surveillance. The people may use social media to question their government. At the same time, governments can use these media to monitor and control their citizens. It is necessary for a new form of political and social discourse to emerge between governments and governed that is capable of promoting constructive outcomes beneficial to all.

Young Arab people are increasingly demanding a greater share of power in relation to how their societies operate. In some countries, governments have responded quite positively to such pressure. The emergence of dialogue concessionary to disparate viewpoints is critical if outcomes satisfactory to all parties are to be achieved. For instance, in Saudi Arabia the major confrontation between the rulers and authorities, religious institutions and their leaders, and civil and political activists has been reduced when citizens call for limited reforms rather than wholesale regime change. Kuwait has a relatively open political system compared to other Arab Gulf States, as it is the only semi-constitutional monarchy, and here youth groups and women have been calling for a constitutional monarchy with extended powers for the legislature.

Political Activism

The position in Saudi Arabia was examined in Chapter 2 where Chaudhary discussed the role of social media in the context of pro-democracy lobbies. Any suggestion here that these movements sought or might have hoped to achieve major political reconstruction was over-optimistic and indeed unrealistic given the current status of the country's mode of governance and the major concerns of its citizens. A Western-style democracy is unlikely to make a good fit for the Kingdom, although some concessions relating to information sources and flows and equalisation of rights and opportunities for different segments of the population would be welcomed by the people and could be accommodated safely by government. Pressures for social reform pre-date the internet era, however, and cannot be traced to the door of social media.

In the early 1990s, the Saudi realm witnessed political activism which, although not fundamentally questioning the Islamic foundation of the royal family, *did* push for change in political practices. The House of Saud has continued to control public order by countering dissent, political challenges and any questioning of its authority. Theoretically, Islam has been declared to be incompatible with democracy although further analysis to verify this mutual exclusivity is still required. Following the 'Arab Spring', there remains ambiguity over whether there is a common form of democracy that would fit comfortably within specific Arab communities.

In Saudi Arabia, there are several distinct identities such as ethnicity, nationality and ideologies that need to be questioned in order to achieve transformations. Within this region, religious identity is as important as political identity. Finding a new identity that fits political aspirations while not conflicting with a more immutable religious identity remains a major challenge. Although it may in theory be possible to conceive of political structures that might be created to promote democracy, it remains doubtful whether the processes to which they give rise would be consonant with dominant religious values and expectations.

Chaudhary concluded that social media have encouraged the creation and acceptance of identities that could produce some political and cultural transformation in Saudi Arabia. In support of this argument, the regime has indeed changed following the Arab uprisings in 2011. Where it has accommodated political and social change, however, this has not amounted to the wholesale importation of Western-style democracy. Many online Saudis believe that social media have played a vital role in their empowerment. They feel they are more connected to their communities via the social media sites. However, the realm remained quiet in terms of dissent and protests during the 2011 uprising, as the analysis by Khalid Al-Tawil and Daniel Drezner indicated.[4] Furthermore, the Saudi government has also used social media to spread its ideological perspective, mainly Wahhabism, on many issues and to override any dissenting ideological voices.

The analysis presented in Chapter 3 by Omair Anas looked at the how Arab social media were used to move from revolutionary euphoria to cyber-realism and how this affected the relationship between citizens and their Arab governments. Social media, in this context, are understood as a message. Social media are characterised in part in terms of their user-generated content. Yet, governments, their agencies and large corporate interests have also established a considerable presence in this environment. This phenomenon therefore asks questions about the true salience of the voices of ordinary people in social media settings. Social media can be as useful to the powerful as to the powerless. Governing regimes in the Arab world monitor social media activities and can enact legislation to restrict the way these platforms might be used. As such, the social media become an extension of state policing. Knowledge of such activities can by itself be sufficient to discourage ordinary citizens from voicing their true thoughts and feelings online.

The way in which governments can take control of social media to ensure that extant political systems are reinforced has been illustrated well by the case of Bahrain. This was discussed in Chapter 4 by Marc Owen Jones who examined the potential problems posed by social media to diplomacy in Bahrain and how the Bahraini government attempted to utilise social media to influence the nature of public political debate. During the early days of the Bahrain uprising of 2011, social media were used and exploited to underpin the ethically diplomatic strategies. It seems that the Bahrain government has interfered in the social media scope and militated against ethical peer-to-peer diplomacy. Despite the rise of social media and the opportunities for ethical P2P diplomacy, the Bahraini government and its allies have been able to engage in a form of P2P diplomacy that remains focused on cultivating Bahrain's image as modern, liberal and finance-friendly in the Middle East.

In a state with a government widely perceived by many of its inhabitants to be illegitimate, diplomatic efforts undertaken by the state bring with them their own questions of legitimacy. If a country's own unelected ministries, dominated by members of the ruling family, cannot be said to have a mandate to conduct international relations on behalf of a willing population, then the actual line between unofficial and official acts of diplomacy become increasingly nebulous. However, the government has a disproportionate amount of resources compared to those opposing internal forces typically advocating social justice, and this allows it to distort the information continuum in its favour through the use of PR, P2P diplomacy and reputation management strategies. Given Bahrain's inability to be entirely autonomous in its foreign policy, policy objectives are subordinated to the ambitions of powers such as the US, whose relationship with the conservative Saudi regime stymies the emergence of democracy in the region.

Opening Up News Sources

The opening up of information flows through the internet and other digital communications technology developments in the Arab world has inevitably created fresh appetites, especially for news, that can be difficult for national Arab governments to deny. Increasingly, research evidence has emerged to show that new, information-bearing media are being adopted with great enthusiasm, especially by younger members of Arab populations. This phenomenon is illustrated by Abdul-Karim Ziani and Mokhtar Elareshi in Chapter 5. They trace the development of the use of mobile phones as a new platform for gathering a wide range of information about local communities. Young people in the Arab world emerged as the most enthusiastic adopters of technology in the region, especially in their use of mobile phones. Arab people use mobile phones for communication, information and entertainment purposes. Use of new advanced technology linked to 4G and Wi-Fi equipment has triggered high demand for more varied and high-quality content. Mobile phones, as increasingly popular points of transactions, have brought social and economic benefits to local citizens' lives. Mobile phones have also benefited national economies by promoting pan-Arab and global business. Their popularity among ordinary people as interfaces for the internet and social media sites has also generated a growing appetite among users for fresh news sources and agendas.

Against this background, Ziani and Elareshi presented the findings of a detailed study of mobile phone and internet news usage in the GCC region. They revealed that young Arabs retain an appetite for consuming news and now use their smart technology devices to do so. This study showed that young Arabs engage with local as well as international news but often seek to become more active in the news production and commentary processes. The widespread use of the transactional capabilities of mobile devices also meant that the technology further promoted local economies by creating new channels through which businesses and their customers can interact.

In Chapter 8, Elareshi and Al-Jaber provide further evidence about the use of new media for news and the impact of this phenomenon on the use of longer-established news media sources. Their evidence derived from surveys of news consumers across Bahrain, Qatar and Saudi Arabia. The authors found that people in these states derived their news from multiple platforms. The internet and social media have influenced news consumption habits, however. For some people the older news media have been displaced by new news sources online. Traditional media such as television have not been abandoned, but patronage has switched to new suppliers on broadcast platforms. International pan-Arab stations have become popular and many of these are also very active online.

The study also found that citizens of Gulf States were satisfied with their news media, and most of them indicated that the overall quality of news reporting in their countries had improved. There are indications that a more diversified range of suppliers and a more competitive news market have sharpened news production practices and generated better-looking presentation formats and more substantive reports.

Equality Issues

In a further analysis of social media and mobile technologies, Bulla and Buie reported in Chapter 6 that UAE citizens welcome these devices for a host of personal, social and transactional reasons. The UAE is recognised as one of the world's most advanced nations as far as technology is concerned. Mobile phones are a significant personal apparatus in the regime. Sheikhs, citizens and expat workers alike all use social media to communicate with others and to link to the wider world. One other significant development has been the enthusiastic use of social media by the country's leaders to reach out with personal messages to their citizens. Local citizens can in turn stay in touch with their leaders by following them on Twitter or Facebook.

Bulla and Buie also looked at the UAE's broad cyber-crime law, its definition, and how this law has been applied in specific cases. The authors described how people in the Emirates use multiple mobile technologies for different purposes. While some social media sites are significant in the news-gathering context, others are used mainly for person-to-person communications. In a sense, such diverse applications indicate a social construction approach to new media use, with online technologies and applications being adapted for specific social purposes to which local users deem them best suited.

It has been observed already that social media have been adopted by specific interest groups in the Arab world in order to further their own specific political, social or cultural agendas. In a world that has not been characterised by gender equality, women have become increasingly active users of social media to promote specific causes designed to open up social and professional opportunities for their gender. This is the subject covered by Fatima AlSalem in Chapter 7. AlSalem examines Kuwait and situates her initial discussion in the context of the political participation of women in this country. Women's involvement in politics has been a focus of ongoing debate in the Arab world as a whole. The events of the past few years have affected Kuwaiti women's social and political rights, with more women now being permitted to vote, voice their opinions and organise social movements.

The emergence of the internet opened up opportunities for women to engage with news agendas. Traditionally, women in countries such as Kuwait were not major consumers of news via the traditional mass media. Women, especially those who were better educated, began to consume e-newspapers online when they had previously eschewed print versions. As women joined the ranks of news consumers it is perhaps not surprising that their political consciousness was also raised. Their exposure to political debate no doubt also fed their appetites for greater direct involvement in and influence over political processes. Through social media, women also found an environment in which they could more readily communicate with one another about political matters and the affairs that most concerned them. Such interactions enabled them to be better placed to orchestrate their own political movements.

Optimistically, then, the internet has radically changed the way of participating in politics, as it offers a vast amount of information and can create a sense of empowerment and spaces for expression and mobilisation. Accessibility to political information does not always correlate precisely with actual participation and there is a need for further study of the types of political activities in which people engage online. Although oil-rich countries such as Kuwait do not suffer from physical barriers to accessing the internet, which is widely available, there are other cultural barriers to full online inclusion in local political affairs. For example, AlSalem found that women in Kuwait have still been influenced by their families in terms of their abilities to participate in politics. Thus, conventional factors that have restricted women's political involvement remain active. In these settings, men are able to act to limit the extent of women's political engagement. In this context, women have developed many communities of social relationships outside their families. Online social media have facilitated this process. Thus, online social communities have compensated for the lack of local family support for women's public involvement and participation. However, there is still a long way to go before women achieve political parity with men.

Freedom or More Control

In many non-democratic nations around the world, the introduction of the internet has been welcomed with the hope that with it will come a gradual relaxation of government control over the flow of information and the eventual adoption of more democratic processes for electing those who govern. This outcome is not always achieved. In some autocracies, the internet and accompanying social media have been co-opted as additional tools of social control. In Chapter 9, Marc Owen Jones offered another look at the use of social media in this context. His analysis focused on the situation in Bahrain. He examined how social media, in particular Twitter, have assisted the Bahraini government to maintain the traditional hegemony.

Jones found that the Al Khalifa regime has used social media for the purpose of surveillance, spying, censorship and propaganda. Jones placed his initial discussion in the broader context of change experienced across the GCC region, emphasising the use of Twitter as a source of information and communication available potentially to all. He usefully distinguished between the terms 'surveillance' and 'sousveillance' whereby citizens can monitor and reflect upon the actions of their governments while their governments in turn monitor them.

As a result, internet users in Bahrain have been repeatedly targeted by government through legislation and regulation, as well as through more active agencies. For example, cybercafés are strictly regulated and subversive websites are blocked based on Articles 19 and 20 of Bahrain's press rules. Some new media laws appear to legitimise tighter state control over the media. Further, the erosion of trust is a crucial part of the effects of surveillance, and as things stand, pro-democracy activities still face severe difficulties when trying to find spaces for expression. In this sense, social media are no different from the offline world in terms of the freedoms they offer to activists seeking political reforms. Thus, a battle for cyberspace has been fought between the principles of devolved citizen empowerment and centralised control. As such, the social media have become tools of both emancipation and repression.

The capacity of social media to bring about political reforms in the Arab world is broadly reflected upon in Chapter 10, where Samah Ahmed examines the impact of social media in the GCC region. The chapter offers a wide-ranging overview of the communication landscape and policy in the region and how government agencies have adapted to social media. E-government programmes have been successful in the region. For example, the Dubai government is in a unique position to leverage and encourage its citizens to go online for news and information about their region and for social engagement in their communications and service delivery strategies.

It seems that some GCC States have taken substantial steps in adopting and using social media sites. For example, guidelines for using social media by government departments are in place. Young GCC activists are more likely to pursue political agendas via the internet than older opposition elements and older generations. For these governments, social media have become a statement source of societal pressures, and the message to nationals is clear. Again, however, lack of technology, resistance to change, and cultural norms all add to the various barriers the GCC continues to face.

Conclusion

Social media in the Arab world received a great deal of attention due to their purported role in relation to events across the region now widely known as the 'Arab Spring'. Despite claims that social media sites played a crucial part in enabling activists to orchestrate protests and other actions that led, in some Arab nations, to changes of government, others have argued that their role in this context has been overstated. Regardless of whether microblogs such as Twitter and social networks such as Facebook *did* provide the tools for wholesale political change, there is ample evidence that these platforms have become widely used across the Arab world.

Social media sites have grown in use as internet penetration has deepened in this region. These sites are used by ordinary people, political activists, governments and large corporations alike. Their applications are manifold. They have emerged as increasingly important sources of news and information. They represent platforms for political debate. They have, in some Arab countries, facilitated closer contact between rulers and ruled. They also provide tools capable of empowering politically disenfranchised groups.

Social media can represent forces for social change. Their power in this context depends upon the will and skill of their users, however. It is also framed by the regulatory systems imposed by governments on the way such sites are permitted to operate. Acceptance of the messages of online lobbyists seeking political change will often depend upon the nature of the change being sought. In some Arab countries, complete regime changes have been witnessed since 2011. In other Arab countries, however, any such attempts have been rapidly and effectively suppressed. Nonetheless, social media have apparently created a softening of the positions of some regimes in the region, such that they are now more open to lobbying for gradual reform provided that such change does not pose a direct threat to the ruling elites. In a sense this process can be regarded as a willingness to enable a gradual release of pressure for change before it builds to a point where it becomes explosive.

The power of social media derives from the scale of their user bases. The major social media sites, such as Facebook, have subscribers worldwide. Users can link readily to other users, and political messages generated by a single individual can spread rapidly to millions. On this platform it is difficult if not impossible for governments to exercise complete control over the flow of information even from within their own countries. This means that the usual government gatekeeping controls over information are rendered impotent. In his now famous book *The Facebook Effect*, David Kirkpatrick states that 'if we are to consider Facebook as a state it will be the third largest country in the world after China and India' – referring to the number of users. As of January 2011, when the 'Arab Spring' started,

Facebook had more than 600 million active users.[5] Indeed, the impact is much more serious than that. A single page on Facebook, a Tweet, or a video on YouTube could draw worldwide public attention. It should be added that we are only at the beginning of a technological revolution as the internet becomes a universal tool of interactive communication.

Whether they like it or not, Arab governments have had to concede that the world of the online social media has radically altered communication power structures. In response, they have adopted these sites for their own purposes as sources for monitoring public opinion and the activities of those who might seek to depose them. In addition, they have also had to cede some of their centralised control over communications systems and allow a broadening of information agendas. These changes within the Arab world reflect worldwide developments that have occurred in dominant political orders. Democratic systems modelled on Western liberalism have evolved across the planet. In response to this, however, the democratic model has not yet attained complete dominance. Governments in some old autocratic regimes, such as Russia, have tightened their centralised grip on political processes and the flow of information. Others such as China have given an appearance of loosening centralised control but this has been restricted to certain economic systems, while politically the choices for citizens remain limited.

The emergence of the internet and its open communications systems has created a networked world in which individual citizens can link to one another freely. This observation is true in many parts of the world, but not everywhere. There are settings in which physical access to the internet does not mean the same as feeling free to use it without constraint. Autocracies have discovered they can use these information networks as policing tools to monitor the behaviour of their citizens. Awareness of this fact alone can cause restraint among citizens in their use of online communications systems. There are, of course, individuals who will nonetheless seek to defy such government restraints, and the ability of social networks to enable these individuals to reach massive audiences very quickly is not lost on governments – even the most autocratic of regimes.

Two common trends in these processes of political transformation signal a new historic landscape, according to Wesley Longhofer and Daniel Winchester.[6] First, none of them could have taken place without new communication technologies. Thus, while technology is not the cause of the transformation, it is an indispensable facilitator medium. In fact, it is what constitutes the historical novelty of this multidimensional transformation. Second, all these change processes have taken place via massive information networks.

The most important direct impact of information networks on political and social structures concerns the way in which they have changed power relationships. Historically, power was embedded in organisations and institutions, organised around a hierarchy of centres, and in the case of the Arab political system centralised in the hands of the ruling elites. Networks dissolve centres; they disorganise hierarchy and make materially impossible the exercise of hierarchical power without processing instructions in the networks, according to the network morphological rules. Thus, contemporary information networks of capital, production, trade, science, communication, and human and political rights bypass the national state, which, by and large, has ceased to be a sovereign entity.

The traditional, twentieth-century Arab political systems found it hard to grasp or accept these complex settings. As a result, some have already been removed by the tide of revolution; others, awaiting their turn, are still misleadingly talking about national sovereignty, the supremacy of national laws and the right of the state to use excessive force to subdue society. Arrogance, ignorance and the lust for wealth and power have all made it difficult for Arab regimes to understand the multifaceted transformation that began two decades ago. Some still need to understand that the impact of the social media cannot be challenged by bullets, torture or abuse. It is a political phenomenon that ought to be dealt with by political means (power-sharing, more participation and good governance). Gone are the days when rulers could rule with mere force.

The internet, especially via social media sites, has been used as a powerful symbol of the mobilisation of local people, and it has had a powerful influence across the Arab world in the wake of the 2011 uprisings. However, the role of social media is still ambivalent in terms of the technological and temporal context in which they are being used. Evidence presented in this book has indicated that social media in the Arab world can be regulated to fit with current government agendas, but this may not stem the tide of change being orchestrated in online theatres. Democracy is still far away for many parts of the Arab world. Nonetheless, social media provide tools that can be utilised by those who seek political change, at least to gain a louder voice. Gaining government compliance with demands for change, however, will take a long time and is most likely to be achieved through gradual negotiated settlements and concessions that are regarded by all parties as non-threatening.

The acceptance of political change as negotiated via the internet will also depend upon acceptance of the internet itself as a non-threatening environment. Not all online behaviour is responsible. The internet can be a site that enables the production and circulation of content that offends social, political and religious sensibilities, incites violence or threatens personal security. It can also be a site through which public protest can lead to personal harassment, the arrest of those identified as perpetrators, and the temporary closure or summary removal of user services.[7]

There is a demand for greater freedom and expression in the GCC region; for example, in Bahrain the Shi'i opposition has been seeking power-sharing, has complained of sectarian partiality, and has urged the government to address the financial situation. In Oman, the internet has been a site of complaints about rising unemployment, the cost of living and corruption among government officials. Others have called for the ending of the system of 'political apartheid' based on racial and tribal discrimination.

The Bahraini movement in 2012 in Pearl Square or the 'Dignity of a Nation' movement in Kuwait, respectively, reveal a new phase in the modern political communication of GCC countries. It is apparent that social media have provided valuable platforms for the exchange of information and for moderate political mobilisation in the GCC region. Some GGC countries such as Bahrain, Qatar and UAE have embraced online communications because they have sought to attract international investment in their technology systems. They have encouraged citizens to use the internet in this context. Yet, at the same time their governments have acted to block thousands of sites on the internet because they are uncomfortable with their citizens being exposed to them. Often, sites are considered undesirable by the authorities for religious, cultural or political reasons. Sometimes these concerns may have legitimate roots, such as in the case of banning pornographic sites. However, these online restrictions can extend to sites that do not contain inherently harmful content but simply material with which the government disagrees.

These restrictions conflict with the alleged informational openness of the internet. In the Middle East, it means that citizens lack the freedoms of people in other parts of the world to select their own online content. The aim is simple. Governments seek still to control the information diet of their citizens, just as they did with traditional mass media. The problem with this approach is that it may ultimately create more tensions among citizens who naturally expect internet access in order to receive a wider information diet.

Notes

1 Philip N. Howard and others, 'Opening Closed Regimes: What Was the Role of Social Media during the Arab Spring?', *Seattle*: (PIPTI, 2011), pp. 1538–2464 <http://pitpi.org/index.php/2011/09/11/opening-closed-regimes-what-was-the-role-of-social-media-during-the-arab-spring/>.

2 Melisssa Wall and Sahar El Zahed, '"I'll Be Waiting for You Guys": A YouTube Call to Action in the Egyptian Revolution', *International Journal of Communication*, 2011, 1333–1343.

3 Lisa Anderson, 'Demystifying the Arab Spring Parsing the Differences between Tunisia, Egypt, and Libya', *Foreign Affairs*, 90 (2011), 2–7.

4 Khalid Al-Tawil, 'The Internet in Saudi Arabia', *Arab IP Centre*, 2001 <http://www.arabipcentre.com/the-internet-in-saudi-arabia.php>.

5 David Kirkpatrick, *The Facebook Effect: The Real Inside Story of Mark Zuckerberg and the World's Fastest-Growing Company* (London, UK: bookmarque, 2010).

6 Wesley Longhofer and Daniel Winchester, *Social Theory Re-Wired: New Connections to Classical and Contemporary Perspectives* (Oxon: Routledge, 2012), p. 160.

7 Roger Dickinson and Barrie Gunter, 'What Is the Future for News in the Arab World?', in *News Media in the Arab world: A Study of 10 Arab and Muslim Countries*, ed. by Barrie Gunter and Roger Dickinson (London, UK: Bloomsbury, 2013), pp. 173–188.

Bibilography

Abdalla, Nadine, 'Social Protests in Egypt before and after the 25 January Revolution: Perspectives on the Evolution of Their Forms and Features', *Dossier*, 2012 <http://www.iemed.org/observatori-en/arees-danalisi/arxius-adjunts/anuari/med.2012/abdalla_en.pdf>.

Abdallah, Mariam, 'Saudi Arabia: Boycotting Twitter to Save It', *Al-Akhbar-english*, 31 January 2012 <http://english.al-akhbar.com/node/3783>.

Aday, Sean, Henry Farrell, Deen Freelon, Marc Lynch, John Sides, and Michael Dewar, 'Watching from Afar: Media Consumption Patterns around the Arab Spring', *American Behavioral Scientist*, XX (2013), 1–21 <doi:10.1177/0002764213479373>.

Aday, Sean, Henry Farrell, Marc Lynch, John Sides, and Deen Freelon, *New Media and Conflict after the Arab Spring* (Washington, DC: United States Institute of Peace, 2012).

Ahmed, Qanta, 'Saudi Arabia's Struggle with Social Media: Twitter Clowns and Facebook Fatwas', *The Blaze*, 2013 <http://www.theblaze.com/contributions/saudi-arabias-struggles-with-social-media-twitter-clowns-and-facebook-fatwas>.

Ajbaili, Mustapha, 'Egypt TV Presenters Tout Twitter Ban over Anti-Sisi Hashtag', *Al-Arabiya TV News*, 2014 <Egypt-TV-presenters-tout-twitter-ban-over-anti-Sisi-hashtag.html>.

Al-Arabiya TV, 'Egypt TV Presenters Tout Twitter Ban over Anti-Sisi Hashtag', 2014 <http://english.alarabiya.net/en/media/television-and-radio/2014/03/31/Egypt-TV-presenters-tout-twitter-ban-over-anti-Sisi-hashtag.html>.

——'Paralyzed Saudi Pleads for Help on Twitter, Receives Attention and Money', 2014 <http://english.alarabiya.net/en/variety/2014/05/12/Paralyzed-Saudi-pleads-for-help-on-Twitter-receives-attention-and-mon>.

Al Dhaheri, M.S, F. Al Gafli, S. Al Nuaimi, and N. Al Shateri, 'Public Image in the UAE' (Abu Dubai, 2014).

Al-Jazeera, "The Stream-Bahrain Foreign Minister Criticises Al Jazeera Documentary on Twitter." *Youtube*. N. p., 2011. Web. 20 February 2015.

Al-Jazeera.net, 'Egypt State Media Changes Sides', 2011 < http://english.aljazeera.net/news/middleeast/2011/02/201121361556414860.html>.

——'Bahrain Sentences Twitter Users to Prison', *Al-Jazeera.net*, 2013 <http://www.aljazeera.com/news/middleeast/2013/05/2013515122729865611.html>.

——'Egypt's Twitter Hashtags Declare Defiance', 2014 <http://m.aljazeera.com/story/201448154324428189>.

Al Jenaibi, Badreya, 'Use of Social Media in the United Arab Emirates: An Initial Study', *Global Media Journal-Arabian Edition*, 1 (2012), 3–27.

Al Olaimy, Leena, "'Just Bahrain' Not Welcome at Checkpoints." *Mahmood's Den.* N. p., 2011. Web. 5 March 2015.

Alahmad, Safa, 'Reporting Saudi Arabia's Hidden Uprising', *BBC*, 2014 <http://www.bbc.com/news/world-middle-east-27619309>.

Alajimi, Mohammed, *Kuwaiti Women and Political Participation: A Scientific Analysis*. (Beirut, Lebanon: Dar AlJadeed, 2000).

——*Political Participation in Kuwait. A Study of Reality and the Future* (Cairo, Egypt: Aldar Alalamiya, 2009).

Albarran, Alan B., and Arrese Angel Reca, *Time and Media Markets* (Mahwah, NJ: Lawrence Erlbaum Associates, 2003).

Aldweelah, Abeer, 'The Degree of Political Awareness among Kuwaiti Working Women in Higher Education and Its Effect on Students', *Kuwait Center for Research and Studies*, 2009.

Alijla, Abdalhadi, 'Social Networking Sites: Public or Private Sphere', 2014 <http://www.jadaliyya.com/pages/index/16828/arabicl>.

Al-Jaber, Khalid, and Barrie Gunter, 'Evolving News Systems in the Gulf Countries', in *News Media in the Arab World: A Study of 10 Arab and Muslim Countries*, ed. by Barrie Gunter and Roger Dickinson (New York, NY: Bloomsbury, 2013), pp. 21–40.

Aljabre, AbdulAziz, 'Social Networking, Social Movements, and Saudi Arabia A Review of Literature', *ARPN Journal of Science and Technology*, 3 (2013), 161–168.

Al-Khouri, Ali, 'Population Growth and Government Modernisation Efforts: The Case of GCC Countries', *IRACST- International Journal of Research in Management & Technology*, 2 (2012) <file:///C:/Users/AVSGuest/Downloads/Population Growth and Government Modernisation Efforts.pdf>.

Alqabra, S., 'Social Cohesion in Kuwait: From Establishment to the Current Movements in 2011', *Almesbar Studies and Research Center*, 2012, pp. 14–49.

Al-Qaisi, Khulood, 'Mobile-Phone Subscriber's Motivations for Using Mobile System in Jordon' (Unpublished master's dissertation, Jordon University, Jordon, 2000).

Al-Sayegh, Fatima, 'The Impact of Social Media on UAE Society', *The Emirates Center for Strategic Studies and Research*, 2013 <http://www.ecssr.ac.ae/ECSSR/print/ft.jsp?lang=en&ftId=/FeatureTopic/Fatma-AlSayegh/FeatureTopic_1698.xml>.

AlShayji, Abdulla, 'Kuwait: A Democratic Model in Trouble. Carnegie Endowment for International Peace. Analysis on Arab Reform', *Carnegie Endowment for International Peace*, 2009 <http://carnegieendowment.org/2009/02/03/kuwait-democratic-model-in-trouble/f9l5>.

Bibilography

Alturki, Lisa, 'Arab Women in the Nineteen-Twenties Presence and Identity', *Beirut: AlWihda AlArabiya Study Center*, 2010.

Anas, Omair, 'Changing Profile of Media in the Arab States', *Global Media Journal*, 2 (2013), 28–46.

Anas, Omair, 'Facebook Campaigns in the Arab Uprisings: The Role of "Kulluna Khaled Said"', in *The Arab World: The Role of Media in the Arab World's Transformation Process*, ed. by Christoph Schmidt (Bonn: DW Akademie: International Media Studies, 2013).

Anderson, Lisa, 'Demystifying the Arab Spring Parsing the Differences between Tunisia, Egypt, and Libya', *Foreign Affairs*, 90 (2011), 2–7.

Anduiza, Eva, Marta Cantijoch, Aina Gallego, and Josep Martin, 'Online Resources, Political Participation and Equality', in *Paper presented at the American Political Science Association annual conference* (Boston, MA, 2008), pp. 28–31.

Anduiza, Eva, Marta Cantijoch, and Aina Gallego, 'Political Participation and the Internet', *Information, Communication and Society*, 12 (2009), 860–876.

Annual Statistical Abstract, 'Population: Kuwait Annual Statistical Report', *Press and Publication Department at Kuwait Statistical Bureau*, 2011 <http://www.csb.gov.kw/Socan_Statistic_EN.aspx?ID=19>.

Aoki, Kumiko, and Edward J. Downes, 'An Analysis of Young People's Use of and Attitudes toward Cell Phones', *Telematics and Informatics*, 20 (2003), 349–364 <doi:10.1016/S0736-5853(03)00018-2>.

Arab Advisors Group, 'Reports on the Arab World's Communications and Media Markets', 2005 <http://www.arabadvisors.com>.

Asiri, Abdulredha, *The Political System in Kuwait: Principles and Practices* (Kuwait: Alwatan, 2007).

Attias, Shay, 'Israel's New Peer-to-Peer Diplomacy', *The Hague Journal of Diplomacy* 7 (2012): 473–482.

Augustus, Richard, *The Puzzle of Political Reform in the Middle East* (Oxford: Oxford University Press, 2009).

Auter, Philip, Mohamed Arafa, and Khalid Al-Jaber, 'Identifying with Arabic Journalists: How Al-Jazeera Tapped Parasocial Interaction Gratifications in the Arab World', *International Communication Gazette*, 67 (2005), 189–204.

Ayish, Muhammad, 'Virtual Public Relations in the United Arab Emirates', *Public Relations Review*, 2005, 381–388.

Bakir, Vian, *Sousveillance, Media and Strategic Political Communication: Iraq, USA, UK* (London: Continuum, 2010).

Barakat, Rabie, *New Media in the Arab World: A Tool for Redesigning Geopolitical Realities* (Lebanon: Lebanese American University, 2011).

Barton, Ben, and Marthalee Barton, 'Modes of Power in Technical and Professional Visuals', *Journal of Business and Technical Communication*, 7 (1993), 138–162 <doi:10.1177/1050651993007001007>.

Batane, Tshepo, 'Internet Access and Use among Young People in Botswana', *International Journal of Information and Education Technology*, 3 (2013), 117–119 <doi:10.7763/IJIET.2013.V3.246>.

Bimber, Bruce, 'The Internet and Political Transformation: Populism, Community, and Accelerated Pluralism', *Polity*, 31 (1998), 133–160.

——'Information and Political Engagement in America: The Search for Effects of Information Technology at the Individual Level', *Political Research Quarterly*, 54 (2001), 53–67.

Bimber, Bruce, and Lauren Copeland, 'Digital Media and Traditional Political Participation over Time in the U.S.', *Journal of Information Technology & Politics*, 10 (2013), 125–137 <doi:10.1080/19331681.2013.769925>.

Blinkoff, Robbie, 'The Mobiles: Social Evolution in a Wireless Society: Context-Based Research Group', 2001 <http://www.contextresearch.com/context/z.study.cfm>.

Blumler, Jay, 'The Role of Theory in Uses and Gratifications Studies', *Communication Research*, 6 (1979), 9–36.

Boellstorff, Tom, *Coming of Age in Second Life* (Princeton, NJ: Princeton University Press, 2008).

Bogart, Leo, *Press and Public: Who Reads What, When, Where, and Why in American Newspapers* (Hillsdale, New Jersey: Lawrence Erlbaum Associates, 1989).

Bolin, Göran, 'The Labour of Media Use', *Information on Communication & Society*, 15 (2012), 796–814.

Bond, Emma, 'Managing Mobile Relationships: Children's Perceptions of the Impact of the Mobile Phone on Relationships in Their Everyday Lives', *Childhood*, 17 (2010), 514–529 <doi:10.1177/0907568210364421>.

Boyd, Danah, and Nicole Ellison, 'Social Network Sites: Definition, History, and Scholarship', *Journal of Computer-Mediated Communication*, 13 (2007), 210–230 <doi:10.1111/j.1083-6101.2007.00393.x>.

Brownlee, Jason, 'Low Tide after the Third Wave: Exploring Politics under Authoritarianism', *Comparative Politics*, 34 (2002), 477–498.

Bruns, Axel, 'Gatewatching, Not Gatekeeping: Collaborative Online News', *Media International Australia Incorporating Culture and Policy: Quarterly Journal of Media Research and Resources*, 2003, 31–44.

——*Gatewatching: Collaborative Online News Production* (New York, NY: Peter Lang, 2005).

Cannarella, John, and Joshua Spechler, 'Epidemiological Modeling of Online Social Network Dynamics', *Princeton University*, 2014 <http://arxiv.org/pdf/1401.4208v1.pdf>.

Canton, James, *Managing the Game-Changing Trends That Will Transform Your World* (Boston, MA: Da Capo Press, 2015).

Caroll, William, and Robert Hackett, 'Democratic Media Activism through the Lens of Social Movement Theory', *Media Culture Society*, 28 (2006), 31–44 <doi:10.1177/0163443706059289>.

Castells, Manuel, *The Rise of the Network Society* (Oxford: Blackwell, 1996).

——'Communication, Power and Counter-power in the Network Society', *International Journal of Communication*, 1(2007), 238–266.

——*Communication Power* (New York, NY: Oxford University Press, 2009).

Castells, Manuel, Mireia Fernandez-Ardevol, Jack Linchuan Qiu, and Araba Sey, *Mobile Communication and Society: A Global Perspective* (Boston, MA: MIT Press, 2007).

Chung, Deborah, and Chan Yoo, 'Audience Motivations for Using Interactive Features: Distinguishing Use of Different Types of Interactivity on an Online Newspaper', *Mass Communication and Society*, 11 (2008), 375–397.

Colombo, Silvia, 'The GCC Countries and the Arab Spring: Between Outreach, Patronage and Repression', in *Paper prepared for the Istituto Affari Internazionali* (Rome, Italy, 2012).

Comunello, Francesca, and Anzera Giuseppe, 'Will the Revolution Be Tweeted? A Conceptual Framework for Understanding the Social Media and the Arab Spring', *Islam and Christian–Muslim Relations*, 23 (2012), 453–470.

Cook, Jordan, 'Social Media, American Interests, and the Arab Spring', *Dalhousie Journal of Interdisciplinary Management*, 9 (2013) <doi:10.5931/djim.v9i1.3354>.

Correa, Teresa, Amber Hinsley, and Homero de Zuniga, 'Who Interacts on the Web? The Intersection of Users' Personality and Social Media Use', *Computers in Human Behavior*, 26 (2010), 247–253 <doi:10.1016/j.chb.2009.09.003>.

Dabashi, Hamid, *The Arab Spring: The End of Post Colonialism* (New York, NY: Zed Books, 2012).

Dahlgren, Peter, 'The Internet, Public Sphere, and Political Communication: Dispersion and Deliberation', *Political Communication*, 22 (2005), 147–162.

Deloitte, 'Arab States Mobile Observatory 2013', 2013 <http://www.gsma.com/spectrum/arab-states-mobile-observatory-2013/>.

Dennis, Everette, Justin Martin, and Robb Wood, 'Media Use in the Middle East: An Eight-Nation Survey', 2013 <http://menamediasurvey.northwestern.edu/>.

Desmukh, Fahad, 'The Internet in Bahrain: Breaking the Monopoly of Information', *Foreign Policy*, 2010.

——'Bahrain Government Hacked Lawyers and Activists with UK Spyware', *Bahrain Watch*, 2014 <https://bahrainwatch.org/blog/2014/08/07/uk-spyware-used-to-hack-bahrain-lawyers-activists/>.

Dickinson, Roger, and Barrie Gunter, 'What Is the Future for News in the Arab World?', in *News Media in the Arab world: A Study of 10 Arab and Muslim Countries*, ed. by Barrie Gunter and Roger Dickinson (London, UK: Bloomsbury, 2013), pp. 173–188.

Di Gennaro, Corinna, and William Dutton, 'The Internet and the Public: Online and Offline Political Participation in the United Kingdom', *Parliamentary Affairs*, 59 (2006), 299–313.

Dijk van J. A. G. M., *De Netwerkmaatschappij, Sociale Aspecten van Nieuwe Media [Dutsh]*, 3rd edn (Houten NL, Zaventem BEL: Bohn Stafleu van Loghum, 1997).

Dimmick, John, Jaspreet Sikand, and Scott Patterson, 'The Gratification of the Household Telephone', *Communication Research*, 21 (1994), 643–663 <doi:10.1177/009365094021005005>.

Dixon, Suzi, 'Facebook "Used to Hunt down Bahrain Dissidents"', *The Telegraph*, 4 August 2011 <http://www.telegraph.co.uk/expat/expatnews/8681230/Facebook-used-to-hunt-down-Bahrain-dissidents.html>.

Dodge, Toby, 'From the Arab Awakening to the Arab Spring: The Post-Colonial State in the Middle East', *LSE Ideas*, 2012, pp. 5–11 <http://www.lse.ac.uk/IDEAS/publications/reports/pdf/SR011/FINAL_LSE_IDEAS__fromTheArabAwakeningToTh eArabSpring_Dodge.pdf>.

Dooley, Brain, "Troll" Attacks on #Bahrain Tweets Show Depth of Government Attempts to Silence Dissent', *The World Post*, 2011 <http://www.huffingtonpost.com/brian-dooley/troll-attacks-on-bahrain_b_1099642.html>.

Drezner, Daniel, 'Weighing the Scales: The Internet's Effect on State-Society Relations', *The Brown Journal of World Affairs*, 16 (2010), 31–44.

Duffy, Matt, 'Media Laws and Regulations of the GCC Countries: Summary, Analysis and Recommendations', *Doha Centre for Media Freedom*, 2013 <http://www.dc4mf.org/sites/default/files/gcc_media_law_en_0.pdf>.

Dunne, Aine, Margaret-Anne Lawlor, and Jennifer Rowley, 'Young People's Use of Online Social Networking Sites: A Uses and Gratifications Perspective', *Journal of Research in Interactive Marketing*, 4 (2010), 46–58.

Eisenstadt, Shmuel, *Traditional Patrimonialism to Modern Patrimonialism* (London: Sage Publications, 1973).

Elareshi, Mokhtar, *News Consumption in Libya: A Study of University Students* (Newcastle: Cambridge Scholars Publishing, 2013).

Elareshi, Mokhtar, Abdul-Karim Ziani, and Barrie Gunter, 'The Use of Mobile Phone and Internet in Getting Local News in GCC Regions: A University Student Study', *Journal of Media and Communication Studies*, 3 (2015), 001–010.

Elareshi, Mokhtar, and Barrie Gunter, 'News Consumption among Young Libyan Adults: Are New Satellite TV News Services Displacing Local TV News', *Arab Media & Society*, 2010.

El Khouli, Mohamed, 'The Most Important Negative Aspects of Suing Social Networking Affecting the Family Stability in Abu Dhabi – a Pilot Study', *International Journal of Engineering and Technology*, 5 (2013), 85–90.

Ellison, Nicole, Charles Steinfield, and Cliff Lampe, 'The Benefits of Facebook "Friends": Social Capital and College Students' Use of Online Social Network

Sites', *Journal of Computer-Mediated Communication*, 12 (2007), 1143–1168 <doi:10.1111/j.1083-6101.2007.00367.x>.

Elmasri, Mohammad, 'Egypt's Campaign of Elimination: Pro-June 30 Analysts and the Quantitative Rationalization for Egypt's Coup', *Open Democracy*, 2014.

El-Nawawy, Mohammed, and Adel Iskander, *Al-Jazeera: How the Free Arab News Network Scooped the World and Changed the Middle East* (US: Westview Press, 2002).

Eltantawy, Nahed, and Julie Wiest, 'Social Media in the Egyptian Revolution: Reconsidering Resource Mobilization Theory', *International Journal of Communication*, 2011, 1207–1224.

Etling, Bruce, John Kelly, Robert Faris, and John Palfrey, 'Mapping the Arab Blogosphere: Politics, Culture and Dissent', *Research Publication No. 2009-06* (Cambridge, MA: Harvard University, 2009) <www.cyber.law.harvard.edu/cyber.law.harvard.edu/files/Mapping_the_Arab_Blogosphere>.

Fahad, Maryam, *Arab Media Outlook*, 2011.

Fortunati, Leopoldina, 'The Mobile Phone: An Identity on the Move', *Personal and Ubiquitous Computing*, 5 (2001), 85–98 <doi:10.1007/PL00000017>.

Foucault, Michel, *Discipline and Punish: The Birth of the Prison* (New York: Vintage Books, 1977).

Fraser, Nancy, 'Transnationalizing the Public Sphere on the Legitimacy and Efficacy of Public Opinion in a Post Westphalian World', *Theory, Culture & Society*, 24 (2007), 7–30 <doi:10.1177/0263276407080090>.

Freedom House, 'Freedom on the Net: Bahrain', 2011.

——'Freedom in the World 2013', 2013 <http://freedomhouse.org/report/freedom-world/freedom-world-2013#.U0uSdfm-1cY>.

——'Freedom in the World: Kuwait', 2013 <https://freedomhouse.org/report/freedom-world/2013/kuwait#.VRk4hvnF-Sp>.

——'Freedom on the Net 2013: Bahrain', 2013 <https://www.freedomhouse.org/sites/default/files/resources/FOTN 2013_Bahrain.pdf>.

——'Freedom on the Net: Egypt', 2014 <https://freedomhouse.org/report/freedom-net/2014/egypt>.

From Protection Group International (PGI), 'Olton', 2012 <http://www.olton.co.uk/services/reputation-management>.

Gandy, Oscar H. Jr, *The Panoptic Sort: A Political Economy of Personal Information* (Boulder, CO: Westview Press, 1993).

Gant, Diana, and Sara Kiesler, 'Blurring the Boundaries: Cell Phones, Mobility and the Line between Work and Personal Life', in *Wireless World: Social and Interactional Aspects of the Mobile Age*, ed. by Barry Brown, Nicola Harper, and Richard Green, 2001, pp. 121–131.

Garrett, R. Kelly, 'Protest in an Information Society: A Review of Literature on Social Movements and New ICTs', *Information, Communication and Society*, 9 (2006), 202–224.

Gelvanovska, Natalija, Michel Rogy, and Carlo Rossotto, 'Broadband Networks in the Middle East and North Africa, Accelerating High-Speed Internet Access', *The World Bank*, 2014 <http://www.worldbank.org/en/region/mena/publication/broadband-networks-in-mna>.

Ghanem, Renad, 'Social Media Connecting People', *Saudi Gazette*, 2012 <http://www.arabnews.com/what-happened-twitter>.

Ghannam, Jeffrey, *Social Media in the Arab World: Leading up to the Uprisings of 2011* (Washington, DC: Center for International Media Assistance, 2011).

——*Digital Media in the Arab World One Year after the Revolutions* (Washington, DC: Center for International Media Assistance, 2012).

Ghonim, Wael, *Revolution 2.0: The Power of the People Is Greater than the People in Power: A Memoir* (New York: Houghton Mifflin Harcount, 2012).

Gillespie, Marie, 'BBC Arabic, Social Media and Citizen Production: An Experiment in Digital Democracy before the Arab Spring', *Theory, Culture & Society*, 2013, 1–39.

Gillmor, Dan, *We the Media: Grassroots Journalism by the People, for the People* (O'Reilly Media, 2006).

Gladwell, Malcolm, *The Tipping Point: How Little Things Can Make a Big Difference* (Boston: Little, Brown and Company, 2006).

Goldstone, Jack, 'Understanding the Revolutions of 2011: Weakness and Resilience in Middle Eastern Autocracies', *Foreign Affairs* 3, 2011 <http://www.foreignaffairs.com/articles/67694/jack-a-goldstone/understanding-the-revolutions-of-2011>.

Govers, Robert. 'Brand Dubai and Its Competitors in the Middle East: An Image and Reputation Analysis', *Place Branding and Public Diplomacy* 8 (2012): 48–57.

Grossman, Lawrence, *The Electronic Republic: Reshaping Democracy in the Information Age* (New York: Penguin Books, 1995).

Gugler, Josef, 'The Urban Character of Contemporary Revolutions', *Studies in Comparative International Politics*, 17 (2002), 60–73.

Gunter, Barrie, *Television versus the Internet: Will TV Prosper or Perish as the World Moves Online?* (Oxford: Chandos Publishing, 2010).

Gunter, Barrie, and Roger Dickinson, 'News Developments and Changes to News Consumption Patterns in the Arab World', in *News Media in the Arab World: A Study of 10 Arab and Muslim Countries*, ed. by Barrie Gunter and Roger Dickinson (New York, NY: Bloomsbury, 2013), pp. 135–152.

——'The Changing Nature of News and the Arab World', in *News Media in the Arab World: A Study of 10 Arab and Muslim Countries*, ed. by Barrie Gunter and Roger Dickinson (New York: Bloomsbury, 2013), pp. 1–20.

Gunter, Barrie, Vincent Campbell, Maria Touri, and Rachel Gibson, 'Blogs, News and Credibility', *Aslib Proceedings*, 61 (2009), 185–204.

Haddon, Leslie, *Information and Communication Technologies in Everyday Life: A Concise Introduction and Research Guide* (Oxford, UK: Berg, 2004).

Hafez, Kai, 'The Role of Media in the Arab World's Transformation Process', in *Bound to Cooperate – Europe and the Middle East II*, ed. by Christian-Peter Hanelt and Almut Möller (Bielefeld: Verlag Bertelsmann Stiftung, Gütersloh, 2008).

Hamada, Basyouni, 'Satellite Television and Public Sphere in Egypt: Is There a Link?', *Global Media Journal*, 7 (2008).

Hermida, Alfred, Seth C. Lewis, and Rodrigo Zamith, 'Sourcing the Arab Spring: A Case Study of Andy Carvin's Sources on Twitter during the Tunisian and Egyptian Revolutions', *Journal of Computer-Mediated Communication*, 19 (2014), 479–499.

Hindman, Matthew, *The Myth of Digital Democracy* (Ptinceton, NY: Princeton University Press, 2010).

Hofheinz, Albrecht, 'Arab Internet Usage: Popular Trends and Public Impact', in *Arab Media and Political Renewal: Community, Legitimacy and Public Life*, ed. by Naomi Sakr (London: I.B.Tauris, 2007), pp. 56–79.

Horne, John. "Tn Tn Ttn and Torture in Bahrain: Puncturing the Spectacle of the "Arab Spring"" *The Bahrain Uprising*, ed. by Marc Owen Jones and A Shehabi. London: Zed Books, 2015.

Hourani, Albert, *A History of the Arab Peoples* (London, UK: Faber and Faber, 2013).

Howard, Philip N, Aiden Duffy, Deen Freelon, Muzammil Hussain, Will Mari, and Marwa Mazaid, 'Opening Closed Regimes: What Was the Role of Social Media during the Arab Spring?', *Seattle:* (PIPTI, 2011), pp. 1538–2464 <http://pitpi.org/index.php/2011/09/11/opening-closed-regimes-what-was-the-role-of-social-media-during-the-arab-spring/>.

Hroub, Khaled, 'Internet Freedom in the Arab World: Its Impact, State Controls, Islamisation and the Overestimation of It All', *Culture and Society*, 2009, 267–271 <http://www.iemed.org/anuari/2009/aarticles/a267.pdf>.

Humphreys, Lee, 'Who's Watching Whom? A Study of Interactive Technology and Surveillance', *Journal of Communication*, 61 (2011), 575–595 <doi:10.1111/j.1460-2466.2011.01570.x>.

Ibahrine, Mohammad, 'Mobile Communication and Sociopolitical Change in the Arab World', in *Handbook of Mobile Communication Studies*, ed. by James E. Katz (London: Massachusetts Institute of Technology, 2008), pp. 257–272.

Ibish, Hussein, 'The Bahrain Uprising: Towards Confrontation vs Accommodation', *A Henry Jackson Society Strategic Briefing*, 2011 <http://www.henryjacksonsociety.org/cms/harriercollectionitems/Bahrain1c.pdf>.

Ihlen, Oyvind, Betteke Ruler, and Magnus Fredriksson, *Public Relations and Social Theory: Key Figures and Concepts* (New York, NY: Routledge, 2009).

International Labour Organisation, *Global Employment Trends* (Geneva, Switzerland: ILO, 2008).

Internet World State, 'Oman', *Internet World State*, 2012 <http://go.hrw.com/atlas/norm_htm/oman.htm>.

——'Internet World Stats, Usage Population and Statistics', *Miniwatts Marketing Group*, 2014 <www.internetworldstats.com>.

——'Internet World Stats, Usage Population and Statistics', *Miniwatts Marketing Group*, 2014 <www.internetworldstats.com>.

ITU, 'World Telecommunication/ICT Development Report 2014: Measuring ICT for Social and Economic Development', 2014 <http://www.itu.int/ITU-D/ict/publications/wtdr_06/index.html>.

Jagun, Abi, Richard Heeks, and Jason Whalley, 'The Impact of Mobile Telephony on Developing Country Micro-Enterprise: A Nigerian Case Study', *Information Technologies and International Development*, 4 (2008), 47–63.

Jensen, Michael, James Danziger, and Alladi Venkatesh, *Electronic Democracy in America: Civil Society, Cyber Society and Participation in Local Politics* (Irvine: Center for Research on Information Technology and Organization, University of California, 2005).

Jones, Marc Owen, 'Bahrain Activists' Trouble with Trolls', *Index on Censorship Uncut*, 2012 <http://uncut.indexoncensorship.org/2012/05/bahrain-marc-owen-jones-twitter-trolls/>.

——'Putting a Price Tag on Repression', *Your Middle East*, 2012 <http://www.yourmiddleeast.com/opinion/marc-owen-jones-putting-a-price-tag-on-repression_14547>.

——"Social Media, Surveillance, and Social Control in the Bahrain Uprising." *Westminster Papers of Communication and Culture* 9.2 (2013): 69–92.

——"Bahrain's Celebrity Anti-Diplomacy." *Your Middle East*, 2014.

——'Social Media, Surveillance, and Spying in the Bahrain Uprising', *The Bahrain Uprising*, ed. by Marc Owen Jones and A. Shehabi (London Zed Books, 2015).

Joseph, Sarah, 'Social Media, Political Change, and Human Rights', *Boston College International & Comparative Law Review*, 35 (2012), 145–188 <http://lawdigitalcommons.bc.edu/cgi/viewcontent.cgi?article=1667&context=iclr>.

Kapiszewski Andrzej, 'Saudi Arabia: Steps toward Democratization or Reconfiguration of Authoritarianism', *Journal of Asian and African Studies*, 41 (2006), 489–482.

Karam, Imad, 'Satellite Television: A Breathing Space for Arab Youth?', in *Arab Media and Political Renewal: Community, Legitimacy and Public Life*, ed. by Naomi Sakr (London: I.B.Tauris & Co Ltd, 2007), pp. 80–95.

Katz, Elihu, Jay Blumler, and Michael Gurevitch, 'Uses and Gratifications Research', *The Public Opinion Quarterly*, 37 (1973), 509–523.

Kaviraj, Sudipta, 'An Outline of the Revisionist Theory of Modernity', *European Journal of Sociology*, 46 (2005), 497–526 <doi:10.1017/S0003975605000196>.

Kenix, Linda, 'Blogs as Alternative', *Journal of Computer-Mediated Communication*, 14 (2009), 790–822.

Kenski, Kate, and Natalie Stroud, 'Connections between Internet Use and Political Efficacy, Knowledge, and Participation', *Journal of Broadcasting & Electronic Media*, 50 (2006), 173–192 <doi:10.1207/s15506878jobem5002_1>.

Khondker, Habibul, 'Role of the New Media in the Arab Spring', *Globalisations*, 8 (2011), 675–679.

Kirkpatrick, David, *The Facebook Effect: The Real Inside Story of Mark Zuckerberg and the World's Fastest-Growing Company* (London, UK: bookmarque, 2010).

Klandermans, Bert, 'Mobilisation and Participation: Social and Psychological Expansions of Resource and Mobilization Theory', *American Sociological Review*, 49 (1984), 583–600.

Klandermans, Bert, and Dirk Omega, 'Potentials, Networks, Motivations and Barriers: Steps towards Participation in Social Movements', *American Sociological Review*, 52 (1987), 519–531.

Kohut, Andrew, Carroll Doherty, Michael Dimock, and Scott Keeter, 'Key News Audiences Now Blend Online and Traditional Sources: Audience Segments in a Changing News Environment', *Pew Research Center*, 2008, 43.

Kohut, Andrew, Richard Wike, James Bell, Juliana Horowitz, Katie Simmons, Jacob Poushter, and others, 'Social Networking Popular across Globe: Arab Publics Most Likely to Express Political Views Online', *Pew Research Center*, 2012 <http://www.pewresearch.org/daily-number/arab-publics-turning-to-social-networks-to-express-political-views/>.

Kraidy, Marwan, 'Reality Television and Politics in the Arab World: Preliminary Observations. Annenberg School for Communication', 2006 <http://repository.upenn.edu/asc.papers/303>.

Kyem, Peter, and Peter LeMaire, 'Transforming Recent Gains in the Digital Divide into Digital Opportunities: Africa and the Boom in Mobile Phone Subscription', *The Electronic Journal on Information System in Developing Countries*, 28 (2006), 1–16.

Lahlali, El Mustapha, 'Arab Media Discourse: Breaking Taboos', *International Journal of Afro-Asiatic Studies*, 13 (2011), 157–166.

Lawrence, Eric, John Sides, and Henry Farrell, 'Self-Segregation or Deliberation? Blog Readership, Participation, and Polarization in American Politics', *Perspectives on Politics*, 8 (2010), 141–157.

Leccese, Mark, 'Online Information Sources of Political Blogs', *Journalism and Mass Communication Quarterly*, 86 (2009), 578–593.

Lee, Waipeng, and Eddie C. Y. Kuo, Internet and displacement effect: Children's Media Use and Activities in Singapore, *Journal of Computer-Mediated Communication*, 7(2002), 0. DOI: 10.1111/j.1083-6101.2002.tb00143.x.

Lin, Kuan Yu, and Hsi Peng Lu, 'Why People Use Social Networking Sites: An Empirical Study Integrating Network Externalities and Motivation Theory',

Computers in Human Behavior, 27 (2011), 1152–1161 <doi:10.1016/j.chb.2010.12.009>.

Ling, Rich, 'We Will Be Reached: The Use of Mobile Telephony among Norwegian Youth', *Information Technology and People*, 13 (2000), 102–120 <doi:10.1108/09593840010339844>.

Linz, Juan, 'Totalitarian and Authoritarian Regimes', in *Handbook of Political Science*, ed. by Fred Greenstein and Nelson Polsby (Colorado: Lynne Rienner Publications, 2000).

Livingstone, Sonia, Leslie Haddon, Anke Gorzig, and Kjartan Olafsson, 'Risks and Safety on the Internet: The Perspective of European Children', *EU Kids Online*, 2011 <www.eukidsonline.net>.

Longhofer, Wesley, and Daniel Winchester, *Social Theory Re-Wired: New Connections to Classical and Contemporary Perspectives* (Oxon: Routledge, 2012).

Lotan, Gilad, Erhardt Graeff, Mike Ananny, Devin Gaffney, Ian Pearce, and Danah Boyd, 'The Revolutions Were Tweeted: Information Flows during the 2011 Tunisian and Egyptian Revolutions', *International Journal of Communication*, 2011, 1375–1405.

Lynch, Marc, 'Political Science and the New Arab Public Spheres', *Institute for Public Knowledge*, 2012 <http://publicsphere.ssrc.org/lynch-political-science-and-the-new-arab-public-sphere/>.

Lyon, David, *Surveillance Society: Monitoring in Everyday Life* (Buckingham: Open University Press, 2001).

MacKinnon, Rebecca, *Consent of the Networked: The Worldwide Struggle for Internet* (New York, NY: Basic Books, 2012).

Madden, Mary, Amanda Lenhart, Maeve Duggan, Sandra Cortesi, and Urs Gasser, 'Teens and Technology 2013', *Pew Internet & American Life Project*, 2013 <www.pewinternet.org/Reports/2013Teens-andTech.aspx>.

Madianou, Mirca, and Daniel Miller, *Migration and New Media: Transnational Families and Polymedia* (London, UK: Routledge, 2012).

Mann, Steve, '"Reflectionism" and "diffusionism": New Tactics for Deconstructing the Video Surveillance Superhighway', *Leonardo*, 31 (1998), 93–102.

Mann, Steve, Jason Nolan, and Barry Wellman, 'Sousveillance: Inventing and Using Wearable Computing Devices for Data Collection in Surveillance Environments', *Surveillance & Society*, 1 (2003), 331–355.

Marczak, William, John Scott-Railton, Vern Paxson, and Morgan Marquis-Boire, 'When Governments Hack Opponents: A Look at Actors and Technology', in *Paper presented at the 23rd USENIX Security Symposium 20–22 August* (San Diego, CA, 2014) <http://www.icir.org/vern/papers/govhack.usesec14.pdf>.

Massey, Kimberly, 'Analysing the Uses and Gratifications Concept of Audience Activity with a Qualitative Approach: Media Encounters during the 1989 Loma Prieta Earthquake Disaster', *Journal of Broadcasting and Electronic Media*, 39 (1995), 349.

Matthiesen, Toby, *Sectarian Gulf: Bahrain, Saudi Arabia and the Arab Spring That Wasn't* (California: Stanford University Press, 2013).

McLuhan, Marshall, *Understanding Media: Extensions of Man* (New York, NY: McGraw-Hill, 1964).

McQuail, Denis, *McQuail's Mass Communication Theory* (London: Sage Publications, 2005).

Meraz, Sharon, 'Is There an Elite Hold? Traditional Media to Social Media Agenda Setting Influence in Blog Networks', *Journal of Computer-Mediated Communication*, 14 (2009), 682–707.

Metzger, Miriam J., Andrew J. Flanagin, and Lara Zwarun, 'College Student Web Use, Perceptions of Information Credibility, and Verification Behavior', *Computer and Education*, 41 (2003), 271–290 <doi:10.1016/S0360-1315(03)00049-6>.

Miliany, Khulood, 'The Impact of the Internet on Saudi Students' Use of Television' (Unpublished doctor's dissertation. University of Leicester, UK, 2013).

Mitchell, Timothy, *Colonising Egypt* (Berkeley: University of California Press, 1991).

Mohsen, Shopie, 'The Role of New Information and Communication Technologies and Social Media during the Arab Spring' (Unpublished master's dissertation, University of Ottawa, Canada, 2013).

Morozov, Evgeny, *The Net Delusion: The Dark Side of Internet Freedom* (Jackson, TN: Public Affairs, 2011).

Mourtada, Racha, and Fadi Salem, 'Social Media, Employment and Entrepreneurship: New Frontiers for the Economic Empowerment of Arab Youth?', *Arab Social Media Report*, 2012 <http://www.dsg.ae/en/publication/Description.aspx?PubID=307&PrimenuID=11&mnu=Pri>.

Mourtada, Racha, and Paul Salem, 'Social Media in the Arab World: The Impact on Growth, Women and Social Change', *Arab Social Media Report*, 2012, pp. 269–274 <http://www.iemed.org/observatori-en/arees-danalsi/arxuis-adjuncts/anuari/med.2012/mourtada salem-en>.

Newman, Melanie, and Oliver Wright, 'PR Firm's Plan to Target Sting after Gig Boycott', *The Independent*, 8 December 2011 <http://www.independent.co.uk/news/uk/politics/kazakhstan-pr-firms-plan-to-target-sting-after-gig-boycott-video-6273824.html>.

Newsom, Victoria, Lara Lengel, and Catherine Cassara, 'Local Knowledge and the Revolutions: A Framework for Social Media Information Flow', *International Journal of Communication*, 2011, pp. 1303–1312.

Norris, Pippa, *A Virtuous Circle: Political Communications in Post-Industrial Societies* (New York, NY: Cambridge University Press, 2000).

——*Digital Divide: Civic Engagement, Information Poverty, and the Internet Worldwide* (Cambridge, UK: Cambridge University Press, 2001).

Osorio, Benat, Soumitra Dutta, and Brunov Lanvin, 'The Networked Readiness Index 2013, Benchmarking ICT Uptake and Support for Growth and Jobs in a

Hyperconnected World', *World Economic Forum*, 2013 <http://www.searo.who.int/entity/health_situation_trends/country_profiles/e_health/wef_gitr_2013_nri_structure.pdf>.

Oxford Business Group, 'The Report: Oman', 2014 <http://www.oxfordbusiness-group.com/oman-2014>.

Ozcan, Yusuf, and Abdullah Kocak, 'Research Note: A Need or a Status Symbol? Use of Cellular Telephones in Turkey', *European Journal of Communication*, 2003, 241–254 <doi:10.1177/0267323103018002004>.

Palmgreen, Philip, and J.D Rayburn II, 'Uses and Gratifications and Exposure to Public Television: A Discrepancy Approach', *Communication Research*, 6 (1979), 155–180.

Pempek, Tiffany, Yevdokiya Yermolayeva, and Sandra Calvert, 'College Students' Social Networking Experiences on Facebook', *Journal of Applied Developmental Psychology*, 30 (2009), 227–238 <doi:10.1016/j.appdev.2008.12.010>.

Portio Research, 'Latest Mobile Stats', *Mobile Thinking*, 2013 <http://mobithinking.com/mobile-marketing-tools/latest-mobile-stats/e#lotsofapps>.

Poster, Mark, *The Mode of Information: Poststructuralism and Social Construct* (Chicago, IL: University of Chicago Press, 1990).

Powell, Juliette, *33 Million People in the Room: How to Create, Influence, and Run a Successful Business with Social Networking* (New Jersey: FT Press, 2009).

Qian, Hua, and Craig Scott, 'Anonymity and Self-Disclosure on Weblogs', *Journal of Computer-Mediated Communication*, 12 (2007), 1428–1451 <doi:10.1111/j.1083-6101.2007.00380.x>.

Radsch, Courtney, 'Blogosphere and Social Media', in *Seismic Shift: Understanding change in the Middle East* (Washington, DC: The Henry L. Stimson Center, 2011), pp. 67–83.

Rainie, Lee, and Andrew Kohut, 'Tracking Online Life: How Women Use the Internet to Cultivate Relationships with Family and Friends', *The Pew Internet Project*, 2000 <http://www.pewinternet.org/reports/pdfs/Report1.pdf.>.

Rainie, Lee, and Barry Wellman, *Networked: The New Social Operating System* (Cambridge, MA: MIT Press, 2012).

Reese, Erlich, 'In Saudi Arabia, Shiite Muslims Challenge Ban on Protests', *NPR*, 2013 <http://www.npr.org/2013/03/23/175051345/in-saudi-arabia-shiite-muslims-challenge-ban-on-protests>.

Rheingold, Howard, *The Virtual Community: Homesteading on the Electronic Frontier* (New York: Harper Collins, 1993).

——*The Virtual Community: Homesteading on the Electronic Trontier* (New York: MIT Press, 2000).

Rinke, Eike, and Maria Roder, 'Media Ecologies, Communication Culture, and Temporal-Spatial Unfolding: Three Components in a Communication Model of the Egyptian Regime Change', *International Journal of Communication*, 2011, 1273–1285.

Rinnawi, Khalil, 'Cyber Uprising: Al-Jazeera TV Channel and the Egyptian Uprising', *Language and Intercultural Communication*, 12 (2006), 118–132 <doi: 10.1080/14708477.2012.671607>.

Roos, J.P., 'Sociology of Cellular Telephone: The Nordic Model (300,000 Yuppies? Mobile Phone in Finland)', *Telecommunications Policy*, 17 (1993), 446–456.

Rubin, Alan, 'Media Uses and Effects: A Uses and Gratifications Perspective', in *Media Effects: Advances in Theory and Research*, ed. by J. Bryant and D. Zillman (NJ: Erlbaum, 1994), pp. 417–436.

Ruggiero, Thomas E., 'Uses and Gratifications Theory in the 21st Century', *Mass Communication and Society*, 3 (2000), 3–37.

Rugh, William, 'Do National Political Systems Still Influence Arab Media?', *Arab Media & Society*, 2007 <http://www.arabmediasociety.com/?article=225>.

Saad, Ashraf, and Noshin Kilany, 'Kuwaiti Women and Their Green Chair Struggle', *Arabic Sky News*, 2012 <http://www.skynewsarabia.com/web/article/56899/>.

Sabbagh, Karim, Mohamad Mourad, Wassim Kabbara, Ramez Shehadi, and Hatem Samman, *Understanding the Arab Digital Generation* (Dubai: Booz & Company and Google, 2012).

Saco, Diana, *Cybering Democracy: Public Space and the Internet* (Minneapolis: University of Minnesota Press, 2002).

Saideman, Stephen, 'Conclusion: Thinking Theoretically about Identity and Foreign Policy', in *Identity and Foreign Policy in the Middle East*, ed. by Shibley Telhami and Michael Barnett (Ithaca, NY: Cornell University Press, 2002), pp. 196–200.

Salem, Fadi, and Racha Mourtada, 'Civil Movements: The Impact of Facebook and Twitter', *Arab Social Media Report*, 2011 <www.unpan1.un.org/intradoc/groups/public/documents/dsg/unpan05080>.

——'Social Media in the Arab World: Influencing Societal and Cultural Change', *Arab Social Media Report*, 2012 <www.arabsocialmediareport.com/user-Management/PDFD/ASMR 4 updated 29 08 12>.

——*Arab Social Media Report*, Dubai, July 2012 <www.dsg.ae/en/imagees/ASMR4finaltopost.pdf>.

——'Transforming Educationin the Arab World: Breaking Barriers in the Age of Social Learning', *Arab Social Media Report*, 2013 <http://www.arabsocialmediareport.com/UserManagement/PDF/ASMR_5_Report_Final.pdf>.

——'Citizen Engagement and Public Services in the Arab World; The Potential of Social Media', *Arab Social Media Report*, 2014 <http://www.mbrsg.ae/getattachment/e9ea2ac8-13dd-4cd7-9104-b8f1f405cab3/Citizen-Engagement-and-Public-Services-in-the-Arab.aspx>.

Salem, Fadi, Racha Mourtada, May Al-Dabbagh, and Ghalia Gargani, 'The Role of Social Media in Arab Women's Empowerment', *Arab Social Media Report*, 2011.

Salem, Fadi, Racha Mourtada, and Sara Alshaer, 'The Arab World Online (2014): Trends in Internet and Mobile Usage in the Arab Region', *Arab Social Media Report*, Dubai, 2014 <http://www.mbrsg.ae/getattachment/ff70c2c5-0fce-405d-b23f-93c198d4ca44/The-Arab-World-Online-2014-Trends-in-Internet-and.aspx>.

Salem, Paul, 'Kuwait: Politics in a Participatory Emirate', *Carnegie Endowment for International Peace*, 2007, 3 <http://carnegieendowment.org/files/cmec3_salem_kuwait_final1.pdf>.

Samir, Mohammed, 'The Official Page of Egyptain Army on the Facebook', 2012 <https://www.facebook.com/Egy.Army.Spox>.

Sanou, Brahima, 'ITU World Telecommunication /ICT Indicators Database. ICT Facts and Figures', *ITU*, 2013 <https://www.itu.int/en/ITU-D/Statistics/Documents/facts/ICTFactsFigures2014-e.pdf>.

Scarpino, John, and Ali Alshif, 'The Impact of Social Networks on Saudi Residents Living in the United States', *Issues in Information Systems*, 14 (2013), 72–81.

Schanzer, Jonathan, and Steven Miller, *Facebook Fatwa: Saudi Clerics, Wahhabi Islam and Social Media* (Washington, DC: FDD Press, 2012).

Scott, D. Travers, 'Pundits in Muckrakers' Clothing: Political Blogs and the 2004 US Presidential Election', in *Blogging, Citizenship and the Future of Media*, ed. by Mark Tremayne (New York, NY: Routledge, 2007), pp. 39–57.

Shirky, Clay, *Here Comes Everybody: How Change Happens When People Come Together* (London: Penguin Books, 2009).

——'The Political Power of Social Media', *Foreign Affairs*, 2011 <http://www.foreignaffairs.com/articles/67038/clay-shirky/the-political-power-of-social-media>.

Shoemaker, Pamela, and Stephen Reese, *Mediating the Message* (White Plains, NY: Longman, 1996).

Silver, Vernon, 'Gamma Says No Spyware Sold to Bahrain; May Be Stolen Copy', *BloombergBusiness*, 2012 <http://www.bloomberg.com/news/2012-07-27/gamma-says-no-spyware-sold-to-bahrain-may-be-stolen-copy.html>.

Silver, Vernon, and Benjamin Elgin, 'Torture in Bahrain Becomes Routine with Help from Nokia Siemens', *BloombergBusiness*, 2011 <http://www.bloomberg.com/news/2011-08-22/torture-in-bahrain-becomes-routine-with-help-from-nokia-siemens-networking.html>.

Silverstone, Roger, and Eric Hirsch, *Consuming Technologies: Media and Information in Domestic Spaces* (London, UK: Routledge, 1992).

Simsim, Mohammed T., 'Internet Usage and User Preferences in Saudi Arabia', *Journal of King Saud University – Engineering Sciences*, 2011, 101–107.

Singh, Priyanka, and Yagya Dwivedi, 'Social Media and Awareness in Global Society', *International Journal of Humanities & Social Sciences*, 1 (2013), 48–56 <http://www.academia.edu/4243682/social_media_and_awareness_in_global_society>.

Socialbakers, 'Facebook Brands Stats – Saudi Arabia Fans Only', *Socialbakers*, 2015 <http://www.socialbakers.com/facebook-pages/brands/country/saudi-arabia/>.

Sopher, Christopher K., 'Younger Thinking: An Evaluation of Young America and the Future of News Media and Civic Life', 2010 <http://youngerthinking.com/upload/ResearchPaper-reduced.pdf>.

Sponder, Marshall, *Social Media Analytics: Effective Tools for Building, Interpreting, and Using Metrics* (New York: McGraw-Hill, 2012).

Swanson, David L., 'Gratification Seeking, Media Exposure, and Audience Interpretations: Some Directions for Research', *Journal of Broadcasting & Electronic Media*, 31 (1987), 237–254.

Tewksbury, David, 'Differences in How We Watch the News: The Impact of Processing Goals and Expertise on Evaluations of Political Actors', *Communication Research*, 26 (1999), 4–29 <http://crx.sagepub.com/cgi/reprint/26/1/4>.

The Economist, 'Arab Satellite Television: The World through Their Eyes', 2005 <http://www.economist.com/PrinterFriendly.cfm?Story_ID=3690442>.

The Pew Research Center, 'News Media Consumption Survey', *The Pew Research Center for The People & The Press*, 2008.

Thorpe, Vanessa, 'Radio Times Poll Provokes Online Battle for Baftas', *Guardian*, 2012.

Thulin, Eva, and Bertil Vilhelmson, 'Mobiles Everywhere: Youth, the Mobile Phone and Changes in Everyday Practice', *Young: Nordic Journal of Youth Research*, 15 (2007), 235–253 <doi:10.1177/110330880701500302>.

Thurlow, George, and Katherine Milo, 'Newspaper Readership: Can the Bleeding Be Stopped, or Do We Have the Wrong Patient?', *Newspaper Research Journal*, 14 (1993), 34–44.

Tolbert, Caroline, and Raamona McNeal, 'Unraveling the Effects of the Internet on Political Participation', *Political Research Quarterly*, 56 (2003), 175–185 <10.1177/106591290305600206>.

Trade Arabia, 'Al-Wasat Journalists to Stand Trial in Bahrain', *Trade Arabia*, 2011 <http://www.tradearabia.com/news/MEDIA_196756.html>.

Tremayne, Mark, Nan Zheng, Jae Lee, and Jaekwan Jeong, 'Issue Publics on the Web: Applying Network Theory to the War Blogosphere', *Journal of Computer-Mediated Communication*, 12 (2006), 290–310.

Tufekci, Zeynep, and Christopher Wilson, 'Social Media and the Decision to Participate in Political Protest: Observations from Tahrir Square', *Journal of Communication*, 62 (2012), 363–379 <doi:10.1111/j.1460-2466.2012.01629.x>.

Tully, Claus J., 'Growing up in Technological Worlds: How Modern Technologies Shape the Everyday Lives of Young People', *Bulletion of Science, Technology and Society*, 23 (2003), 444–456 <doi:10.1177/0270467603260812>.

Underwood, Martin, 'UAE and Social Media: Dangers out in the Open', *The National*, 2013 <http://www.thenational.ae/news/uae-news/uae-and-social-media-dangers-out-in-the-open>.

United Nations, 'E-Government Survey 2012: E-Government for the People', *United Nations*, 2012 <www.unpan1.un.org/intradoc/groups/public/documents/un/unpan048065>.

——'United Nations E-Government Survey 2012: E-Government for the People', *United Nations Department of Economic and Social Affairs*, 2012 <http://www.un.org/en/development/desa/publications/connecting-governments-to-citizens.html>.

Verclas, Katrin, and Patricia Mechael, 'A Mobile Voice: The Use of Mobile Phones in Citizen Media', 2008 <www.mobileactive.org>.

Wall, Melisssa, and Sahar El Zahed, '"I'll Be Waiting for You Guys": A YouTube Call to Action in the Egyptian Revolution', *International Journal of Communication*, 2011, 1333–1343.

Wallin, Matthew. 'The Challenges of the Internet and Social Media in Public Diplomacy', *American Security Project* (2013).

Weaver, David, 'What Voters Learn from Media', *Annals of the American Academy of Political and Social Science*, 546 (1996), 34–47.

Wei, Ran, 'Motivations for Using the Mobile Phone for Mass Communications and Entertainment', *Telematics and Informatics*, 25 (2008), 36–46 <doi:10.1016/j.tele.2006.03.001>.

Weinberger, David, *Small Pieces, Loosely Joined* (Cambridge: Cambridge University Press, 2002).

Wendt, Alexander, *Social Theory of International Politics* (Cambridge: Cambridge University Press, 1999).

Wheeler, Deborah, 'The Internet and Youth Subculture in Kuwait', *Journal of Computer-Mediated Communication*, 8 (2003) <doi:10.1111/j.1083-6101.2003.tb00207.x>.

Wheeler, Mark, and Iian Kapoor, 'Should Celebrities Promote Charities?', *New Internationalist*, 2012.

Wiktorowicz, Quintan, *Islamic Activism: A Social Movement Theory Approach* (Bloomington: Indiana University Press, 2004).

Willnat, Lars, 'The Impact of Internet News Consumption on Mass Media Use', in *Paper presented at the annual meeting of the International Communication Association* (Dresden, Germany, 2006) <http://www.allacademic.com/meta/p90915_index.html>.

Willnat, Lars, Joann Wong, Ezhar Tamam, and Annette Aw, 'Online Media and Political Participation: The Case of Malaysia', *Mass Communication and Society*, 16 (2013), 557–585 <doi:10.1080/15205436.2012.734891>.

Wilson, Christopher, and Alexandra Dunn, 'Digital Media in the Egyptian Revolution: Descriptive Analysis from Tahrir Data Sets', *International Journal of Communication*, 2011, 1248–1272.

Wittel, Andreas, 'Digital Marx: Toward a Political Economy of Distributed Media', *tripleC*, 10 (2012), 313–333.

Wolfsfeld, Gadi, Elad Segev, and Tamir Sheafer, 'Social Media and the Arab Spring: Politics Comes First', *The International Journal of Press/Politics*, 18 (2013), 115–137 <doi:10.1177/1940161212471716>.

World Population Review, 'Kuwait Population Review', 2013 <http://worldpopulationreview.com/kuwait-population-2013/>.

Wright, Charles, *Mass Communication: A Sociological Perspective*, 3rd edn (New York: Random House, 1986).

Wu, Shaomei, Jake M. Hofman, Winter A. Mason, and Duncan J. Watts, 'Who Says What to Whom on Twitter', in *Paper present at the 20th International Conference on World Wide Web* (New York, NY: ACM, 2011), pp. 705–714.

Xenos, Michael, and Patricia Moy, 'Direct and Differential Effects of the Internet on Political and Civic Engagement', *Journal of Communication*, 57 (2007), 704–718.

Yuan, Yangyang, and Gerald Kosicki, 'Citizen Use of Internet and Traditional News Media Sources: What's New about New Media?', in *Paper presented at the annual meeting of the International Communication Association, Marriott Hotel* (San Diego, CA, 2003).

Zhang, Juyan, 'Public Diplomacy to Promote Global Public Goods (GPG): Conceptual Expansion, Ethical Grounds, and Rhetoric', *Public Relations Review* 35.4 (2009): 382–387.

Index

Printed and bound by CPI Group (UK) Ltd, Croydon, CR0 4YY
14/09/2026
02216527-0001